Wrestling with Gravy

Wrestling with Gravy

A LIFE, WITH FOOD

JONATHAN REYNOLDS

RANDOM HOUSE TRADE PAPERBACKS
NEW YORK

To the long and enduring line
of Remicks and Reynoldses,
particularly those descending upon
and emanating from Quincy, Massachusetts,
and Fort Worth, Texas

2008 Random House Trade Paperback Edition

Published in the United States by Random House Trade Paperbacks,
an imprint of The Random House Publishing Group,
a division of Random House, Inc., New York.

RANDOM HOUSE TRADE PAPERBACKS and colophon are trademarks
of Random House, Inc.

Originally published in hardcover in the United States by Random House,
an imprint of The Random House Publishing Group,
a division of Random House, Inc., in 2006.

LIBRARY OF CONGRESS CATALOGING-IN-PUBLICATION DATA

Reynolds, Jonathan.
Wrestling with gravy: a life, with food/Jonathan Reynolds
p. cm.
ISBN 978-0-8129-7288-7
1. Cookery.   2. Reynolds, Jonathan.   I. Title.

TX714.R496 2006
641.5—dc22   2006041765

Printed in the United States of America

www.atrandom.com

2 4 6 8 9 7 5 3 1

Book design by Simon M. Sullivan

I don't mind dying broke.
I just don't want to be broke the day before.

—Donald W. Reynolds

Be careful, Jonnie!

—Edith Remick Reynolds

Contents

Introduction: Exhuming the Lede

~~~~~~~~~~

I'VE WRITTEN ABOUT food on the sly since the age of twenty-nine, never expecting any of it to see the light of day. In an attempt to make order of what was then a chaotic life, I began making candid diary entries about restaurants and dinners where I'd been either guest or host, noting not only what was on each menu but evaluating it and the event's surroundings—and occasionally throwing in the emotions and current events that went with it. If I traveled to London or Atlanta or Alleghany County, North Carolina, or Los Angeles or Manila, I'd take notes about the people and the food (though there wasn't much to write about in Manila except for the mangoes). Between jobs, I'd watch afternoon television cooking shows—The Julia, of course, and Graham Kerr—for their technique and recipes. I'd kept a sports scrapbook as a kid, cutting out pictures and (rarely) articles about stars in every conceivable sport—I even had a few pages of swimmers—and now reverted to childhood practice, only this time filling the scrapbook with recipes and (really rarely) photographs. I was sure this was a sideline interest, possibly a psychotic one, so I kept it secret. I should have realized that as I was spending more time describing the preparation for the small dinners I threw for eight to twelve people than on the script I was supposed to be working, and more time on the preparation itself than on the descriptions, food was becoming more than a way of not dying. It didn't occur to me that making scribbles in little notebooks would one day inadvertently prepare me to turn future scribbles into magazine columns.

A "lede" is newspaperese for the eye-catching topic of a story, the burying of which in someplace other than the first sentence or two is a sure sign of the amateur and a probable loss of the reader's attention. It is spelled as it is so as not to be confused with "lead" as in "leaden," perhaps for fear it might be mistaken as criticism of the writing. By squirreling away these notebooks, I was not only burying one of my life's ledes, I was burying the whole story.

Often, these dinners included some televised event—the Oscars, a World Series, the landing on the moon—to ensure that the guests wouldn't be bored if I was out of the room and they didn't like one another or, more frequently, to keep them happy when dinner was two or three hours late. In 1972, my longtime friend the abstract painter Gary Stephan and his girlfriend Linda Patton and I watched every night of the Summer Olympics—a joyful occasion until the terrorists arrived, then a riveting and somber one. I made all the food every night, liberally mixing cuisines—a bananas Foster preceded by *petits pois* braised with lettuce, preceded by Chinese woolly lamb (chunks of shoulder with cellophane noodles).

Food is controllable, while most of life isn't. And cooking is power: If you're the chef, you're determining what people eat. Cooking encourages freedom and invention, but if you're stuck, you can always fall back on a formula inside a cookbook or something cribbed from Batali on the Food Network. I cook most when feeling helpless: When I've been fired from a job or not hired for another, or a woman didn't phone back or did but said, "I don't think this is working," I'd zip to the stove, seek out Jeremiah Tower's blueberry *financier,* see if I could make a duck-liver mousse, find a new kind of heat to throw into a gumbo, and invite noisy people over. Not only would they be a distraction from my romantic or professional agony of the moment, but by being in charge of others for a few hours, I could be in charge of me for a few hours.

My first paid writing jobs were for David Frost's and Dick Cavett's television shows—the most exciting daily jobs I've ever had. In 1969, Frost was determined to change American television and so approached it like a journalist: get this story, that scoop, this embarrassment to surprise a guest, this confrontation between audience and pundit, all in the mold of an entertaining talk show like Johnny Carson's. Cavett was more cerebral and less rabble-rousing but appreciated guests who didn't usually appear on television. (He was much praised for an appearance by Noël Coward and the Lunts—which irritated him, since he knew they meant little in terms of national ratings.) At the Frost and Cavett shows, I booked and pre-interviewed a guest or two each day and, as a result, met just about everyone I ever wanted to: politicians, writers, movie stars, artists, singers, directors, Colonel Sanders his own self, and even occasionally the Right Woman. I strongly recommend this line of work for at least a year or two to everyone with a crush on adrenaline.

It was also immensely satisfying because whatever I wrote was usually seen on national television that very night. This instant gratification was ruinous for a writing career, and spoiled me for every other medium. When I was—*ahem*—excused from the Cavett show in 1972 and was seriously out of work for the first time in my life at the age of twenty-nine, I took up writing plays and movies—a Sisyphean task, considering my natural disinclination for self-motivation. After the razzle-dazzle of daily television, and now facing an electric typewriter in the stillness of my living room, either there was no feedback at all or it would dribble in months after the work was completed. I don't have now, and didn't have then, sufficient self-confidence to shore up a fathomless need for reinforcement, so I took up cooking. It was instantly creative, sensual, filled my tiny apartment with wonderful smells, and became a much-admired way to avoid writing. Other writers would say to me, "So that's how *you* don't write. Cool." And the reinforcement was as instantaneous as a daily talk show's, unless I was preparing thousand-year-old eggs.

Serendipitously, I learned that women find a man cooking seductive. I'm not sure why. Perhaps it's the surprise, or the role reversal, or some revelation of this warm fuzzy we men are secretly supposed to have if only we'd admit it, or the implied altruism—"He's taking the time to whip up that *riz à l'impératrice* just for *me*"—but every woman I've asked, married or un-, claims that a man cooking specifically for her is aphrodisiacal.

The converse is not true. Most men still find women who cook specifically for them scary, grasping, desperate, and clearly in search of a lifelong mate. Worst of all, it's expected—like men fixing the satellite dish. Women need to *not* cook for thirty or forty years so it becomes a novelty again.

My evidence is empirical. Two instances spring to mind. I wish I could brag about them over beers, but due to substantial defects in my personality, both failed to evolve into anything lasting longer than a few hours. The first woman, although sufficiently smitten by what I prepared, wouldn't go out with me for another five months, and that date was the last. Something terrible must have happened between the pear frangipane tart and breakfast, and I never knew what it was, though I am still willing to learn.

I'd been infatuated with the second woman for five years. After I made dinner, she, too, seemed smitten by my cooking just for her. I kissed her passionately after the dessert and could sense her breath shorten through her nose. I slipped my hand between her legs with ease—usually an encouraging sign. But just as the tension became deliciously unbearable and undergarments could no longer contain our heaving flesh, an alarm went off in her cortex, and she refastened snaps and clips, smoothed her skirt, and abruptly departed to meet another guy. She'd made an additional date at ten o'clock! The lucky beneficiary of all my toil and sweat was greeted with a well-fed, well-primed sleeping companion for whom he had to do no heavy lifting at all. True to form, I didn't see her again for ten years, when she wouldn't even hold hands.

Neither of these instances was calculated. I loved cooking and selflessly (well, sort of) wanted to thrill these young racehorses with vibrant new tastes. And since I wasn't making a dime at the time, it was actually quite a bit cheaper to stay home with a bottle of plonk and a *bavarois Clermont* than to go to a restaurant, even if it meant sweating over the soup for hours beforehand. Besides, taking a woman to a restaurant on a first date is about as original as carrying her books, and about as stressful as the night the *Times* critic comes to your play.

A man has to be truly obnoxious to impress a woman at a restaurant on a first date because he really has to perform. He's got a limited time frame and limited physical possibilities: About all he can do is talk and either show off about the wine or embarrass the waiter or in some way be completely thrilling. Women like to be thrilled.

But wielding a cleaver and sautéing diver scallops in his own kitchen, well, the work speaks for itself. He can bop around, show off scrapbooks and music, dance, do push-ups, and generally dazzle with displays of his possessions.

If you're lucky, there's a moment on a date when her eyes will forget the background and focus on you. She'll laugh at an idiosyncrasy, or you'll mesh on some point—a dislike of skiers, the weirdness of the name *Verizon*, a fear of heights, the realization that, despite Hollywood screenwriting rules, real people usually *aren't* sympathetic—something. Even if all you make is farfalle with jarred tomato sauce (don't show her the jar), you will have her focus.

During my second single life, which only recently ended without remorse in a second marriage, I devised the following:

TEN RULES FOR SEDUCING A WOMAN BY COOKING HER DINNER
(which may also apply to men cooking for men and women cooking for women—I don't know)

1. Find out if the seductee is allergic to anything. Find out what she loves but seldom gets, and get it.

2. Make something ambitious. Although I generally prefer simplicity at a restaurant, the perfectly cooked chicken breast isn't going to accomplish what you want unless your date is Rose Levy Beranbaum.

3. Balance the meal. You don't want it all heavily sauced, or neither one of you will feel thin enough to take your clothes off.

4. Serve something exotic—like cardoon. Though popular in France and Italy, and available here from late spring till early fall, it has never become popular in this country. It looks like celery, tastes like artichoke, and will make you seem a man of the world.

5. Have plenty of cayenne pepper on hand. Cayenne masks every conceivable cooking mistake except oversalting and burning. The former you can fix with sliced raw potato or a teaspoon of sugar and vinegar. If you burn something, you may be pleasantly surprised to find that she thinks you did it on purpose. Or you can always say, "I caramelized it."

6. Try to pull off at least one impressive cooking flourish. Throw things around in a wok or set something on fire. Don't froth anything—that's been over for years. Pour something from a great height,

like mint tea in a Moroccan restaurant. Think Baryshnikov, not one of those grunting tennis players.

7. Never consult a cookbook in public. Memorize the recipes or write them on little cards and hide them around your apartment, the way Marlon Brando did in *Last Tango*.

8. Clean your apartment to a better-than-postgraduate level.

9. Make sure the woman you're cooking for doesn't have another date at ten o'clock.

10. Make these:

Chicken La Tulipe

La Tulipe was a wonderful restaurant on Thirteenth Street just off Sixth Avenue in New York that made a feast of a single chicken and had the pride to name it after itself. It is as close to an aphrodisiac as the date rape laws currently allow.

1 ½ ounces dried morels
2 tablespoons Cognac
2 tablespoons butter
1 ¼ cups light cream or crème fraîche
1 teaspoon salt, divided in half
Pinch of cayenne
One 3 ½-pound chicken, rinsed (neck, giblets, and liver removed)
¼ teaspoon pepper
¼ cup dry white wine

1. Preheat oven to 450 degrees. Wash morels carefully with cold water, making sure you get all the sand and grit out. Let morels soak in Cognac 15 minutes. Drain, reserving liquid.
2. Sauté morels in 1 tablespoon of the butter for 5 minutes; then add ½ cup of the light cream and reduce by half. Stir in ½ teaspoon of the salt and the cayenne.

3. Rub chicken with remaining butter and sprinkle with remaining salt and the pepper. Spoon morels into the body cavity. Roast chicken on one side for 15 minutes, baste, and then roast on the other side 15 minutes and baste again. Finally, roast it breast-side up for 20 minutes.

4. Remove chicken from the oven. Throw away most of the fat from the pan, add the wine and mushroomy Cognac, deglazing, and flambé immediately. *Make sure your guest sees this move.* Reduce over high heat.

5. Shake morels and juices from the chicken into the pot, add the rest of the light cream, and simmer for 5 minutes, until thickened. Taste for seasoning.

6. Cut the chicken into 8 serving pieces, arrange them on a platter, and pour the morel sauce over them. If it's that kind of evening, limit yourselves to two pieces each (see Rule Three on page xiii).

YIELD: 2 big servings.

BRAISED CARDOON

(or, Less Exotic but Still Formidable, Leeks)

4 cardoon stalks, peeled, split lengthwise, cut into 2-inch pieces, and
   washed well (or leeks, cleaned of all internal grit)
1 cup beef broth
1 tablespoon butter, in bits
Salt and freshly ground pepper

1. Preheat oven to 450 degrees. Grease a 1-quart baking dish. Cut cardoon crosswise into ½-inch pieces. Place in baking dish.

2. Bring beef broth to a boil and pour over the cardoon, top with butter, and sprinkle with salt and pepper.

3. Cover tightly with foil and bake 40 minutes, until tender.

YIELD: 2 servings.

BAKED FIGS

This is a freely adapted version of a recipe by Alain Senderens, the noted Parisian chef of Chez Lucas-Carton.

6 firm, ripe fresh figs, stems removed
1 ½ tablespoons butter, melted
1 ½ tablespoons sugar
Vanilla ice cream (or 1 cup raspberries, ½ cup heavy cream, and ¼ cup
    confectioners' sugar)

1. Preheat oven to 375 degrees and grease a medium-size baking dish.
2. Place figs in the baking dish and brush with butter and sprinkle with sugar. Bake 15 minutes, until bubbly and lightly caramelized.
3. With scissors or a knife, make an X in the top of each fig so that it opens like a flower.
4. Serve figs hot with ice cream, or with raspberries folded into heavy cream whipped with confectioners' sugar.

YIELD: 2 servings.

Wrestling with Gravy

Cut to the Chase

~~~~~~~~

MY PARENTS BATTLED through an acrimonious divorce right at the end of the war that supposedly made their generation the Greatest. They were almost central-castingly perfect opposites: Don Reynolds was short and fat, and at first meeting seemed like a hick from the dustbowls of Oklahoma and Texas; Edith Remick was a tall, dark-haired beauty, a refined and privately schooled graduate of Smith who had been brought up in Quincy, Massachusetts. She was given to upper-middle-class maladies like mild depression, frequently saw doctors for no apparent reason, and spent an inordinate amount of time resting at home. He was a whirlwind, she a lovely and fragile icicle.

In the late thirties, he briefly owned part of a Quincy newspaper. One of his biggest advertisers was an upscale department store specializing in men's clothing, named Remick's. They met at a company picnic, and he swept her off her feet. She'd never seen anyone like him: such energy, such surprising smarts, such wild visions of the future. And such a sexual drive. I don't know whether he loosed her panties the very first night or was forced to wait till marriage—but I would bet the ranch, if I had one, that it was on his mind, raging, from the moment they met and every moment thereafter. He told her—and her family—that he intended to live in Quincy for the rest of their lives together.

Within a month of their marriage, he sold his interest in the Quincy newspaper and announced that they were moving to Texas. He didn't ask her and hadn't forewarned her or anyone in the family; he just announced it, and off they went. Men could get away with things like that then. He then proceeded to hit the road in search of additional businesses. My sister, Nancy, was born in San Antonio in 1938, and the three of them moved to Fort Smith, Arkansas, where he established the Southwestern Publishing Company, a solely-owned enterprise that operated half a dozen small newspapers. I was born in February 1942, barely two months after the attack on Pearl Harbor, and Dad was drafted shortly after that. He grumbled about the army but finagled his way to Europe, where all the glamour was.

He returned home from adventures in London, France, and Australia, restless to continue his empire-building. Despite a wound received while being flown somewhere for *Stars and Stripes* (the military newspaper), he'd had a great time during the war, traveling everywhere and hobnobbing with bigs. As he was fond of saying, "It was a hell of a war, but better than no war at all!" After about five minutes of peacetime America, he looked at the open landscape and concluded he'd outgrown Mother, and definitely had outgrown children. He hit the road for good in pursuit of new ventures, thinking Mother was living with my sister and me back in Texas because that's where he'd last left us and that's where her letters were postmarked. Once Mother decided on a divorce—an iconoclastic choice in those days, unless you were a Hollywood star—all Dad had to do to protect his rapidly increasing wealth was stay out of Texas so he wouldn't be served with divorce papers.

Or so he thought. But Mother snuck us into Arkansas, where his headquarters was located. To establish residence, we hid out for six dusty months in Blytheville because she might have been recognized in Little Rock or Fort Smith. I remember surviving a tornado, watching Mother alone at an outdoor ironing board, and seeing a dog kill a rabbit. Nothing else.

With the help of a very determined lawyer named Fred Schlater, Mother found out Dad was driving into Arkansas late one night and hired a midnight paper-server to surprise Dad with divorce documents right there on the highway.

Angry? I was only three or four and didn't see the ambush, but he must have stomped around the countryside kicking up dust and biting dogs for weeks. He was so furious about the trap she'd laid—cop cars! Middle of the night! Those lying postmarks!—that he wouldn't talk to her, except in a courtroom, for eleven years. Her treachery filled him with such righteous indignation that he felt he didn't have to see us more than fifteen minutes a year on moral grounds.

He stayed in the Southwest and frequently saw his son by his second marriage, Don Junior (Mother was his third of four wives), while Mother reared Nancy and me in New York. I do remember that once he began rolling in dough, he exaggerated his childhood poverty so as to make his substantial, self-made adult wealth all the more mythic.

The world operated by one set of values, and Dad lived by another, which changed whenever he wanted it to. And he bragged about that set! He believed in his right to complete self-expression regardless of whom it hurt; and he had the vision of an artist. He's one of the reasons I've thought artists are natural Republicans—they have vision and, like the best entrepreneurs, will do anything they must to realize it. Dad benefited thousands of people by employing them and gave everyone good benefits and low-cost loans for education. He was the only stockholder of his company, which meant he had to answer to no one.

I envied his fearlessness, his creativity, and his lack of concern for what others thought of him. I was tugged—yanked—between two radical extremes: on the one hand, a father who lived like a circus acrobat, balancing upside down on one finger atop a unicycle that he pedaled along a tightrope several thousand feet in the air; and on the other, a terrified, cautious, and passive mother who cared excessively what others thought. Envied him, simulated her. Saw no faults in him and in her nothing but. Perhaps it was because I was surrounded by her family and can remember seeing his only once.

Alice Waters Cooks Her Turkey Too Long

~~~~~~~~~~~~~~~~~~~~

FOR CHILDREN, the end-of-year holidays—Thanksgiving, Christmas, New Year's—are cause for celebration bordering on delirium. For adults, they often signal obligation, and border on panic and fear of disappointment.

By the time I was aware of Thanksgiving, at about six, the Remicks were as fractured as the Tyrones in *Long Day's Journey into Night*, though without the drugs or booze. Grammie was a determined widow, Mother was filled with repressed rage, and she and her brother, Bus, were both divorced at a time when it was considered a sign of mental disturbance, and Maymie, her sister, was what used to be called a spinster and possibly lesbian before it was fashionable. But we all temporarily regrouped for Thanksgiving in Quincy, as though posing for the cover of *The Saturday Evening Post*.

The highest compliment Grammie could pay a turkey was to say that its skin was just like wrapping paper. She'd always ask, "Would you like some wrapping paper, dear?" The turkey in those days seemed all right to me but hardly worth the long train ride. The sides were much more fun: candied sweet potatoes, sweetened cranberry jelly from the can, peas with sugar, corn with sugar, stuffing with sugar, endless pies of apple, mince, and canned peach. Unlike most nostalgics who revert to their childhoods for soothe, I've never had any of those exact recipes since: sweet potatoes and all the rest are much better without all the treacle. I wasn't paying much attention to food then—except for the single candy Grammie always offered each of us at meal's end from the Whitman's Sampler she kept in a cupboard. To me,

Thanksgiving was just the holiday without presents. It wasn't until much later that I discovered that eating was one of its pleasures, and that you could have your wrapping paper—and turn turkey into a destination.

A superbly roasted turkey (or any other poultry, for that matter) is welcome at any time of year. Even though they're bland, I love what these beautiful birds represent all the year round and rush to embrace new methods of preparation even in the summer because turkeys remind me of holidays as a child, and I want to re-create that feeling for others—an impossibility, of course.

Any day in May, when the suicide-and-euphoria holidays of the previous winter are a distant memory (as in childbirth, the pain forgotten or nobody would go through it again), is probably the perfect time to talk about cooking a turkey. Procrastinators can rejoice that they have 190+ days to plan but not execute, and the better-adjusted among us can analyze at leisure instead of rushing to the stove, ripped magazine recipe in hand, on Thanksgiving or Christmas morning, when it's too late. And tortured perfectionists like Barbra Streisand can practice, practice, practice.

The difficulty, as we have been told almost daily for the last quarter-century, is to cook the bird's drumsticks and thighs sufficiently without turning the white meat into washcloth.

All sorts of well-intentioned tricks are suggested for moisturizing the breast meat. Julia Child was said to massage butter between the breast and the skin, which lubricates the breast but makes the texture of the meat greasy and the taste overly buttery. Martha Stewart dips cheesecloth in melted butter, then drapes it over the white meat, but the melted butter fails to penetrate the more-or-less-waterproof skin. Alice Waters soaks the entire fowl in a home-concocted brine for seventy-two hours. This step is indeed helpful, though it takes so much time that you need to plan days ahead for even the simplest fowl. And she then defeats her noble aim by keeping the bird in the oven too long, drying it out.

There are two solutions. For those with successful hedge funds, buy two turkeys and cook one for the white meat and the other for the dark, then discard the overcooked white of one and the undercooked dark of the other. The rest of us can follow John Hess's method and have our twelve-pound dinner out of the oven in two hours, our sixteen-pounder in two and a half, and a twenty-pounder done perfectly in three.

Based on Hess's recipe, which appeared in *The New York Times* more than thirty years ago, a twelve-pound turkey is stuffed, slathered with a stick of butter, roasted at a very high temperature, first on one side, then the other, and basted every twenty minutes or so. True, all the basting is a nuisance, and the smoke caused by the high temperature may result in a visit from New York's Bravest, but this is a small price to pay for a standing ovation and the likelihood of hotel-room keys dropped in your direction by Casablanca models. Our bird will have juicy breasts, pinkless legs, and skin that crackles in your mouth like a UPS parcel.

Two important don'ts. First, don't truss the animal, whether you stuff it or not. Trussing is a matter of aesthetics: The perfectly bound, coquettishly trussed bird reminds me of a '50s debutante at a cotillion, not a hair out of place; untrussed, it looks like a ravished slut, disheveled and eager for more. But if you bind the turkey legs together, fifteen to thirty minutes must be added to the cooking time so the insides of the thighs and legs can reach the proper temperature—and at that point about the only thing you can do with the white meat is spackle the bathroom. If the purpose of trussing is to contain stuffing in the body cavity, a simple pin through the skin flap will do that; if the butcher has removed the flap, cover the opening with foil.

Second, don't, as some suggest, pour water into the roasting pan to prevent it from scorching, or you'll inadvertently steam the bird. Two tablespoons of oil will do the trick—as well as neutralize the burning properties of the stick of butter.

GRAMMIE NEVER PREPARED our Thanksgiving turkey, and I don't know how it was cooked. She had what used to be called a maid who did the culinary work. In those days, you could tell which hemisphere of the country you were in by how the maid was addressed: if she was called "Miss" or "Mrs.," you were in the northern; if "Amise" or "Thelma," the southern.

Magically, Grammie's Mrs. O'Bannion would appear at exactly the right moment when the family—which included my sister, Nancy, and me now—was finished or ready for seconds.

"How does Mrs. O'Bannion know we're finished?" I asked Grammie time after time, which amused her no end. Over many Thanksgivings and summer holidays, I'd ask how Mrs. O'Bannion knew her entrance cue, and Grammie wouldn't tell me, just smiled slyly. I became increasingly frustrated and dazzled by this telepathy.

Finally, after an hour of pleading that threatened to last one entire Thanksgiving day, she decided that if she didn't tell me I might either 'splode or become an even greater danger to society than I turned out to be. "Look," she said, pointing to a bump in the rug near her chair. She pressed it with the ball of her foot, and Mrs. O'Bannion whooshed through the swinging door.

"What? What did you do?"

Grammie laughed. So did everyone else. "Go into the kitchen," she said.

I did, and after a moment heard a buzz. I didn't get it.

Then I did!

I ran back into the living room. "It's a buzzer! You operate it with your foot! It's hidden under the rug!"

"Yes, dear."

Nancy, three and a half years older, rolled her eyes. "Duh," she said, two or three decades before it became hip again.

I didn't care—I had discovered one of the wonders of electricity! If not electricity itself! "May I do it?"

"Yes."

I sat in her chair and toed the buzzer's button about thirty times, just stopping before everyone went insane. "That's enough, dear," Grammie finally said. "Now sit down and have some wrapping paper."

To serve ten people and have leftovers for sandwiches, here are two methods:

Two Ways to Roast a Turkey

1. Strangle and pluck a 12-pound turkey, preferably an anarchist that has been allowed to run around and eat grain whenever it wants. Remove whatever is inside (usually a neck and giblets) and cut off the wing tips, reserving them.

2. *Method One:* Twenty hours before cooking, swish 2 cups of kosher salt in 2–3 gallons of cold water until dissolved (no need to heat it) and submerge the turkey for 12 hours in this brine, using a weight to keep it underwater. (Waters suggests a more complicated mixture, but since the bird is rinsed thoroughly after brining, it just adds unnecessary work.) Either put this brining turkey in the fridge for those 12 hours or more, or if there's no room and the temperature is 33 degrees Fahrenheit or better and you live on a low floor, put it on the windowsill; or put lots of ice cubes in the brine, adding more when they melt. Skip to step 5.

3. *Method Two:* Instead of brining, after removing the neck, giblets, and wing tips, follow the recipe for Internal Turkey Brine (page 12), and inject the result into the turkey, as instructed. This will keep the bird as moist as the brining process does and gives it more flavor.

4. Pat the skin dry and refrigerate overnight (or at least 12 hours) so the skin will tighten and dry, increasing its eventual postalness.

5. Begin your stock by deeply scoring whatever was inside the turkey (except the liver, which may be chopped, sautéed, and added to a stuffing) and the wing tips and tossing them into a pot. Add a sliced carrot, a sliced celery stalk, a large quartered onion, and a handful of parsley and cover with water or with poultry, veal, or beef stock. Simmer for 3 hours, replenishing the liquid if it gets low or too salty. Because you are in charge, when the stock is done you get to eat the neck, which is delicious. You may also eat the vegetables, which are pretty tasty, too.

6. One hour before cooking the turkey, remove it from the fridge to bring it to room temperature and preheat the oven to 450 degrees. Pour a couple of tablespoons of oil into a roasting pan and either oil or use a nonstick V-shaped, nonadjustable rack. (Adjustable racks are too unreliable and may collapse under the turkey's weight.)

7. Stuff the turkey and rub its skin with a stick of softened butter. Place it on its side on the rack, place the rack in the roasting pan and the roasting pan into the blistering oven. Roast for 30 minutes. If smoke filters out of your oven, enjoy its spiritual qualities unless something actually catches fire. (If, however, your kitchen, the pan juices, or the turkey's skin ever approach blackness, turn the oven down to 400, or even 375 degrees.)

8. Baste the turkey with the pan juices. Then take the pan out of the oven, and with wads of paper towels (or large forks) placed at either end, turn the turkey over onto its other side, baste it, and put it back in the oven. (Turning the thing can get pretty ungraceful, so try not to be photographed right now, and don't try to turn the turkey at oven level unless you're wearing a truss. Instead, lift the pan from the oven rack, closing the oven door with your left heel; place the pan on a steady surface and wrestle the bird to its other side however you can.) Set the timer for 20 minutes and baste every 20 minutes, four times—your total cooking time will now be 110 minutes. Rotate the by-now-mahoganied beauty breast-side up, basting everything in sight.

9. Take the turkey's temperature in the fattest part of its thigh. It should read 135 to 145 degrees. (If it doesn't, leave it in a few more minutes.) If it does, take it out immediately and put it on a platter—it will continue to cook for the next 20 minutes or so while you make the sauce.

10. No flour or thickener is used in the sauce because it tastes better without. Pour off half the fat from the bottom of the roasting pan and place the pan over high heat (possibly two burners). Add 1 cup of the strained turkey stock and deglaze the pan, dislodging everything with a wooden spoon. Taste for saltiness and intensity—sometimes the sauce can go in those directions. If it does, add another cup of stock and reduce. If it is still too intense or salty, thin with a little water. Add ½ cup Cognac, white wine, or dry sherry and bring to a boil or set it afire to cook off the booze. This will not make more than 1 ½ cups of sauce—a tablespoon or two per serving, which is all that's needed. Some strain this concoction, but I prefer being surprised by tasty little scraps on top of my white meat.

When you roast the turkey on its sides, gravity drips what little fat exists in the dark meat into the white; like the basting, this helps moisten the meat. Some suggest cooking the bird breast-side down until the last 30 minutes, then browning the breast, but this makes basting about six times as difficult and the back of the turkey the brownest part of the body.

With the technique above, you'll be out of the kitchen an hour earlier than you have been at previous feasts. Your turkey will be sensual with juice, your wrapping paper will crackle, and you'll be ready to do battle with the next national holiday—the Academy Awards.

Internal Turkey Brine
¾ cup chopped onion
¾ cup chopped celery
3–6 tablespoons chopped garlic
4 tablespoons unsalted butter
2 tablespoons (or more) chopped hot peppers from pepper vinegar
2 tablespoons Worcestershire sauce
1 tablespoon plus 1 teaspoon salt
1 tablespoon cayenne
1 tablespoon black pepper
1 cup chicken stock

1. Sauté onion, celery, and garlic in butter until tender. Add hot peppers and Worcestershire sauce, then stir in the salt, cayenne, and black pepper. Add the chicken stock and bring to a boil.
2. Strain into a bowl, pressing the solids to extract as much juice as possible, to yield about 1½ cups.
3. With monster hypodermic, inject the turkey's breast in five places and each leg and wing in one place.
4. Pat the skin dry and refrigerate overnight, or 6–12 hours.

John Hess's Sausage, Black Olive, and Walnut Stuffing

(Adapted from The Taste of America *by John L. Hess and Karen Hess, Viking, 1977)*
I've been making this basic stuffing for decades, and when I don't overcook it, it's marvelous. When I do, I add a little stock or fat to moisten it.

1 pound bulk pork sausage
1 turkey liver, minced

1 cup chopped onions
½ cup very thinly sliced celery
1 teaspoon chopped fresh thyme
1 loaf good bread, sliced
1 cup mild, pitted California-style black olives, sliced
1 cup walnut pieces
½ cup chopped Italian parsley
2 tablespoons Cognac or 4 tablespoons Madeira, port, or dry sherry
Kosher salt and freshly ground black pepper to taste
½–1 cup turkey stock, depending on desired moistness

1. Place the sausage and the turkey liver in a large heavy pan over medium heat, stirring until cooked and the sausage meat is well broken up, about 12 minutes.
2. Add the onions, celery, and thyme and cook, stirring frequently, until the onions are tender and pale yellow, about 10 minutes.
3. Toast the bread slices and dice; you should have about 3 cups. Place the sausage mixture in a bowl and add in the bread.
4. Mix in the olives, walnut pieces, Italian parsley, Cognac, salt, and pepper.
5. Add enough stock so the stuffing will hold together in the bird.

YIELD: About 4 cups.

If Alice Waters cooks her turkey too long, it's about the only thing in the culinary world she's ever done wrong. If most of the great professional chefs have been men for the last century, most of the great cookbook writers (and therefore influences on the home kitchen) have been women. Julia Child, Marcella Hazan, Madhur Jaffrey, Diana Kennedy, Eileen Yin-Fei Lo, and of course Elizabeth David, Jane Grigson, and the Fannie Farmer conglomerate spring to mind. There are many crossovers, of course—Mario Batali, Eric Ripert, and Thomas Keller helm kitchens and write excellent books. But none has done both to the degree Alice Waters has over the last thirty years. Her restaurant Chez Panisse in Berkeley is responsible for the California-cuisine explosion, and her cookbooks have spread the gospel to benighted urbanites the world over. She continues to be at the forefront of sustainable farming and cooking.

Now, good as the turkey above is, if you've got room for a vat of boiling oil and a propane tank to fire it, I strongly suggest deep-frying a turkey. Although bringing four to five gallons of oil to a bubble can take as much as forty-five minutes, the turkey takes only three and a half minutes per pound to deep-fry, little or no oil is absorbed because of the turkey's skin, and the resulting meat is the best turkey you'll ever taste. Though Louisianans have been boiling their birds for decades, I read about it in a piece for *The New Yorker* by Calvin Trillin and have since made about fifty of them without a single hitch in either flavor or conflagration. However, the potential for fire and oil-mess is great, which means you *must* do this procedure outdoors. Equipment made specifically for deep-frying turkeys (but useful for other preparations) is available at www .cabelas.com and many other outdoor outfitters.

Deep-Fried Turkey

(Adapted from The Prudhomme Family Cookbook *by Paul Prudhomme, William Morrow, 1987)*

One 14-pound turkey
4–5 gallons of peanut oil or lard
Internal Turkey Brine (page 12), minus the cayenne pepper
1 tablespoon cayenne or favorite Cajun spice

1. Follow instructions for Internal Turkey Brine, but omit the cayenne for now.
2. After injecting the turkey, with your bare hands, rub the cayenne into the turkey's breast *under the skin*.
3. You can either refrigerate, uncovered, 8–24 hours to dry out the skin or fry it immediately.
4. When you're ready to fry the turkey, remove it from the refrigerator, place it in the empty fryer, and cover completely with water. Then empty the pot, measuring the water.

5. Fill the fryer with the same amount of oil or lard, attach the extra-long thermometer to the pot, and heat the oil to 350–375 degrees.
6. Pierce the turkey with its holder and lower slowly into the oil.
7. Boil the turkey for 49 minutes or slightly longer (3–3 ½ minutes per pound).
8. Remove the turkey, let the excess oil drain off, and rest it on a platter for 10–20 minutes. Slice and dive in!

GRAMMIE WAS ALICE COOPER (yup) until she married Alfred Remick at the turn of the last century. Alfred was one of several brothers who owned Remick's, at the time a dry-goods store frequented by working men in Quincy. Although Alfred and Alice had three children—my mother, Edith, my uncle Bus, my aunt Mary, known as Maymie—their marriage was said to be relatively loveless. Alfred was a bayzo—fond of bay rum—and frequently could be heard by neighbors bellowing songs late at night as he wound his way up the hill from Remick's to the family house at 26 Fairmount Way. These noisy returns home infuriated Alice and got him banished from the bedroom. *Withholding* and *passive-aggressive* were not yet terms in fashion, simply because no professional jargonists knew Grammie. Ice. Silence. Cut-off.

But when Alfred died suddenly of a heart attack in his fifties, Grammie was heartbroken and went into deep mourning. She didn't exactly wear black the rest of her life like her mentor Queen Victoria, but she never married again. I don't think it occurred to her. By the time I knew her, she seemed loving and affable, with an easy, subdued laugh and the softest, wrinkliest skin. Her gift for inducing guilt was passed down to my mother, Edith, and it gave them both pleasure and the illusion of control.

Alfred left the store to his widow and three children, to be managed by the man in the family, Bus. He was a senior at Harvard and uninterested in the retail business but dutifully took on the assignment. Over the years, he turned Remick's into not only a success but the fashion center of downtown Quincy. He redesigned the interior, making its focal point a long, gracefully curved staircase, at the top of which he hung an enormous oil of Alfred. The portrait gave the store an aura of tradition, history, and permanence; the staircase and up-to-date fixtures transformed it from a boots-and-overalls store for the working stiff to an elegant emporium for the upper-middle-class aspirant. He improved the quality of the merchandise on sale, specializing in above-average men's haberdashery. He knew his customer base well enough not to attempt Armanitude, and was happy to be considered a competitor of Brooks Brothers. In the fifties, Bus mechanized the store windows at Christmas, as Saks and Lord & Taylor and B. Altman's had done in New York. None of these successes was accomplished without considerable personal sacrifice.

Most Elegant Fowl

~~~~~~~~

FATHER OF ACTRESS Lee and would-be rancher Bruce, stepfather to three, and maternal uncle to my sister, Nancy, and me—Bus Remick was the most elegant man ever to grace the boulevards of New York, Boston, and Quincy, Massachusetts. Even given the hyperbole of memory, he remains the only person I never saw ruffle.

He loved good food, all the arts (on principle), laughing—slow, rolling baritone—his children, two wives at the appropriate times, and the retail business. He knew who he was; his view of the world was balanced, though occasionally Republican and decidedly anti-Kennedy, and his devotion was unconditional, as you'll see.

His real name was Frank, and his nickname was short for Buster, which he was called because he had once been a chubby kid—no remnant of which remained by the time I met him. Ever since I can remember, he looked like the love child of Cary Grant and William Holden and smoked cigarettes beautifully, using a long holder.

As a teenager, I didn't know what class I'd been born into or that there were classes. Certainly, the Remicks were middle class, and Bus's retail success and increasing prominence in the Quincy business community nudged the family toward upper-middle-classness. Dad was decidedly lower class by birth, but by virtue of all his money and the divorce settlement wrested from him by Mother, Nancy and I were New York City private-school kids and probably somewhere between middle and upper-middle. In any case, we both resented it—from the safe distance of being in it. Nancy wanted to dance pro-

fessionally, and I emulated all the pop-idol bad boys, from Elvis to James Dean
to Brando, dying to carry a switchblade, don a black leather jacket, and ride a
motorcycle—though I was as far from being a tough guy as anyone at the
Allen-Stevenson or Trinity schools who didn't learn to ride a bicycle (let alone
a hog) till he was twenty-two could be. Still, as a teenager, I loved Brando's
line (or rather the screenwriter John Paxton's line spoken by Brando) in *The
Wild One*.

GIRL
What're you rebelling against, Johnny?

BAD BRANDO
Whaddaya got?

I'd made a study of cigarette-smoking styles and found myself torn between the soigné technique of Uncle Bus (from the Noël Coward School of
Smoking) and how I imagined my father would have smoked—ciggie between thumb and first two fingers—if he had. And then there was the tortured cigarette manipulation of James Dean, which was mighty attractive. At
a New Year's Eve party when I was fourteen, I toyed with Pall Malls and a
holder and got a date, which I assumed was because the holder (or possibly
the Bermuda shorts and knee-length socks) made me look grown up. I continued with the holder for a week or so before the whole process just became too
unwieldy. But Uncle Bus always made it look smooth.

When, years later, he was forced to give it up because of a series of heart attacks, and his doctor advised gum as a stand-in, he became the suavest of
chewers, slowly and subtly massaging the gum, never popping it or biting it
frenetically, so that in his mouth even this activity looked magnolious.

The beaming black-and-white photograph of him on his mother's anti-
macassared Victorian tabletop in her dark Quincy parlor, brass buttons and
gold braid spiking his double-breasted navy uniform, made him look more
dashing—and a lot less show-bizzy—than Gary Cooper or Adolphe Menjou.
His clothes were understated, though expensive. He frequented the theatre,
loved the ballet even before my sister danced in the New York City Ballet
under Balanchine. When in New York, he took me several times to Birdland,

where, in sheer volume (let alone transcendence), the Count Basie Band with Joe Williams would have humbled the mongrel children of Limp Bizkit and Nine Inch Nails. We laughed every time we entered the place. Over the entrance was inscribed "Through These Portals Pass the Most." When I'd visit my uncle in his bachelor digs in Boston between his marriages, he'd put on a platter late at night, turn off the lights, and teach me how to listen to music: in the dark and L-O-U-D.

Bus had dreamed of high finance in London and Paris, but when his father died, he found his role in life: George Bailey, the character played by Jimmy Stewart in *It's a Wonderful Life*. If Bus hadn't agreed to run Remick's, his mother and two older sisters might have become penniless. Certainly, they were frightened. He embraced responsibility, took over the reins of the business for the sake of the women . . . and discovered he loved it. He held the company reins till shortly before he died of heart failure in 1983. Although needled by my father to open other branches of Remick's, or at least move out of downtown Quincy before it died, he remained civic-minded and kept only the one store, on Hancock Street. When it became successful, he took a box at Fenway.

This is how elegant he was: After Mother divorced, she sued Bus for paying her less than what she felt was her fair share of the family store, and Bus, not yet fifty, had his first heart attack. For years afterward, until a judge dismissed the case as frivolous and declared the price fair, Bus suffered considerable New England guilt. When I was twelve and found my eighty-third school in a row incompatible (actually, it found me), Mother had the nerve to phone him and ask for help as a paternal surrogate; Dad was empire-building out west and had little interest in counseling his children. He felt the million bucks Mother "stole" from him was sufficient contribution.

By rights, Bus didn't owe his litigious sister the time of day. She had brought him much misery and had nearly broken up the Remicks of Quincy—both commercially and personally. And he was trying to ease his own children through his divorce. But shortly after her phone call, Bus flew down to New York, never said a word against her, and introduced me to my first red wine, pheasant under glass, and steak without ketchup.

Though we moved to New York when I was six, my experience with "fine dining" had been limited to Mother's infrequent forays to Longchamps and

Schrafft's, which meant putting on a tie, Wildrooting down my hair, and sitting up straight (squirming actually) just in order to eat a "chopped sirloin" that wasn't nearly as good as the monster ground chuck at Hamburger Heaven next door. (It still isn't; chuck makes a better burger than sirloin.)

At home, I nourished myself with No-Cal cream soda, a forerunner of the diet-soda mania, and often requested Anne Pudding, named after a maid we had. The recipe is as follows:

ANNE PUDDING

1 slice pound cake
½ cup vanilla sauce, from powder
½ cup Nestle's milk-chocolate bits, more if I could get them

1. Put pound cake on plate.
2. Warm vanilla sauce and pour over pound cake.
3. Smother with chocolate bits.

YIELD: 1 serving.

So when Uncle Bus took me solo to the dining room of the old Westbury Hotel on Madison Avenue, I went eagerly—he was fun to be with, and he listened.

Until that night, he had seemed a pleasant, if distant relative, who was married to an energetic and breathtaking blonde and who was raising two golden children much more popular than I thought my sister and I were. I realized later we didn't see much of that side of the family because of Mother's lawsuit.

I didn't know what a pheasant was, but I'd heard it referred to in plays and books as the epitome of Upper East Side excess, and it appeared on the Westbury's menu. The restaurant's interior was considerably tonier than any I'd been to previously—filled with red velvet banquettes, golden lighting fixtures, perhaps a crystal chandelier. I wore a tie.

Mother certainly wouldn't have allowed me to have pheasant—too sybaritic and too expensive. But testing adults was the only behavior I felt comfortable with, and Uncle Bus was not only an adult, but also one who needed testing to see if he would leave like Dad. I had to ask. "What if I ordered the pheasant under glass?" Bus didn't raise an eyebrow at the expense or question my judgment.

"That's why I had them put it on the menu," he said. His eyes were playful. He had aced the test.

The bird didn't look nearly as glamorous as the "under glass" had promised. Instead of plumage and trumpets, here was a beige poultry breast under what I called gravy ("sauce," Uncle Bus said lightly), covered with a cloudy glass dome. When the waiter lifted the lid, I backed away to avoid the steam, but Uncle Bus waved the bird's perfume toward his nose. "That's the point, you see. The glass concentrates the aroma, so that you can smell it. Beautiful, isn't it?"

A bolt of lightning crashed through the Westbury's ceiling. Smelling was part of eating? Food could be . . . beautiful? It was the first time I realized food could be something more than fuel. I quickly waved my hands in imitation of Uncle Bus's, hoping to catch some of the pheasant vapor, but it had dissipated. "Just so you know for next time," he said.

If memory serves, the taste was bitter—not as bland or tender as the chicken and turkey my adolescent palate was accustomed to—and it was made worse by the unfamiliar taste of Cognac, softened though it was with cream and butter. In fact, Uncle Bus rescued me—the first of many times—by trading plates. When I asked for ketchup for the steak he'd given me, he said gently, "The meat is so good, maybe this once you should try it without." There were qualities of meat besides ground and not ground? I never ketchupped not-ground meat again and ever since have shunned sauces that overwhelm what they are supposed to complement.

I assumed his marching orders were to tell me to behave in school, which he did. But instead of questioning past performance, he said, "Do any of the subjects interest you?" After I'd dismissed them all, as befitted my professionally disgruntled student persona, he asked me about English.

"We're reading *A Tale of Two Cities*, which is pretty good, and I'm really good at diagramming sentences."

Math? "We just started percentages, and I'm actually pretty good at them."

American history (his major at Harvard)? "I can't wait to get to the Civil War!" He went through science and art—his minor—and music, and it turned out that I actually liked them all. "I'm glad to hear that," he said, "because you have so much to offer."

End of crit! He had tricked me into realizing I *did* like school and into wanting to do better at it! He didn't have to mention my underachievements in behavior. He must have known that taking pleasure in academics would straighten me out. I told him about Elvis, whom he thought fascinating, unlike any other person his age. And he loved the pheasant, a taste I've since acquired through diligence and education.

Uncle Bus didn't leave, and he was the best father substitute a boy, and then a man, could ask for. And the permission to order pheasant under glass was liberating: I wasn't ridiculous, my judgment was worth considering, and in his eyes I was on my way.

Pheasant Under Glass

Although this preparation is difficult to find on restaurant menus these days, it's a magnolious way of serving the bird. (Isn't magnolious *a mellifluous word? I use it as often as I can.)*

1 whole large pheasant breast, split and boned
2 tablespoons freshly squeezed lemon juice
½ teaspoon freshly ground black pepper
2 tablespoons unsalted butter
6 dried morels, brushed off
2 large shallots, peeled and chopped
2 large white mushrooms, wiped clean, trimmed, and sliced thin
2 tablespoons brandy
⅓ cup dry white wine
⅓ cup heavy cream

1 ½ teaspoons chicken demi-glace

Pinch cayenne pepper

1. Flatten pheasant breasts slightly with a mallet or rolling pin, then rub with 1 tablespoon of the lemon juice and season with black pepper.
2. Melt 1 tablespoon of the butter over medium-high heat in a 9-inch skillet. When it foams, sear the pheasant, skin-side down, about 5 minutes per side. Remove to a plate, cover, and keep warm.
3. Wash morels carefully with cold water, making sure you get all the sand and grit out. Steep the morels in ½ cup hot water for about 5 minutes. Drain and strain, reserving the soaking liquid. Discard stems and slice caps thinly.
4. Melt the remaining tablespoon of butter in the skillet and sauté the shallots for 2 minutes, until golden, then add the morels and mushrooms for 1 minute. Remove to a bowl and keep warm.
5. Boil the reserved morel-soaking liquid with the brandy and white wine until reduced by half, about 1 minute, then whisk in the cream and demi-glace and boil about 1 minute, until sauce is thickened and smooth. Whisk in the remaining lemon juice and the cayenne.
6. Place the pheasant breasts skin-side up on hot serving plates and top each with half the mushroom mixture, then the sauce.
7. Enclose each breast with (ideally) a glass cover. Alert your guests to the olfactory possibilities, so they don't blow the experience the way I did. Once they are seated and you have their attention, lift the cover and fan the essence toward them, if necessary.

YIELD: 2 servings.

IT TOOK MOTHER a while to get her money from Dad. She'd been awarded one third of his business in the 1947 judgment, but what good did that do if he reinvested every penny of profit back into the business? He paid himself a modest salary, but, as the only shareholder, he could allow himself an expense account that included homes, cars, fat watches, servants, fireplaces, travel, food, and the moon, with no one to say no. He loved showing off his belongings, and as soon as he could get a plane, he got one, then another, then jets, ultimately winding up toward the end of his life with his own 727, in which he installed a king-size bed.

I didn't understand any of this. Except for the dusty months in Blytheville, I didn't know what our circumstances meant. We moved to New York and a small apartment on Fifth Avenue in '48 or '49. Nancy went to Brearley, I to Allen-Stevenson—both private schools. I think it was hard on Mother, and I imagine she borrowed from her mother and sister.

Then in 1952, not long after she initiated the suit against Bus, Mother went back to court and convinced the judge that she was being rooked by her ex-husband. The judge awarded her a million bucks, and we immediately moved into a splendid three-bedroom duplex at 4 East 72nd Street. We had *two* TVs in a time when one was a luxury, an enormous living room, a separate dining room, and maid's quarters, which were occupied by a live maid. At ten, I was as savvy about money as I was about where babies came from—as far as I was concerned, the stork brought both. A friend visited and told me he didn't have a TV. I was incredulous and offered him some of my allowance. When I'd visit someone who lived in less elegant surroundings, I assumed his parents lived there by choice, and I'm sure I said some variation of "Jeez, you really should live in a better place" several times. I don't know why I was so thick in figuring out how the world worked. The curse is, I'm even thicker now.

I was curious about many things—TV, sports, movies, comic books, why some kids liked me and why others didn't, how grown-ups behaved, and more sports. But money? It was just lying around—for everybody, wasn't it? Blessed by New England guilt, Mother was ashamed of it, secretly felt she didn't deserve it (despite protestations of "I earned every penny, living with your father"), and so was tight-fisted. We never discussed it, and Dad—who was an encyclopedia on it—never bothered to clue me in about it or sex or much of anything else. I managed to learn something about sex and everything else, but never about money.

The Shot Heard 'Round the World

GROWING UP IN NEW YORK, I was such a Yankee fan that in the fourth grade I nicknamed myself Allie because of the great pitcher. When the real Allie Reynolds threw two no-hitters in the same season, I was ecstatic, furtively hoping people would mistake me for him—a little early schizoid behavior, since I was nine and he was thirty-six. Only slightly more realistically, I hoped strangers would think I was his son. .

In that fall of '51, while we still lived in the lightless uptown apartment, the New York Giants and Brooklyn Dodgers were locked in the most dramatic pennant race ever. The Giants fell into the cellar early in the season and clawed their way to a tie with the Dodgers on the last day of the regular season. The commissioner decreed a best-of-three playoff for the pennant, and the city could talk, breathe, or eat nothing else.

The Giants won the first game of the playoff, the Dodgers the second, and they just about closed down the federal government for the final game. Despite their early integration of black ballplayers, the Giants were the white, blue-collar team, and the Dodgers were the black street fighters from uncivilized Brooklyn. The Yankees, of course, were the plantation owners who didn't deign to integrate until Elston Howard joined the club in 1955—eight years after Jackie Robinson had broken the barrier with the Dodgers.

The final game of the playoff was on October 3, 1951. I woke up that morning and told Mother I couldn't walk.

"What?" she said, amazed.

"I can't walk . . . see?" I slid around our faux-marble linoleum floor in my pajamas. She looked at me as if I were insane.

"Of course you can walk. Now get up and go to school."

"No, I can't walk." I made several theatrical attempts to stand but just couldn't. "I guess I'll have to stay home." She lifted me by the arms, but I became dead weight. "I want to walk, Mother, but I can't. I don't understand this," I said, suppressing my glee over this brilliant scheme to stay home and watch the game.

Nancy came in to breakfast. "What's the matter with Jonnie?"

"He can't walk," Mother said, laughing. Nancy had other things on her mind and thought this was about as important as an earache. "Well, I've got to go to school." She left. Mother had appointments out of the house, but our colored maid, Thelma, was coming.

"I know exactly what you're doing," Mother said. I think she was impressed by my ingenuity and amused by its foolishness. "You want to watch the ball game. Well, you can't. Our television is broken, and you can't go to the Crouses' next door. So you might as well go to school."

I couldn't very well admit I was faking, so I said, "But, Mother, I can't walk."

"Well, then, we better get you to a hospital," she bluffed.

"No, no, why don't we wait and see what I'm like this afternoon?"

"All right, that's enough—get up."

"But, Mother, I can't walk." I valiantly attempted to stand again and crumpled.

Whatever the equivalent of "Yeah, right" was then, she said it, and tried sixteen or seventeen times to get me up to my feet, but I was too proud to admit defeat. Finally, she left and wrote Thelma instructions not to let me leave the apartment.

I got tired of zipping around on my knees pretty quickly. Without TV, there wasn't much to do, and I had to be convincing as a cripple. Thelma was round and jolly, and when she arrived, I told her, "I can't walk." She laughed out loud. "That's the craziest thing I ever heard!" she said, and dusted the venetian blinds. The day dragged on. I kept acting the stricken victim, even in my room with the door closed.

Nancy, who was also a baseball fan, returned from school at three and immediately headed for the Crouses' working TV. By now, I was bored and anxious and wished I'd gone to school. At least I would have been able to see the last few innings like Nancy. In an hour, she returned.

"What happened?" I asked breathlessly.

"Oh, it was very exciting. The Giants were behind four to two in the bottom of the ninth, two men on, one out, and Bobby Thomson came up and hit a home run." My God, the Giants had won the pennant! The Giants had won the pennant! The most famous home run in baseball history, subsequently called "the shot heard 'round the world," and I had been sliding around on the floor . . .

Almost immediately I recovered and stood up.

"What was this not-walking anyway?" Nancy said.

"I wanted to see the game," I admitted and asked her to explain the game in detail.

It's hard to remember that there was a time before instant replays, VCRs, and DVDs. Occasionally, I was lucky enough to see Bobby Thomson on film at the local Trans-Lux movie theatre around the corner as he rounded third and dove into a swarm of euphoric teammates at home plate. When a team wins a division or a pennant or the Series these days, it's mandatory that the dugout empties and the players enthuse; but in those days, the enthusiasm was spontaneous and for real.

I wondered several times afterward, What should I have done to be allowed to see the game? Told the truth? No, I would have been ordered to school. Gone to school, snuck back early to the Crouses' for the game? No, there'd be hell to pay later. Been picked up by the school bus, ducked out while everyone entered the building, gone to the Polo Grounds? No, I was nine, had no money, and didn't know how to get there. Chosen a more believable affliction? There was no perfect answer.

Two years later, I found the nerve to ask the headmaster at Trinity, where I'd transferred—a gruff, megalomaniacal hunchback—if I could be excused from classes to attend opening day at Yankee Stadium. To my astonishment (and the whole sixth grade's), he said yes. Although many of the players were before my time, I knew the Yankee numbers up to 30 by heart, and still do:

Billy Martin was number 1, then Crosetti, the Babe, Gehrig, DiMaggio, Bobby Brown, Mickey, Yogi, Hank Bauer, the Scooter, Johnny Sain, Gil McDougald, no number 13, Gene Woodling . . . then skip a few. Raschi was 17, Allie 22, and Lopat 30. Twenty-two years later, I wrote my first play, *Yanks 3 Detroit 0 Top of the 7th*, about a Yankee pitcher having a nervous breakdown on the mound in the seventh inning of a perfect game.

I was a spoiled kid in many ways, but none more than as a Yankee fan. They just won everything. So we Yankee sons believed this was our destiny, too. Sort of like America, 1945–1963. (Very good for self-image, very bad when it turned out they could also lose, because it meant so could we.) The few times when they did lose (say, not winning their fifth World Series in a row) became cause for tortured soul-searchings: What had we done wrong? Why was God mad at us? And just as I didn't know that I was living a privileged childhood until it was too late to enjoy it, I didn't realize till too late that the Yankees weren't going to finish first forever. I was a fair-weather fan, it turns out; when they began failing—and I began growing up—the disillusionment was so crushing that I turned on them. Sort of like kids and parents.

I had brief success as a player—at age nine or ten, I pitched a no-hitter at camp. But I was a lousy batter, and whenever I played in the outfield, couldn't judge where a fly ball would descend. I'd invariably run toward the plate be-cause that's where the ball seemed to be at that instant, then realize as it sailed overhead that I needed to run back, and it was too late; or I'd run back to protect myself from that error and have to race into the infield to even have a chance at it. Made me crazy.

As I grew and the players got better, balls came at me faster, and by the time I was in my early teens I was actually scared to death of a pitched base-ball—not so much because I might be hit by one but because I'd swing goofily at one three feet from the bat. So I usually determined to swing as the pitcher was winding up—not exactly a scientific choice unless you're a gambler bet-ting they can't *all* be balls. But I remained a fan—and a talker.

I don't really remember the food in the Bronx. Like Jughead in the *Archie* comics, I preferred hamburgers to hot dogs, made alliances with boys who felt the same, and shunned those who liked dogs. I ate franks at the stadium only because the burgers were so bad. (Still are, at every ballpark—in order to murder bacteria, they're cooked beyond defeat.) But on recent visits to a few ballparks, I've been impressed how good the food is at the newer places and stunned to discover how sorry the food is at our local arenas.

After mother's milk, the three greatest cuisines in the world are French, Chinese, and Junque. (Italians, Japanese, and Myanmarians may argue the first two, but nobody disagrees with the third.) I'll go to the sainted Popeye's with anyone at any time. I'll follow those visits with a fistful of White Castle cheeseburgers or really good biscuits and sausage gravy at the Sparta Restaurant in North Carolina. So it's not with pleasure or from snobbism that I tell you that the food at Shea Stadium is possibly the worst food *in . . . the . . . world*. It's better at Yankee Stadium—but only if you consider that boring trumps putrid.

How did we—supposedly feeders in the culinary capital of America, snubbers of the mighty Ducasse, petulants if we don't get superlatives of everything—fall into such a wretched state? How is it we have allowed our prized ball clubs, with their fat payrolls and staggering TV revenues, to stiff us with near-toxic grub? Why hasn't there been a food riot in seventy-eight years?

It's not like this in San Francisco. At Pac Bell, the relatively new home of the Giants that overlooks the sapphire bay, the menu explodes the notion of traditional ballpark food. More inclusive than the Republican party (well, at its convention), it features Mexican, Thai, Japanese, health, and vegetarian food as well as the more customary hot dogs and popcorn. Chief among them are the scrumptious American or French Gordon Biersch garlic fries, which are so inspired that even during a recent four-run Giant rally, the line to the stand was twenty persons strong. Antithetical to the chili fry, the garlic fry sizzles with a wonderfully concocted fresh garlic-parsley-oil sauce. Pac Bell also serves up surprisingly delicious edamame by the cupful. Admittedly, boiled soybeans would be a tough sell in New York, and we could teach them a thing or two about the pastrami-and-corned-beef sandwich, but whoever is in charge of food has hit several back-to-back grand slams.

The food at Yankee Stadium is exemplified by one teenager's critique of the gloppy and lumpy cheese fries, "But I like fake cheese." But it's Le

Bernardin compared with Shea, where, if you must eat, you better bring a mouth ambulance. The entire menu is truly borderline inedible. Most gruesome of all is a small, sticky-floored and tacky bar named after one of the great wits and cranks of the game—and the man not only responsible for most of the Mets' early popularity but also the one who gave them the sobriquet "Amazin'"—the justifiably legendary Casey Stengel, out from under whose hat once flew a bird. I guarantee you, if Mr. Doubleday (the owner, not the inventor) ever left his leathered and sequined bunker to buy anything here, he'd sell the club.

The game itself interests me less these days. The money is such an obvious factor—the Yankees just buy what they need—which it probably was when I was five and six and twenty-five, but which, like all other financial aspects of life, I chose to ignore till way too late.

Gordon Biersch Garlic Fries

9 ½ ounces olive oil

2 ½ ounces vegetable oil

3 pounds frozen shoestring fries, skin on

1 cup chopped garlic

1 tablespoon kosher salt

¾ cup chopped fresh parsley

1 tablespoon freshly ground pepper

1. Combine the oils and pour ¼ cup of it into a 12–14-inch skillet. Heat until hot and add a third of the potatoes. Cook, covered, stirring occasionally, until browned, about 5 minutes. Drain on paper towels. Repeat with the rest of the potatoes.
2. Crush the garlic and salt with the side of a knife until coarsely puréed. Mix in the parsley and pepper.
3. Add the potatoes to the garlic mixture and toss to coat. Serve hot.

YIELD: 6 servings.

Ship's Edamame (Boiled Soybeans)

6 cups (1 ½ pounds) fresh soybeans in the pod
1 gallon water
2 tablespoons salt

1. Wash the soybeans and drain.
2. Boil the water and add the salt and soybeans.
3. Boil 5–7 minutes, until tender but not soft.
4. Drain in a colander and cool with cold water.
5. Slip out the soybeans from the pod and eat.

YIELD: 6 servings.

Discovering Priapia

~~~~~~~~

MOTHER WAS DEPRESSED most of the time, and I think Nancy and I depressed her more. I'd visit friends in their apartments, and there was usually merriment to be found somewhere, even with the adults. Not in our home. Nancy and I weren't oppressed, or beaten, or deprived of much materially, though there were no Rollses outside. (Dad had those in Arkansas and Oklahoma.) Still, self-pity and defeat clung like humidity to the drapes, lowering the ceiling and replacing the nitrogen in the air. They seeped through our unsuspecting skins right into our marrows and lodged without a fight. Like most children and all dogs, we assumed that the home life we experienced was the norm, and that we were destined to ape its behavior, deepen it, and pass it on to our children. Over the years, I've fought depression like crazy, often beating it back, sometimes succumbing to it. I hate it— my own and whenever I find it in a companion. (I can spot it in anyone who sighs on the phone or drops an eyelid for an extra beat across a football field.) It's as familiar as socks and soon settles in comfortably around me. It's the way the world is supposed to be, and how issues usually work themselves out.

But we weren't as sodden with it as the Crouses next door. Sarah Crouse, who was Mother's age, had four daughters, three of them unmarried and living with her. She, too, was divorced and in her forties, but, unlike Mother, never managed to get out of bed. Whenever I visited Sandra, who was my age, or whenever Nancy visited Linda, who was hers, Sarah was in her nightgown and bathrobe under the covers. She read and slept and talked on the phone with the music of the thirties and forties playing on the *Make-Believe Ballroom* radio show quietly in the background—the family television miles away in the living room and too modern for her. Sarah generally had a glass filled with some brown liquid and ice cubes near her, and when I'd ask Mother why she was always in bed, Mother said, "She's not feeling well." The daughters were alive and full of high spirits, and their father, Otto, a successful lawyer, visited them often, which may have accounted for their resilience.

Years later, I understood why Dad had to get away from all this. He had lofty visions to realize, and with superhuman effort he could muster the energy to bring them to life. He couldn't possibly have done so if he had to bring Mother along with him. It would be like rappelling Mount McKinley with a knapsack full of rocks. And the knapsack was wet.

Leaving the Crouses' apartment and entering ours was like going to a ball-game by comparison. Mother, Nancy, and I had breakfast and dinner together almost every night. (The Crouse girls generally had dinner in their kitchen with their maid.) Mother wasn't interested in food, perhaps because the moment she drank a glass of water or ate five peanuts, they'd appear on her waistline. So in addition to everything else she was avoiding—like the world outside—she kept her distance from food. She tried to re-create a few interesting recipes she'd learned down south, but about all she could execute was a decent fried chicken with cream gravy and a baroque version of bread pudding made with chocolate. Once the divorce settlement became hers instead of a vending machine for Dad's expense account and we'd moved out of the dingy uptown apartment and into the sunny duplex, Anna, the Ukrainian maid, would emerge from her dark lair and serve generally uninspired basics, like well-done little lamb chops, gray chopped steak, and chicken so over-roasted you could dry your hair with it, all primly arranged on the plate with defrosted baby peas and a splot of mashed potatoes.

Unlike Sarah Crouse, Mother fought back against depression. In many ways, she was a pioneer. For six or seven years, she had tenaciously pursued that divorce and finally prevailed, at least financially—to the wonder of Dad and eventual congratulation of her female friends, many of whom had divorced and, in hopes of keeping the peace, settled for whatever their brow-beating husbands offered. The women were invariably shortchanged, and there was never any peace. At least Mother had the pyrrhic victory of making a killing.

At the urging of her lawyer, Fred, and to a degree her ex-husband, she pursued the lawsuit against her brother Bus to the bitter end. That it broke her mother's and sister's hearts and alienated her brother for many years didn't dissuade her from this wrongheaded pursuit, but she saw it through.

She was also the first of anyone we knew to go to a psychiatrist. Laughable as this may seem today, when every other fetus is in some kind of therapy or at least reading a self-help book, only the certifiable or the extremely wealthy indulged in shrinks in the forties and fifties.

Ultimately, she paid fatal prices for her persistence: Dad's flight and fury were gasoline on the flames of her depression, just as her father's sudden death had been kerosene; and the damage done by the lawsuit with her brother was liquid oxygen. Psychiatry became my mother's addiction, at once enlightening her and imprisoning her in her own helplessness. It explained her to herself—and convinced her she was too fragile to make her own way in the world without the weekly, sometimes daily, ministrations of a shrink. When she confided to her two best girlfriends that she was seeing a psychiatrist, they viewed her as slightly odd and began treating her like a wounded china doll.

Self-esteem was called "confidence" in schoolyards then, and mine wasn't done much good when Mother decided I, too, should see a psychiatrist. I was ten or eleven and was instructed by her not to tell anyone—the shame! the shame!—which only reinforced my view of myself as even more of a misfit than I apparently was. I'd had a superb year in the fifth grade at Trinity, flourishing academically and socially under the guidance of a brilliant teacher named McLeod; in the sixth grade, I discovered jealousy and turned on all my friends for their accomplishments in sports, grades, popularity, bravery. The sixth-grade teacher, a man named Duncan, also suffered—from constant comparison to McLeod—and together we had a miserable year.

I'd like to blame my physical cowardice on Mother—she was afraid to do anything, and whenever I was in danger of rolling over in bed the wrong way (let alone playing football), she'd warn, "Be careful! Watch out! That's dangerous!" Certainly her cautious approach to the outdoors colored my view of it, but she wasn't the sole reason. In the fourth grade, I'd rounded an icy corner in the winter, slipped, and got poked just below the eye by the spike of an iron fence. Blood filled the lobby of our apartment building. And though the wound was easily bandaged, it was scary, and the scar lasted twenty years. In the fifth grade, I fell and broke my right wrist on an asphalt basketball court on Randalls Island and was treated at school like a war hero, everyone in the class trying to sign my cast. Nobody had seen someone with a broken bone before! In the sixth, I slipped in my own room and broke my *left* wrist—a far less glamorous venue and injury (though just as painful) and was greeted at school with some hostility and a big ho-hum, as though I had broken that bone to revive my flagging popularity. The sixth-grade cast itched, friends went out to play, and I got fat, despite all the No-Cal cream soda.

It was my own fear of falling that prevented me from learning to roller-skate till I was sixteen or ride a bicycle till I was twenty-two. I still find bicycles terrifying, whether I'm on one or some messenger is. They come at you in the middle of the night, lightless and silent as a sniper's bullet. Everything scared me then, except sex.

Sandra Crouse and I used to sleep at each other's apartments when we were seven or eight or nine, and one night curiosity seized us. We went into the bathroom and examined each other tentatively, both wildly aroused and breathing hard. We had no idea how to calm the tension, of course, and eventually went back to sleep. The next day, she told her mother, and we never had a sleepover together again.

In retrospect, sessions with the shrink were hilarious. They were full-frontal Freud: me at age ten stretched out on a couch, Dr. Becker behind my head, secretly opening his mail. I had no idea what free association meant or what I was supposed to do. The rigors of the philosophy prohibited him from asking direct questions, and it made me more nuts to speak to what I experienced as an empty room. Every now and then, he'd clear his throat and make some rustling noise, and I'd think, "Is he doing what I think he's doing? Is he coughing up phlegm, spitting it into a Kleenex, folding the Kleenex, and putting it back in his pocket? Yikkk!" He became increasingly impatient at my silences, which he considered a lack of cooperation, and I became increasingly anxious at his impatience.

"Why *can't* you remember the first thing that happened to you?" he said after repeated attempts to get at the gold mine of a first memory. I vaguely pictured myself walking into a bathroom, probably in Texas, being intrigued by Mother's dozen or so perfume bottles, and pouring them one by one into the toilet, so I told him that. It became locked in my head as "the first thing I can remember" and was the response I gave to a succession of shrinks, never knowing whether it really *was* the first thing I could remember or only something that came up to ease Dr. Becker's ill temper.

At one session, I fell asleep for the full fifty minutes, and he didn't disturb me—somehow I was supposed to learn a tremendous lesson from this. Trust or something. Mother was furious at this waste of money but sided with Dr. Becker, as she almost always did. To my regular questioning, "But Mother, what am I supposed to say?" the response, "Whatever comes into your head," was no help at all.

Things at Trinity deteriorated. I got angrier at and more resentful of my former friends, and basically turned into Iago, whispering plots behind their backs. They soon found friends who didn't get angry at them and weren't trying to sabotage them in some way. Showing off to new accomplices one lunchtime after some particularly wretched meat product aswim in gravy, I twisted three forks together and threw them into the opening for dirty dishes at the school cafeteria. The lower-school headmaster spotted me, and that together with my general overall pathological behavior became justification for my first NIBbing—Not-Invited-Back-ing. The only difference between being NIBbed and being expelled is that a NIB doesn't go on your record; the student simply decides to change schools. So at twelve, I "decided" to leave the wilds of the Upper West Side for the bucolic pleasures of Garrison, New York.

Boarding school wasn't much of an adjustment for me. When I was four, Mother sent Nancy and me to summer camp because of the nationwide polio scare. I continued to go to camp for the next twelve years, usually for eight weeks at a stretch, once or twice for as many as twelve weeks—longer than most school terms. So after a few minutes of homesickness the first year or two, I became so inured to it that I began counseling the other boys those first few nights. The food was the same at all camps and schools: a choice of hot cereals in the morning (oatmeal, cream of wheat, and the particularly odious farina), pancakes, French toast, reconstituted powdered eggs; lunch featured sandwiches and a bowl of canned pears; dinner was invariably some form of mystery meat—a thing floating in gravy or chipped beef on toast.

Malcolm Gordon was an unusual little school. It took in only twenty-eight boys, ranging in ages from eight to thirteen. The classes were so small—two or three students, max—that they were practically tutorials. It was the first of my three boarding schools, and resulted in the second of my three NIBs.

I was NIBbed at Malcolm Gordon for excessive letter-writing. We were all asked to write a letter of condolence to Arthur Debernarde, who had been attacked by his appendix and was hospitalized. I found the experience so much fun that I proceeded to write him a letter almost nightly—twenty-five or thirty of them over the next six weeks.

I had a great time writing them at the end of study hall every night. They were partially true, partially made up. I remember writing in one an elaborate description of Dad raping Mother, which to the best of my knowledge never happened, at least physically. Mr. and Mrs. David Gordon, who ran the school, encouraged imagination as long as it remained somewhat timid, and saw pederasty under every bed well before any of us students knew what it was. So after a few of my missives, the Gordons began opening them and, rather than reveling in discovering an incipient literary genius, were repelled at the prospect of a serial rapist in their midst, even one who never did any raping.

I had become very fond of the place and felt at home there. I felt betrayed and was stunned when I heard the news of my NIBbing from Mother over spring vacation and tearful when I said good-bye to the headmaster at commencement. (Under threats from Fred Schlater, the Gordons allowed me to finish the year.) I didn't know what it was I'd done wrong, but so great was my shame, it took me more than forty years to tell the story to anyone except a therapist.

I know now but didn't then that as an intensely priapic being, I would have ravished porcupines if that's all that was available in Garrison when I was twelve. When I was thirteen and a half (months are important at that age), my discovery of girls sent me reeling, spiraling, and ejaculating for the foreseeable rest of my life; but between twelve and thirteen and a half, I made the mistake of being surrounded exclusively by boys. This manifested itself not only actively and pragmatically, but literarily.

Lawrenceville used to be for boys only, and as an eighth grader the following year, I discovered written pornography unlike any I've seen since: One of the boys in the dorm got hold of photographs of the pages of a novel called *The She-Devil*, a wallowingly heterosexual romp through the bedrooms of southern France. For twenty-five cents he would rent out photographs *of the pages of the book*. No photos, no drawings—just words. Although we had access to *Playboy, Nugget, Gent*, and other deliriously breast-baring magazines, the suggestive written word was more thrilling than any realistic visual depiction because it hooked the imagination. But despite the swaggering prurience of all these publications, there weren't any actual women around, so I had to make do with what was at hand.

The '50s was not a good decade for homosexuality. It wasn't smart to be a homo then, even if it was through ignorance and lack of choice. (At thirteen, abstinence was not an option.) Every school and camp dedicated to boys was as terrified of homosexuality then as it is of drugs today because it was well-known to be a terrible disease. And the boys—even co-participants—were merciless. And there were many co-participants, as befits a boarding school. The showers were very busy in Thomas House, and I was a serial showerer. I thought all of it was just fun and either gender fair game—*Playboy* under my pillow, some kid with a hard-on in the next cubicle eager for experimentation. It was slightly naughty because sex is supposed to be slightly naughty, and I was relentless. My reputation grew.

One afternoon an attractive fellow named John Uhl from a nearby dorm suggestively lured me downstairs into the office of the lower-school newspaper, *The Recorder*, of which I was the editor, tricked me into confiding that I was perverted (which I did with some theatricality), and then revealed a tape recorder hidden under a desk nearby. I ran from the room, panicked and humiliated, while Uhl and the engineer of the prank, Webster Ford (at last, those scores settled!), proceeded to play the tape at all the lower-school dorms with considerable delight. Although filled with shame, I was able to stand back as if on Pluto and view the whole thing comically—this *was* pretty funny. I was the object of derision for months, and horrid as it felt, it also gave me a sort of swagger; I'd almost laugh at an innuendo said about me or a look exchanged between a couple of kids as though it were happening to someone else.

As if wanting to play the role of buffoon, I arranged my ultimate departure from Lawrenceville by writing a letter to a student I had unsuccessfully propositioned, suggesting we get together and work on some project together. In the back of my mind, I must have thought, "Well, writing letters got me thrown out of Malcolm Gordon, maybe it'll work here, too." And as if Euripides with several darker gods wandered into the lower school one afternoon, I stole a letter from this boy's mailbox, which I'd never done before and haven't done since. It was from his mother, saying that she had shown my letter to the lower-school headmaster, and that her son shouldn't worry—I'd be taken care of quickly. I read this calmly, with no sense of dread but with a tickle of pleasure, put the letter back in the envelope, the envelope back in the mailbox.

I knew for two weeks something drastic was about to happen, and it didn't faze me. A streak of asexual perversion, some naughty glee, was invigorating: "Oh, boy, I'm really going to get it now!" I thought. It wasn't masochism; it was the excitement that titillated. Then on a Sunday afternoon in October of my freshman year, the lower-school headmaster called me into his office.

"Is this serious?" I joked with him on the way downstairs from my dorm.

"Yes, it's serious," he said. It was exciting. But I knew it was about to be very painful.

Mother was in his office crying quietly. Other than that, the room was still. He gently read my letter aloud, then said, "You have a reputation which can't be tolerated. I've talked to Mr. Heely, the headmaster, and he's very upset about this. We can't have you stay here, but it won't appear on your transcript." More silence—except for Mother's sobs.

"When do I have to leave?" I asked.

"Right now. All the boys are out. You need to pack up everything." I did, and Mother had hired a car for the trip back to the city. We never talked about the sexual aspect of the NIBbing—not then, not ever—only what school I would go to next.

Although the actual expulsion was titillating, and I wished I could have stayed to see the look on all those boys' faces when they heard the news, I was miserable and felt tragic. It had also really devastated Mother, whom I never considered.

Years after I unhooked my date's bra for the first time, I continued to slink

around with this shame: Was I secretly queer? Would I be NIBbed from another school, college, job, happy life, heaven? Clearly it was the worst offense
a boy or a man could commit: Look what had happened to me because of it.
And this propensity I had for the arts and aversion to towel-flicking locker-
room prance—wasn't that indicative of effeminacy?

After Lawrenceville, I landed in a tutoring school in New York in hopes of
getting the hell out of high school as fast as I could. It was a silly place: I took
two years' worth of Regents exams in English and history in two months and
suddenly was "ready" to be a junior at age fourteen.

I ENROLLED in an acting school run by John Cassavetes, then a relatively un-
known actor and aspiring director. He was never there, but my teacher was
Burt Lane, who wound up becoming Diane Lane's father. In one memorable
assignment, he'd cast another actor and me in a scene from Robert Anderson's
Tea and Sympathy. I played a college football player who teaches a sensitive college boy who fears he may be gay how to walk in a more manly way. I had
James Dean on the brain then, and was so sensitive and tentative myself that
Lane said at the end, "You two should have been playing opposite parts." Dev-
astating. Stayed with me for about fifteen years.

That my cousin Lee was a movie star by the time I was fifteen had much to
do with my wanting to be an actor. I was attracted to it for all the superficial
reasons: its glam lifestyle; the moody sensitivity of Dean and Brando and
Robert Mitchum; the suave clowning of Cary Grant; the money—was anybody paid more?; the outrageous behavior you were allowed if you reached
stardom; and, of course, all the best-looking women were actresses. My
mother was appalled.

Mother never tired of psychotherapy and trained Nancy and me to turn to
it whenever problems arose. Immediately after the Lawrenceville exit, she
sent me to the Ackerman brothers, two shrinks specializing in lost boys. They
achieved a reputation by espousing a confrontational therapy. I don't remember if it was Nathan or Bernard, but whichever one was bald addressed me fe-
rociously one day by saying, "Look at my head! What does it remind you of?"

"A bald head?"

"No! Something else." I groped for the answer he wanted.

"Uh, my father?"

"No! DOESN'T THIS REMIND YOU OF YOUR OWN PENIS?"

I was terrified. The prospect of a dick as large as his head charging straight for my precious heinie electrified every hair on my body—those on my under-arms, legs, pubes. I ran out of the Ackerman office, and despite their many en-treaties on the phone to capitalize on this "breakthrough," boy did I never go back.

Better Than Fontainebleau Lobster

MOTHER WAS ALFRED and Alice's middle child, beautiful (I'm told), and, even as a child, often withdrawn. Most of her life she felt betrayed by the four men most important to her—her stern, alcoholic father; her wild and entrepreneurial husband; her loving brother; and, I see in retrospect, me. Her father betrayed her by dying when she was barely in her twenties; her husband ran around on her for thirteen years, then abruptly divorced her and abandoned their children; her brother did not betray her at all, but she was convinced by her husband and her lawyer he had. And I took the fun out of having children. I was in combat as a teenager, and was a teenager for a very long time, until recently, really, which is probably why she kicked me out of the house so often.

As a single parent, she was overwhelmed, trying to raise a pair of temperamental and artistic children whose reaction to everything vaguely disciplinary could be measured in liters—sometimes imperial gallons—of defiance. By the early sixties—pre-Beatles, pre-Vietnam, late Freud—plays like *The Glass Menagerie* and *Gypsy* and movies like *Rebel Without a Cause* had created mothers so overbearing they were blamed for everything from juvenile delinquency to the crippling sickness of homosexuality. And since I flirted for about five minutes with both, barbells of guilt rounded her shoulders and made them sag.

When Nancy fled the more conventional life of private-school classes at Brearley and joined the City Ballet, to Mother it was worse than Nancy putting on a pair of stiletto heels and swinging a purse on Eighth Avenue. I wasn't aware of the enormous artistic achievement being blessed by George Balanchine meant till much later, but it ruled and anchored Nancy's life. She didn't want to finish school at all; only after many screaming arguments with Mother did she agree to finish her final year at the Professional Children's School, which would accommodate her rigorous performance and practice schedule. She became estranged from Mother, a split that was never repaired. Her life *was* the ballet, which Mother neither approved of nor understood.

If Nancy stayed pretty much within the law, I didn't always. I started having gin-and-tonics at fourteen, got away with a little shoplifting, stole money from Mother's friends, and, most dangerously, forged her driver's license.

I'd fallen in a big, big way for the photograph of a girl in shorts; her name was Pam and she lived in Miami Beach. She was a friend of a friend, and after boldly phoning her after school one day, I phoned her every day after that. I was determined to see her. With visions of Dad's grandiosity in my head, I wasn't just going to woo her but would knock her off her feet as well as offer up my virginity to her. I decided to fly to Miami, rent a convertible—already heady—and drive her to the beach, where we'd wind up rolling around as Burt Lancaster and Deborah Kerr had in *From Here to Eternity*.

The only problem was . . . I was fourteen. And didn't know how to drive.

Still, I gathered up the money a great aunt left me, ordered a goatee created by Eddie Senz, a leading Broadway makeup man, so I'd look old enough to rent the car (the minimum age was twenty-five), and stole Mother's driver's license. In those days, New York licenses were filled in in ink by the driver, and there were no pictures. I bought ink eradicator and slowly and carefully substituted my name, gender, and weight for hers.

After the Lawrenceville NIB, Mother had hired a companion for me to make sure I didn't get into trouble after school while she worked around the corner at a little pottery shop. She correctly feared I'd either veg out in front of the TV watching *American Bandstand* or come up with some kind of trouble. So she found a male nurse named Scott Olsen, who was not only gay but Extremely Gay. He was tremendous fun, but I don't think Mother quite figured out that an effeminate male role model wasn't exactly what I needed after the Malcolm Gordon and Lawrenceville episodes. Scott knew a lot of second-tier theatrical personalities, frequently said, "Oh, *jamais, jaMAIS*," and never minded when I'd order gin-and-tonics. He smoked and thought it was fine if I did. He roomed with an attractive black man who sometimes answered their apartment door in the nude. In imitation of Scott and his friends, I became more and more affected—while simultaneously pursuing every girl I thought exhibited the remotest chance of taking my virginity. Must have been quite confusing for the girls. And though I longed to be one of the red-blooded normals on *American Bandstand*, I knew if I ever got to Philly for the broadcast, I'd be treated as if I were wearing a clown suit.

I told Mother I was going to Miami Beach for the weekend, and to my astonishment, she said, "Okay, as long as you take Scott with you." It turned out that she'd been so advised by a psychiatrist named Hyman Spotnitz. She already knew I had stolen her license, and the progressive doctor told her, "Let him go. He'll get into a little trouble, but it'll teach him a lesson. How bad could it be?"

Bad enough.

The plane landed in Miami Beach, I spirit-gummed the beard to my chin in the men's room, and Scott and I headed for Hertz. I pulled off renting the car, though almost gave it away when I asked the salesman, "Uh, how do I get this in 'drive'?" He looked at me suspiciously and pointed out the PRNDID2 on the steering column. Scott quietly urged me to let him drive us to the Fontainebleau, which I did.

But not to Pam's house. That I had to do on my own—pantless passion on the beach would not be aided by an older man driving us around. So I managed to get the convertible out of the Fontainebleau lot and pulled onto Collins Avenue. It was a lovely light-blue Chevy convertible with triangles of chrome telescoping from the exaggerated fins to the front doors. Couldn't have been cooler. And the night was breathtaking—sultry, warm, starlit.

I knew I had to turn left in the next few blocks, so I quickly switched on the radio, since that would be part of my entrance. I also had to have a cigarette to make the right impression, and I tried to light one. I realized I had missed the left, so while lighting the cigarette and turning to the right rock 'n' roll station, I impetuously jerked the wheel way to the left, zipped through the intersection out of control, bumped up onto the sidewalk, and scraped the entire right side of the immaculate Chevy to ribbons against a cement wall. It made a hell of a noise.

I wasn't hurt. I jumped out of the car to examine the damage, as I had seen people do in the movies. I had no idea what to do. The chrome had wrapped itself into tight little cylinders on both fins, there was an enormous dent for half the length of the car, and the wall was chalked with blue paint. In case someone was watching, I tried to blame the accident on the Chevy. I kicked the tires two or three times, not realizing that's what you do when buying a car, not wrecking one.

Within about three minutes, two Dade County police cars pulled up, sirens singing and lights flashing. Someone must have seen the accident and phoned it in. I wondered if I should retrieve the goatee and spirit gum, now in the glove compartment, and put it on, but the police were too quick.

"What happened?" an officer asked politely.

"I don't know," I said, acting as though we were old buddies and he surely knew as well as I did how crazy cars could get, sort of like wives. "Pulled over to the left . . . and it shot wide of the turn," I said, blaming the accident on General Motors. Two or three other cops were looking at the wall and the car—now part of the wall—and were whistling and scratching their heads in amazement. They were trying to figure out how such a wide turn was geometrically possible. The beautiful Chevy was totaled.

I'm not sure how I pulled the rest of it off. How could I possibly pass for twenty-five? I was fourteen, with some baby fat, not particularly tall or mature-looking. But I had seen twenty-five-year-olds in the movies and knew something about acting, so I just acted like one. In fact, I probably acted like a fifty-year-old. My demeanor was calm and serious but confident. I kept quiet, as though I had much on my mind. They examined my driver's license. It seemed to satisfy them, but they kept it. They radioed HQ while I sat in one of their squad cars. After half an hour, the pleasant officer said, "The car will be towed—all taken care of. We're going to have to go downtown, but it shouldn't take too long."

I knew I didn't want to go "downtown," whatever that meant. Would they examine the license? Find the goatee and spirit gum in the glove compartment?

"Mmmm, downtown," I said. By now I was wearing a mantle of gravitas that suggested I was missing a cabinet meeting with President Eisenhower.

That certainly would be an inconvenience. "I'd certainly prefer not to do that," I said, looking at my watch. "I'm late as it is. I'd really give anything not to go downtown."

"You would?" the officer said.

"Yes."

"What have you got?" He looked at me pleasantly. He'd been pleasant throughout the whole ordeal.

Thank God for all those movies I'd seen. I knew what he meant right away.

"I've got two hundred dollars in traveler's checks."

"No, sir, no traveler's checks."

"I've got, let's see, eighty to ninety dollars in cash." I was so happy—I was about to become fourteen again. Was this really how the world worked? I was doing it!

"That'll be fine." I gave him the ninety dollars. "Thank you, sir," he said. "Can we drop you somewhere?"

I told him Pam's address, never breaking my fifty- or seventy-five-year-old demeanor. "Lovely night," I said, as though I had grandchildren.

"Yes, sir."

He and his partner dropped me off at Pam's, courteously waiting for her to answer the door. They still had the license. But they didn't have me. Pam took one look at them and was immediately impressed. Was I so important I had a police escort?

"Thank you, men," I said.

"Yes, sir," the pleasant officer said, and drove off.

"Wow, what happened?" Pam asked. All my fingertips had pulses of their own, and they were haywire. I started to tell the story, and a few minutes in took a deeper look at her.

Pam was a dog.

The leggy photo hadn't misrepresented her exactly, but I had foolishly focused on the legs. I'd spent all this money, had a beard made, risked the federal pen for forgery, and endured a police inquisition seventeen hundred miles from home . . . for this? I immediately embraced her and kissed her. She was a good southern girl and wasn't used to this sort of assault. She was polite, and we rolled around on the floor for a while, but she was distinctly uninterested in my advances, and after a couple of hours, began to dislike me. I phoned for a taxi.

"See you tomorrow," I said.

"Yes . . . sure," she said.

Back at the Fontainebleau, I told Scott what had happened. He dropped about six pounds and four pints of blood in three seconds, as pictures of me on a Florida chain gang whizzed through his brain. "I've got to get that license back," he said.

I slept the sleep of the pure, and poor Scott was agitated all night. In the morning, he phoned Mother, who phoned Fred, still her lawyer. They devised some sort of plan. I went out on the beach to enjoy Miami.

But I don't actually like beaches. Windy, hot, too sunny to read, sand sticks to you, sweat collects in your navel. Pam appeared with another couple, who were engaged. In addition to the troubled adolescent stars, I also idolized Frank Sinatra and proceeded as I thought he would in this situation. So I offered Pam and her friends a few drinks and club sandwiches on the beach (turkey, bacon, lettuce, tomato, mayo, sand, toast), and when the guy wasn't looking I made a move on the other girl. She was flattered but not amused. Her fiancé was tough. Pam, who by this time *really* didn't like me, was crushed.

"You're a nice guy," the fiancé said to me, "but keep your hands to yourself." They left.

I had one more day in Miami and nothing to do but watch TV. I ordered lobster from room service for breakfast. It was dry and overcooked. I realized I'd had a rotten time in Miami Beach, and all of it was my doing.

But Scott had an even worse time. He was ready to mainline Miltown, the fifties' trank of choice. He'd spent all of Saturday and Sunday at the police station and was going to stay there until he got that license back. I left on my scheduled flight.

Mother met me at Idlewild Airport—as JFK used to be called—and the following morning I was driven to the Anderson School in Staatsburg, New York. I was told it was the last stop before reform school. I looked forward to

it. It was the first institution I'd been sent to that was coed. And by now I preferred the three cereals—even the farina—and the mystery meat to anything
the Ukrainian maid would serve.

Better Than '56 Fontainebleau Lobster

*The best way to cook a lobster is to smother it in its own juices. But if you steam, roast,
or broil it, the juices will disappear. Try this, which may be prepared in an oven, in a
steamer, or on a grill.*

Two 1 ½-pound lobsters
¼ pound unsalted butter, cut into several pieces
4 cloves garlic, cut into slivers
½ cup chopped fresh cilantro
Handful of seaweed, optional
Salt and pepper, to taste
1 cup melted butter
Juice of 1 lemon

1. If using oven, preheat it to 375 degrees.
2. Stab the lobsters in the throat; this will kill them in the quickest and most
   efficient way.
3. With a nutcracker, crunch claws so they have openings large enough to
   stuff with butter, and make several incisions in the tails.
4. Insert butter slices and garlic slivers into these openings, sprinkle with
   salt, pepper, and cilantro, and drape with optional seaweed, which will
   give a taste of the sea. Wrap completely in aluminum foil.
5. Cook lobster for 20–25 minutes in oven, on outdoor grill, or in steamer.
6. Remove foil and serve with melted butter and lemon juice.

YIELD: 2 servings.

Higher Learning

~~~~~~~~~~~~~~~

ANDERSON DID THE TRICK. It was *filled* with misfits, mostly the misbehaving children of well-to-do parents. It also had its share of epileptics, the palate-clefted, and obsessive-compulsives. By comparison, I was school-president material. In fact, I became school president, an office for which no one who knew me would ever have considered me fit. It wasn't just that much of the student body seemed less able to function, though; the school's founder, V. V. Anderson, had been an industrial psychiatrist at Macy's and had some sense of how to keep order. The discipline was strict: Schedules were the same every day, we went everywhere in groups, no one was allowed to go to another building without a note (except to class). There was absolutely no unsupervised time. The rooms had no doors. The dances with the girls were strictly patrolled; there was no grinding or dirty dancing, absolutely positively no, you're-out-of-here-if-you-do, making out, no holding hands.

It gave me no latitude, exactly what was needed. I became a borderline goody-goody: got good grades, performed acceptably as an athlete, edited a yearbook, started a newspaper, acted in plays, held positions of responsibility. It cost three times as much as Lawrenceville, four times as much as Malcolm Gordon, and was year-round, with vacations between seasons. And it was worth every penny.

Unfortunately, it had no endowment, and when Dr. Anderson and then his son-in-law, the headmaster, died, no one picked up the torch. The school changed course considerably and currently takes only autistic students. Like

Malcolm Gordon, which has closed its doors, it was a singular place catering to a very narrow clientele in a very particular time in history.

A great pal of mine at Anderson was Ronnie Reuben, one of six grandchildren of Arnold, the feisty German immigrant who founded and maintained Reuben's restaurant. From the late teens till the sixties, when it closed, Reuben's was the show-biz-journalist-politico-occasional-mobster restaurant of choice. It was open twenty-four hours a day and was sort of a cross between Katz's Deli, Spice Market, and Nobu. When we were high school juniors, Ronnie introduced me to the most self-indulgent meal I had until I was thirty-three and ate at a German beer hall in Munich, after which I thought I was going to become an involuntary suicide bomber ahead of my time, spreading my own human shrapnel all over the Fatherland. And as you will see, on a Christmas day in the early sixties, Reuben's would be a personal lifesaver.

DURING MY LAST YEAR at Anderson, I thought I was in love with Pat Sutherland, the prettiest girl in school. I had lost—or, more accurately, flailingly flung away—my virginity two years before with a girl named Jo. Jo and I talked incessantly about *Other Voices, Other Rooms; Lolita;* and *On the Road* and decided that though fifteen, we were beats. We also discussed *Love Without Fear,* the paperback sex manual that encouraged use of the "ice-spurred special," the application of crushed ice to certain areas, and made out like mad on her parents' living-room floor in Basking Ridge, New Jersey.

My sexual initiation was not only inept, it was punitive. I had pictured a full afternoon's insatiable lust in my air-conditioned bedroom (Mother at work) followed by a titillating afterglow watching Brigitte Bardot in *And God Created Woman* at the Trans-Lux. I got the air-conditioning right but little else. Gropes, zero preparation, harsh strokes, completion, and depression—all in about ninety seconds. Complete failure! Not a hint of desire the rest of the day. And the spectacle of seeing the usually eroticizing Bardot turned out to be as tormented as De Niro squiring Cybill Shepherd to that porno movie in *Taxi Driver.* And—the punitive part—Jo told me a week later two pieces of news a young man never wants to hear: (a) "I think I'm pregnant," and (b) "I don't think you accomplished the task. I'm still a virgin." Neither, it turned out, was true.

The experience with Pat Sutherland was different. She had previously gone steady with a couple of the badder boys, and I had been with everyone I could talk into clandestinely holding hands. Pat was not only tough (in those days meaning gorgeous, as in the hit song "She's So Tough") but hot (in those days short for "hot to trot," not for gorgeous) and fast (same meaning it has today). She lived in Cuyahoga Falls, Ohio, and Mother allowed me out of her grasp for a few days during a vacation to visit her. Pat and I made incessant teenage love—in a haystack, in the front and back seats of her father's convertible, in her living room when no one was home. Anyplace, it seemed, that didn't have a bed. I finally learned to drive a convertible, and I was besotted with her.

When I visited colleges during my senior year at Anderson, I found that Denison University in Granville, Ohio, was the closest campus to Cuyahoga Falls. With my interesting record of NIBs and tutors and psychos, I wasn't exactly Ivy League material, and Pat wasn't going to college at all. I'd spent my young life in New York, where things can get pretty provincial, and Ohio seemed as far away as California and as exotic as Paris. Secondarily, I was sure I wanted to be an actor, and Denison had an excellent reputation as a theatre school. Hal Holbrook had graduated from there several years earlier. The campus was lovely and friendly. But the main reason I chose it was Pat.

But halfway through the summer, while I was working on a dairy farm in Vermont, she wrote that she was going to marry someone else. I wasn't the least crestfallen—I knew nothing would ever really come of our relationship besides the sex and some admiration that I had the best-looking girl in town on my arm. I went up to Pluto again, as I'd done at Lawrenceville and about thirty times since, and found it darkly hilarious: Here I'd chosen this school because of her, now didn't have her, and was going to the school anyway.

It turned out to be the best choice—or Godtrick—in the world. I wanted to be a fraternity boy, and I wanted to be in the theatre at the same time. Denison was segregated then: The artists (theatre folk, musicians, painters) were down the hill, and everyone else was up the hill. I was one of about one to straddle both worlds, and I loved it. I pledged ΣAE immediately; and because the theatre department had relatively few majors—no more than six the entire time I was there—but did so many plays every year, I was able to appear in about fifty by the time I graduated. This was roughly forty-seven more than my counterparts at Carnegie Tech, Northwestern, and Yale. I played nearly twenty leading roles—about nineteen more than my counterparts. Parts varied thrillingly from Leontes in *The Winter's Tale*, to the Father in Anouilh's *Eurydice*, to Ford in *The Merry Wives of Windsor*, to a Yiddish uncle in *49th Cousin*, Hialmar in *The Wild Duck*, Wilfred Shadbolt in *The Yeoman of the Guard*, a black chauffeur in whiteface in *You Can't Take It with You*. I was in bunches of musicals, and, in summer stock, popular Broadway shows. But whether *Antony and Cleopatra* or *Who Was That Lady I Saw You With?*, they were all approached with the same academic rigor—great introspection, suffering, scenery-chewing. When I understood a role and felt comfortable, I was transported; but far too often, I didn't get a grip on the character and was in torment.

My favorites were the Shaws. The second play I was ever in was George Bernard Shaw's *Too True to Be Good*—and miraculously, I was cast in the lead. This was a larger part than most Shakespearean roles, with language only slightly more modern and no less literate. *Back to Methuselah*, *You Never Can Tell*, *Pygmalion*, *Captain Brassbound's Conversion*: I loved swimming around in the language, wore it well, and attracted girls. What more could an actor ask from a playwright? The experience of being in a play is a much deeper one than simply reading it or seeing it performed. You live the literature, live the soul of the author.

Denison also had a summer theatre on its grounds—nine plays in ten weeks!—and I was in the company for two years, as well as two seasons of stock in Eagles Mere, Pennsylvania, run by Alvina Krause, the legendary acting teacher from Northwestern. If experience alone was the criterion, I was ready for the National Theatre of Great Britain.

I had some girlfriends at Denison, but way more rejections. I may have been scared of falling off a bicycle, but I was fairly fearless as a freshman calling juniors and seniors, who seemed amused by me. Over my college career, I put on forty pounds. I arranged for three illegal abortions in Cleveland, one of them mine, did mediocre work academically except for the theatre and English courses, wrote short stories for the literary magazine—the first about a man named Homer Glottis, who won an eating contest—and it felt so easy I didn't treat it seriously. It wasn't work. Acting was work—I was euphoric one day, depressed the next, like any college kid. There were just too many wild-and-woolly temptations at college to dive into.

Denison required a science, and as an alum of eight or nine years of serious psychoanalysis, I felt uniquely qualified to breeze through this requirement. But I had never met the behaviorists and their Skinner boxes, which proved to be a baffling—and to this day unilluminating—approach to the human mind. (The rat avoids electric shock! The chicken pecks for food when hungry!) It so unilluminated me that I failed the course twice, then finally got a D, necessitating an extra year in Granville. And a splendid year it was. Two semesters of six hours each, which included a course called Camping and Outdoor Life and creative writing. When I asked two of the psych profs if they'd ever had analysis or therapy of any kind, they looked at me as if I'd asked them if they'd ever been eaten by piranhas.

I paid no attention to food, though I ate plenty of it. My memories all fixate on midnight scrambies at the L&K Diner in nearby Newark. I was invited by my friend Rick Boyer to his house in Evanston, where he made something he called Eggs Sauternes—scrambled eggs, butter, and Sauternes wine. I thought to myself, "This is . . . unusual . . . this is . . . *good!*" The taste of it stayed with me.

Eggs Sauternes and, of course, the white apple.

About the only time I can remember not liking onions was a six-month period during and following my fraternity initiation at Denison, when the imaginative sadists at the Ohio Mu chapter of ΣAE put us pledges through what was grandiloquently called Hell Week. Denison was 90%+ Greek in that gentler era when you could still get into college without qualifying as an alcoholic (though you couldn't graduate without that honor). True, rumors abounded of a pledge somewhere in the South who had choked to death on a goldfish or a chunk of raw liver as part of his initiation, but, like the tales about that gearshift and Spanish fly, this was more urban legend than fact. Suffice it to say, the fraternities then were rather benevolent—every house on campus participated in a song contest, competed for grades, and played IMs (intramurals, not Instant Messages). I still find "The Sweetheart of ΣAE" a sweet and naïve and reverential song.

Which is not to say that Hell Week wasn't scary. It was. It actually lasted only a wimpy four days (and I understand that today's equivalent is Hell Day, and that tomorrow's will be Heck Afternoon) and was noted more for its cleverness than for corporal punishment. In addition to memorizing endlessly alliterative and scatological nicknames that were to be bellowed on command, sleeping on the unswept fraternity-house floor about three hours a night, the occasional paddling (we lived), and an inordinate number of practical jokes, we were instructed to wear a fat, raw onion—referred to as a "white apple"—on a string around our necks at all times, including to class, football practice, and ROTC (our neighbors, the Phi Delts, forced their pledges to wear burlap bags under their clothes). Whenever a brother decided we had done something wrong—like thinking for ourselves, or not doing two hundred push-ups in under ten seconds, or just staring into space bleary-eyed from lack of sleep—we were ordered to "take a chomp" of our white apple. Each of us munched through three or four of these monsters a day, which we discovered were not only extremely irritating to the gums but also lingered in our brains, perspirations, and general vapors for several weeks after we'd been activated.

I wasn't savvy enough to know then whether my white apples were Bermudas, Spanish, or big whites—but in retrospect I can tell you for sure that they weren't from Vidalia, Maui, or Walla Walla and weren't the Texas Supersweet variety known as 1015Y—all "sweet" onions with a higher sugar content and less sulfur than the "hot" ones. That's what gives them the sugary taste so enjoyable when chopped or sliced with a German Johnson tomato and a little ranch or Roquefort at Wolfgang's, the best steakhouse in New York (it has rib eye, Peter Luger's doesn't). It's a wonder any of us ΣAEs ever ate another white apple, and it must have been months before we had the nerve to grace our midnight burgers with an uncooked slice. But it's a good thing we persevered, because the absence of alliums—onions, leeks, scallions, shallots, garlic, chives, and their variations—would mean no more French, Italian, Indian, or Chinese food.

Vincent Scotto, formerly a partner at the estimable Scopa, now executive chef and, with his sister Donna, co-owner of Gonzo in New York, includes onions in almost every item on his menu except dessert and must be considered one of our town's leading *onioneurs*. "I love Vidalias raw, but it's a waste to cook them—if you cook a yellow very long and slow, you get the same result," he says. "Walla Wallas and other sweets are good, too, but the difference between all those sweet onions doesn't really blow my skirt up."

His onion salad is not only a modernist sculpture frequently worthy of MOMA's backyard; it constantly surprises the mouth as sweetness alternates with a slight burn. "I love all members of the lily family," he says, perspiring heavily as he works the Lilliputian kitchen at Gonzo, wearing shorts and clogs, frequently wiping down his fashionably hairless pate with a towel. "When I was at Scopa, I started making the salad with Vidalias, but since I couldn't get them all year round, I'd have to take them off the menu, and customers got mad. So I figured out that you can get the same sweetness with a yellow if you cook it long—forty minutes; don't be impatient—over low heat. And leave the skins on till they're done, so as not to lose extra layers."

Slow-cooked in this manner, the tops and bottoms caramelize, but when separated and nested with Parmesan, parsley, and croutons like a Russian doll, only the rims of each ring glisten with char.

VINCENT SCOTTO'S ONION SALAD

4 large yellow onions, unpeeled
10 tablespoons olive oil
Kosher salt to taste
2 slices Tuscan bread, ¾-inch thick
1 clove garlic, unpeeled, halved
¼ cup fresh parsley leaves
¼ cup shaved Parmesan cheese
3 tablespoons fresh lemon juice

1. Preheat a griddle over medium-low heat until hot. Cut off the ends of each onion so that you can see the rings. Cut the onions crosswise into ¾-inch to 1-inch slices, keeping the rings intact and the skins on as much as possible. Use 4 tablespoons of the oil to brush cut sides of the onions and sprinkle them with salt. Grill slices until tender and caramelized, about

20 minutes per side. If they burn, scrape off the charred portion. (A little tastes okay.) Let cool.

2. Meanwhile, grill the bread until toasted, rub on both sides with the cut sides of the garlic, and sprinkle with 2 tablespoons of the oil and some salt. Cut into crouton-size pieces.

3. When onions are cool, remove remaining skins and separate into rings— they will resemble small, bottomless bowls. Divide half among 4 plates, sprinkle with half the parsley, half the Parmesan, and half the croutons. Repeat with the remaining ingredients on top. Drizzle with the lemon juice and the remaining oil.

YIELD: 4 servings.

The Plates Shift

I WAS A JUNIOR in 1963 when JFK was killed. One immediate concern—as it was when Pearl Harbor was attacked and on 9/11—was whether this was a single incident or the first military maneuver in a strategy to bomb, attack, and invade. Because other aspects of the murder became so prominent, it may be hard to remember that we didn't know what was going to happen next; our world had fallen in.

Nikita Khrushchev was every bit as scary as Osama bin Laden and when he banged his shoe on a rostrum at the U.N. and declared with certainty he would bury us, he gave us all just as many nightmares as bin Laden has. Though Khrushchev was talking economics, it was generally interpreted that he meant he would bury us militarily as well, so Kennedy's assassination—in addition to being a personal loss, and an emotional shock that eventually initiated a decade of political activism unseen since the Civil War—was, at least at first, terrifying.

I went into a theatre-history class at Denison that Friday, having heard the president was wounded, and emerged after a surprisingly low-key lecture from the most challenging professor in the school, William Brasmer, to find Kennedy had died. (Brasmer was normally given to bombastic and iconoclastic acting instructions such as throwing a set of keys on the floor and saying, "Make love to them," or firing off a starter pistol so he could observe our reactions.) The difference between "wounded" and "dead" was staggering. An unfortunate incident with optimistic hope of recovery and reversal became the darkest finality. We all could sense this would change our sheltered, privileged lives. We didn't know how, and we didn't know what to do.

On Sunday, two days after the assassination, a bunch of us decided to act rather than wallow in the helpless passivity of a numbed college campus four hundred and fifty miles away from the nation's capital. Six of us scrunched into my 1958 twelfth-hand starter Cadillac and headed for D.C. I had the biggest car, probably because I inherited the Cadillac gene from Dad, who had several new ones, and Uncle Bus, who had a yellow Cadillac convertible. We would drive all night and arrive with little or no sleep in time for JFK's caisson and riderless horse with stirrups reversed to make its way up Pennsylvania Avenue.

We left at 9 P.M. in the dark and knew we had to be back for classes Tuesday.

Duane brought his book about theatrical lighting; Mary Kay, whom I was dating, brought a small makeup kit. She and I were acting together in *Hecuba*, the Greek tragedy by Euripides. She was Hecuba, I Polymestor, whom she blinds for killing all her children. Paul toted underwear, Donna sheet music (she was rehearsing a musical), and Bob brought nothing. I brought a tankful of gas, a couple of maps, and just enough money for more gas, which was then about thirty-two cents a gallon, threatening to go to thirty-three.

Despite the Cadillac's shabby grandeur, the fit was tight, three in back, three in front. The mood was somber, though there was an undercurrent of excitement and the knowledge that we were part of the national experience. We discussed where we might crash for a couple of hours. Donna had friends in D.C.

"How could this have happened?" Paul asked repeatedly. "I don't get it."

"Why did it happen? Who hated him so much?" I asked.

"The Russians," Mary Kay said. "The guy they caught was a Russian."

"They hate us that much?"

"Oh, yes."

" 'President Johnson,' " said Duane. "Sounds funny."

"That poor family," Donna said. "Those little children." She cried easily.

We remained respectful till we crossed into West Virginia, when we began a game of Botticelli. After two or three rounds, we stopped at a gas station where Donna could phone her D.C. friends. We tanked up, then ran next door, where a rival to McDonald's sold us bulging, divinely greasy cheeseburgers in paper bags, more bags of fries, and vanilla shakes. Someone had a fake I.D., so we bought two six-packs of Pabst.

Back on the road, emboldened by beer and comforted by food, we became less noble. Talk degenerated into remarks about other people in *Hecuba*, and their various drawbacks. *Schadenfreude* was a word in '63, and it got nasty. We were bitchy, just like real theatre folk, we thought. The name of the girl playing the second lead came up. "I've always thought she's, you know, depth-decrepit," said Mary Kay. I jumped on her for the use of the made-up word. "Well, you know," she said.

"How can I possibly play somebody blind?" I said. "I've never been blind. I've never really felt any serious pain," I said, forgetting my broken wrists and punctured cheek. Brasmer, the director, had shoved my hands under hot water, then cold, then hot again, to illustrate how pain screams at you, subsides, screams again. It was a brilliant acting lesson—no discussion, just action, and it made the experience visceral.

"Well, how am I supposed to act like all my children have been killed?"

"Mrs. Kennedy just had one of her children killed. Watch her," said Duane.

"I just don't want it to be phony, which I'll be unless I go off and blind myself." This got a laugh.

Brasmer was criticized. Euripides was criticized. How did you deal with the Chorus in Greek plays anyway? So unrealistic.

We crossed into Virginia, and Bob took the wheel. I held Mary Kay's thigh. Duane studied his lighting homework. Paul and Donna started singing, and everyone joined in. Duane fell asleep. We stopped again and got hot dogs. We got testy. We were cramped. We started laughing. We talked about the Kennedys. "What will this mean for Vaughn Meader?" Duane asked, referring to the successful comedian who impersonated JFK for a living. We all laughed and were then puzzled. Yes, what would this assassination do to the comedian?

We pulled into D.C. at about 5 A.M. and drove around for an hour, lost, in search of Donna's friends. We finally found them at daybreak. Donna's friend's parents welcomed us, urged a pile of buttery scrambies and bacon on us, and said we should sleep in the living room. We were all sure we wouldn't be able to fall asleep, then did in about thirty seconds.

We awoke at ten and headed for Pennsylvania Avenue. Thousands lined the streets. It was a cheerful crowd, though not boisterous. We stood for an hour waiting for the president's body. We talked to one another, and to many of the others standing there, and it was pleasant. We were all there for one purpose, and there was no anger. Suddenly I could see the caisson and the horse about a hundred yards away. The crowd turned silent. You couldn't hear a thing. Then, gradually, you could make out the scraping of the caisson wheels and the shoes of the riderless horse, and they became louder and louder, almost amplified. And then there was his casket in front of us, black and shiny and much larger than the man it contained, and it was unbearable. Silence except for the wheels and hooves. Suddenly a large Negro woman shouted out, "You did your job! Your time was short, but you did your job!" and now you could hear sniffles and sobs and clearing of throats all around. The reality was shocking, more shocking than the televised events, and the ride back to campus was relaxed and purifying.

It's important to go to the funerals of people who matter to you. Skipping them because they're unpleasant or watching them on TV if the person is famous doesn't let death scratch you, and it should. And when a funeral's over, the whole thing goes out to sea, and you can let go, if you've been there.

Of course, none of us let go of the repercussions that followed, or will ever forget the sense that even for a few days, the world had slipped out from under us, and we were without gravity and floating toward the moon.

Moonglow

~~~~~~~~~~

S HORTLY BEFORE THEY WERE married in the early sixties, Uncle Bus was rechristened by his second wife, Margaret, who said, "That's enough; that's a kid's name," and got us all to call him Frank.

Frank came to my rescue psychologically, socially, financially, and legally more than once. With Dad performing entrepreneurial calisthenics in Arkansas, Oklahoma, Nevada (by this time he'd bought the largest paper, the *Review-Journal*, and a TV station in Las Vegas), California, Alaska, and Hawaii, it was Frank, simultaneously masculine and effete, who introduced me not only to pheasant under glass and red wine, but to jazz and the proper perspective—all humor—toward *North by Northwest*.

In 1965, I motored across America with a college buddy named Weed. We drove a van with a motorcycle in the back, topping off our senior year at Denison with six weeks of adventures and mishaps from Cincinnati to Salt Lake, L.A., Tahoe, Las Vegas, and the Monterey County jail. One of us would ride the bike during the day (usually Weed, since I clung to my cowardice), and the other drive the van.

I've always liked big cars. They accommodate lots of people and in a pinch the backseat (or, more uncomfortably, the front) functions as a small motel room. Denison had strict rules for dormitory behavior then—no boys in girls' rooms and vice versa; girls in their rooms by eleven on weekdays and by one on weekends. This made physical intimacy quite a challenge, particularly in winter, which was the point.

In my first senior year, I stumbled across what I thought was the perfect solution: a hearse. Big enough in the back for a stretched-out body or two (by definition), cheap, since there were few customers for a used hearse, and certainly attention-getting. I bought one for $750, and when it failed a year later, bought another for $900. They were enormous successes, socially—twenty people to a party! Twenty people *were* a party—and amorously, as girls actually *asked* to see the backseat. But they were unreliable, so I bought a van, which had many of the same attributes. A big red van.

At night, Weed and I would sleep in the van (the second hearse had broken down on the Pennsylvania Turnpike the year before), and thus made the entire round trip for less than $500.

I admired Weed, now a lawyer practicing in Atlanta, not only for his wit and good company but also for his enviable height. He is six foot seven, which made him ineligible for the draft, the luckiest inheritance of genes aside from that of my friend John Schuck, whose allergy to eggs disqualified him.

After an eventful few weeks involving mostly junk food, a little gambling, my initiation into prostitution (on the customer side), something resembling a typhoon in Colorado, and a few days with Dad at Lake Tahoe, we headed to San Francisco, then south. We burgered briefly in Carmel, and the cashier let drop the news that Kim Novak's house was somewhere in the hills nearby.

There isn't much that jettisons me out of control—bullets headed in my direction might; a cardiologist's prescription for unlimited foie gras definitely would—but ever since I developed an un-rein-in-able crush on her at age thirteen, the name or conjuring of Kim Novak has made me delirious. It does even today, when she's in her seventies.

I saw *Picnic* thirteen times at age thirteen. It was a powerful, carnal story, in which a sexy drifter played by William Holden runs off with the sexiest girl in town, played by Kim, after the sexiest scene in all cinema, their dance to "Moonglow and the Theme from *Picnic*."

Kim came to New York to promote the movie, and I phoned *The New York Herald Tribune* to find out she was staying at the Sherry-Netherland (in those days, newspapers were happy to impart information like that; you could even phone the *Times* library at all hours of the day, and the staff librarians would look things up for you, gratis, like an industrial-age Google.com). I tried to woo Kim by sending flowers to her Sherry-Netherland suite three days in a row. This got me a telephone conversation with her that made my hands so sweaty I couldn't hold the phone. Her breathy vulnerability and husky thanks were more than my adolescent heart and knees could take. It also got me grounded for a week, since I'd charged the flowers to mother's account without telling her.

Now, even at twenty-three, being told she was less than twenty miles away in Big Sur, I knew I could never shave in a mirror again if I let this chance not only to meet her and impress her but also to . . . well, I don't exactly know what I wanted to do with or to her. This wasn't a case of lust, you see, and it wasn't simple infatuation. This was love, pure and selfless.

I should have known better. Actually, Weed *did* know better and argued strenuously that we should drop this pursuit—but it was my car. And so, around 9 or 10 P.M., we ventured past all the NO TRESPASSING signs into the Carmel Highlands, where, after an hour's drive, I found a mailbox that miraculously happened to have Kim Novak's *TV Guide* in it. I quickly flashed on what I imagined was a completely acceptable excuse for a stranger knocking on her door shortly before midnight: "Miss Novak, I've come to bring you your *TV Guide*."

She would be in lavender, her favorite color, look slightly wounded, as always, and part her lips, unbelievably grateful. She would invite me in. "Thank you so much—how kind, you young, strong man," she would say in that velvet voice, her platinumized hair shining. She would put on Sinatra or Mathis. (There was a rule left over from the fifties guaranteed to bring about successful seduction: Frank in the summer, Johnny in the winter, or the other way around, I forget which, but it was guaranteed. Even though I may not have wanted to seduce her, there was no harm in *her* seducing *me*.) She would offer pheasant under glass with the martinis, Weed would happily sleep in the van, and Kim and I would talk till dawn. I'd make her laugh huskily; she'd become even more vulnerable, until finally, just as the sun came up, she would invite me to stay for good. Weed could have the car and the motorcycle, free.

Encouraged by finding her mailbox, I insisted that Weed drive a few yards farther, where we came upon two stately houses. Did I really have the nerve to knock on Kim Novak's door? And which house did her door belong to? Until then, I had never acknowledged any obstacle to romance. The Miami Beach experience with Pam had taught me nothing. A year or two before this, I'd fallen for one of the summer-stock actresses who lived in Columbus and, mindless again of potential jail time, driven to her house with a friend, prized open a living-room window, and stolen two pictures of her from the piano. I still have them. I was, once again, thrust impulsively and ineluctably. Suddenly, just as I chose the house on the right, blaring headlights flooded the driveway and the air was filled with the barking of Dobermans. Weed wanted to either disappear or murder me, but I was unfazed. What higher justification could there be for trespassing than passion?

As it turned out, the driver of the car was an elderly woman, and the Dobermans toy poodles. "What are you doing here?" she demanded.

Assuming she would applaud the purity of my ardor, I said, "Looking for Kim Novak. I'm a friend of hers."

"If you're such a friend you'd know she's in Europe," the woman replied. "I'm calling the police." Weed and I were too well reared to yell anything back or run away, and besides, her car blocked ours from getting out. She disappeared into the house, and within minutes, the hands of some muscular representatives of the Monterey County sheriff's department were guiding our heads down into the backseat of their police car. It was the first time I'd seen car doors without inside handles.

Unamused by grand passion, the police took us to the Monterey County jail, where we were photographed and fingerprinted. Bail was set at $750 apiece—a hefty sum in those days. We were ordered impolitely into a cell with six or seven other overnight felons, all of us trying to sleep on one very hard floor. Concrete is unforgiving and retains heat only if there is any, which there wasn't. We spent a fitful and proto-pneumoniacal night. No blankets or pillows, no kind words, and no ways out.

Weed was livid at me, and it was hard to blame him. With a chilling lack of perspective, we were relatively unconcerned about our safety but were absolutely terrified about one thing: What were we going to tell our parents? He knew his would be furious, then hurt. I knew Dad would explode and say, "You got yourself into this—you get yourself out!" Mother would probably send the sheriff rent money to keep me there for another few weeks.

Morning came, and our shivering bodies were fed soupy, gruesome oatmeal and powdered eggs on a steel tray slid under the bars. I knew I was the ringleader and felt bad for my trespassing friend, whom I had virtually kidnapped. It was up to me to come up with a solution, so I did, though quite by accident. I called Uncle Frank, three thousand miles away in Boston. One of his stepdaughters answered and said that he and Margaret were on vacation, golfing.

"Where?"

"Pebble Beach," she replied.

Pebble Beach? Pebble Beach just happened to be twenty-five miles from the Monterey County jail! I had called the right person, all right—he *knew* he was supposed to be at Pebble Beach just in case I got arrested!

Within an hour he and Margaret showed up with two certified checks for $750. He looked at me, amused. "Did you get to see Kim?" he asked.

"No, she's in Europe."

"Well, next time, better intelligence." He was so cool!

He took us to lunch at the Del Monte Golf Course Pro Shop. It may be all we know how to make, but no one knows how to make club sandwiches like WASPs (heavy mayo, crisp bacon, heirloom tomatoes, not too much lettuce, *toast*), and this was the finest meal an ex-con ever had.

That evening, Frank and Margaret and Weed and I returned to the scene of the crime to plead with the victim, her toy poodles, and her lawyer to drop the charges. Frank wanted his bail back, and we wanted to avoid having F.B.I. records for the rest of our lives, not to mention more Monterey County porridge.

Weed and I kept our mouths shut. Frank and Margaret did all the talking. They were quite intimidating, not because they raised their voices or were threatening but because they radiated a sort of aristocratic decency. The woman and her lawyer would somehow be *blessed* if they were allowed to drop the charges, which they did. They even wanted to stay in touch with Frank and Margaret! They were as grateful as I had imagined Kim would have been had I been able to present her with her midnight *TV Guide*.

In our current era, in which argumentative lawyers enrage even those with the noblest intentions, it's hard to imagine another, when refinement could change someone's mind. But that night it did.

I would like to say that Frank fed us pheasant under glass that night, but by then it was pretty much out of date, as would soon be his blue blazer, rep tie, gray flannels, and long cigarette holder. He and Margaret left to continue their vacation with nary a word of criticism. They knew how foolish I felt, which was lesson enough, as I haven't seen the wrong side of a jail since.

Weed and I headed south to visit and covet San Simeon, which I imagined Dad might someday buy, then farther to find Los Angeles aflame in the Watts riots and a world on the brink of catarrh. We didn't go into Watts, of course, but from the freeway could see fire and smoke fill the sky, and the radio told us it was lunatics in fury. The surreal juxtaposition of our prankish, college-kid night in jail with the bloody chaos in L.A. wasn't lost on us, but so shielded from the realities of the times had we been during our idyllic college daze in Granville, Ohio, that in our myopia we could only ask, "Why are they burning down their own neighborhoods?" It took an eerie repetition of those events in south-central L.A. twenty-seven years later, provoked by the decision in the Rodney King trial, for me to get a handle on the enormous rage and frustration and why they were released: The rioters had nothing to lose, and to the participants, riots are one hell of a good time.

One time, many Christmases after our incarceration, my wife and sons and I visited Frank in Boston. He put us up at the Ritz-Carlton—the first and most luxurious one—and over breakfast he laughed about that night in jail. We then ordered a delectable creamed finnan haddie, which had been on the Ritz's menu since the thirties and which turned out to be a perfect foil for the winter outside, shared as it was with this man who took me on as his son.

MONTEREY COUNTY JAIL OATMEAL

Too much water
A lot of instant powdered oatmeal
As much sugar as the screws will let you have

1. Boil the water and stir in the oatmeal. Let steep.
2. Add sugar.
3. Eat with a steel spoon.

YIELD: 1 divided steel plateful.

THE BOSTON RITZ-CARLTON'S CREAMED FINNAN HADDIE

2 pounds finnan haddie (smoked haddock), skinned, boned, and cut into ½-inch dice
2 cups heavy cream
2 egg yolks
Cayenne pepper to taste
Your favorite hot buttered toast points (made from 6 slices of bread)

1. Cover the finnan haddie with water and simmer 6–8 minutes. Drain and keep warm.
2. Boil 1 ½ cups of the cream until reduced by half. In a bowl, beat the egg yolks with the remaining cream and whisk in the hot cream. Return the egg-yolk mixture to the saucepan and whisk constantly until hot but not boiling. Season with cayenne.
3. Divide the haddock over toast points, spoon sauce on top, and serve.

YIELD: 6 servings.

UNCLE BUS DIED in '83, after three or four more heart attacks. I asked him after his penultimate one if there was any pain. "No. My left arm hurt a little, then I woke up in the hospital." He was smiling. It was a great way to go—for him. And murder on the rest of us. I never got to tell him what he'd meant to me and what a shining example he was, and that in the competition between him and Dad for my soul, which neither of them knew anything about, he'd won.

Christians believe death is only the beginning of the good stuff—most religions do. Cheerful way to live. At his memorial service, they played the hymn

> *The strife is o'er,*
> *The ba-a-ttle done.*
> *The victory of life is won.*

The minister said something about his unconditional love. To me, this meant he'd have backed me if I'd spent one night in jail or five years, and I couldn't sing because of the burning in my throat and the tears that blinded me from seeing the words in the hymnal.

Be Like a Noble
Not a Knave
Caesar Uses
Burma-Shave

I LEARNED TO SHAVE from a magazine. *Esquire*, I think it was, or *GQ*, and I think I was in my twenties. Before I read that article, I had tried various techniques, found them all uncomfortable, and in my only attempt to shave upward from the Adam's apple to the earlobe drew droplets of blood at the root of every follicle.

The nonmetaphorical closest shave I ever had was at the hands of a hotel barber in London, who soaked my face in a hot, wet towel, then smoothed on various unguents and creams, stropped his straight razor, then minutely scalped every millimeter of my shaving area. My face felt smooth as a hockey rink after a Zamboni wash but subsequently so sensitive that I couldn't shave for several days. (My closest shave metaphorically was the midnight I fled Francis Ford Coppola's San Francisco mansion, inadvertently setting off the burglar alarm and dodging the police by seconds. But that's another story.)

I subsequently theorized that I had only one thing in common with Richard Nixon—translucent skin that made our beards look blacker than they would have if the skin were different. Nixon reportedly shaved twice a day when he had to make a public appearance, so I tried that a couple of times. My skin broke out in painful pink bumps, and I resolved never again to do anything that man did. So when the shaving recipe appeared, I was greatly relieved, and so was my face.

It wasn't that my father didn't have the knowledge to show me how to shave; he just wasn't around. By the time I was shaving, he was already into his thirtieth or fortieth million, and though you'd think he would be satisfied with that fortune and might have said to himself, "I think I'll feed the hungry in Sudan," or, "I think I'll go east and show my son how to shave," he wasn't and he didn't. Men like this (possibly women, don't know) aren't simply after wealth; they love playing the game. Not unlike Oprah or the Rolling Stones or Rafael Palmeiro, who, having made more money than any of them will ever possibly need, continue to play—and with increasingly record-breaking incomes. After the initial accomplishment—security—big money brings power, independence, a modicum of fame, and the ability to manipulate events. And it's fun! Dad could build an outdoor concert hall in Tulsa not only because it was deductible and good PR for his business in Tulsa but because of the prominence he achieved in town. So it's missing the point to say of a billionaire, "Why doesn't he quit working and do good? Doesn't he have enough money?" The answer is, "No, he doesn't."

He would also say that he *was* doing good. He was employing thousands of people, contributing to the tax base, delivering newspapers to families, wiring homes for cable TV, building concert halls in Tulsa, and benefiting charities.

To this day I don't know what fueled Dad's compulsion to leave such a footprint on the world. Perhaps he was driven by the need to surpass the lower-middle-class material accomplishments of his own father, about whom he felt contempt, embarrassment, and moderate affection. For the last fifty years of his life, Dad never needed to deprive himself of a single sensual experience or material object. But he went to his grave thinking he was deprived of them all.

THE PERFECT SHAVE

Hot water to taste
2 handfuls soap lather
2 squibs brushless shaving cream

1. Wash shaving area with hot water and 1 handful of the lather; leave lather on.
2. After 2 minutes, wash lather off with hot water, then rub in another handful of lather.
3. Massage in brushless shaving cream. Shave (downward if your face is sensitive).

"The Finest Restaurant in the World"

<hr>

DESPITE ALL THE experience I'd gained onstage at Denison and Eagles Mere, somewhere along the way I realized I didn't feel equipped to tackle Shakespeare or many of the British classics with the pros and that I wouldn't learn how to if I stayed in America. I remember cackling over Olivier's film of *Richard III* and being wowed by Albert Finney and Hugh Griffith and Edith Evans in *Tom Jones* and wondering, "How can I ever do *that*?" The times I enjoyed acting were getting fewer and farther between; I began to see actors as puppets, of secondary and tertiary importance to the play, after the author and the director. Miss Krause, the genius from Northwestern, continually stressed that as actors we were in service to the author, that he was the only creator in the process, and that everyone else was an interpreter.

Still, I'd trained all that time as an actor and lacked the imagination to pursue anything else. Much as I enjoyed the small, comfy community that was Granville, I knew there was a considerably bigger world out there. But at the moment, I had to do something to continue my education—there was a war going on in '65, and a draft, and I didn't want to take part in either. I had recently concluded that our involvement in Vietnam was unconscionable, thereby conveniently reinforcing self-interest with morality, not for the last time. I've always had wretched eyesight (glasses at ten, that first year at Trinity) and quickly found I was ineligible to become an officer—but not blind enough to avoid the service altogether. The most attractive option was to spend a year or two pursuing acting in London, and after I auditioned for

LAMDA—the London Academy of Music and Dramatic Art—in New York in the spring, they accepted me.

The idea of London sounded wildly romantic, far-off, and incredibly hip. It was the center of the universe then, thanks to the Beatles, Mary Quant, Richard Lester, and all those British movies made for a dime that were suddenly popular in America. And I thought I'd finally learn the secret of acting.

Mother wanted no part of this and refused to pay for it. Sometime during their marriage, she and Dad had set aside $75,000 to be split between Nancy and me when we became twenty-one. Nancy received her $37,500 at the appropriate age, but when I got there, Mother decided I was too irresponsible to manage it. The terms of the divorce dictated she pay for college—all of $900 per semester—and she liked the control over me it allowed her, as my summer-stock earnings amounted to about $400, total, over four years. However, the terms of the trust insisted that both parents had to agree to withhold the funds, and Dad delighted in not agreeing with her. I don't think he thought about my well-being for a second, only about thwarting her. She, in turn, enjoyed thwarting me—nice little triangle. So when Dad refused to agree, I received the trust, and Mother withheld—this time, in the fiduciary sense. I wound up paying for the last year of college, the shambles of serial Cadillac hearses, the midnight scrambled eggs, the beer. And LAMDA.

In another grandiloquent gesture, Dad gave me a first-class ticket on the S.S. *France* as a graduation present. This was the most spectacular ship on the water, and to be in first class was meant to be the experience of a lifetime—if you were eighty. At this point I didn't know whether he was continuing to open my eyes to the big world outside or competing with Mother—"What did *you* give him, Edith?"—or just showing off. But I was eager to see what would happen.

It was my first time on any kind of cruise, and the ship was indeed magnificent. Grand, stately public rooms, high ceilings, blue carpets, and ultra-*moderne* walls. Fire laws forbade using wood on the interior, so everything was decorated in aluminum, Formica, and plastic. I thought it magnificent. There seemed to be polished brass every three or four inches, officers and crew alike in snappy blue, gold, and white outfits. My cabin was small, but I soon learned all shipboard cabins are small by comparison to land.

Mother accompanied me to the departure and was quietly sarcastic. I didn't blame her when I figured it out some days later. She was confronted with a son she could no longer control, off on a mission of which she didn't approve, traveling on an extravagance she couldn't condone, presented by the man who had ruined her life and who was, at least symbolically, wooing her son away. She should have just put me in a cab.

I saw New York and its West Side piers disappear, and I immediately understood the term "all at sea." I was suddenly attached to nothing solid, literally and figuratively. I didn't know where I was going or, really, why. Didn't know a soul in London; didn't know a soul on board this behemoth.

The *France* was launched in 1960 and instantly became the rage of trans-atlanticers. DeGaulle desperately wanted to compete in the ocean-liner business as France once had with ships such as the *Liberté* and the *Normandie*, but had been outmatched by the *Queens Elizabeth* and *Mary* and the *United States*. He thought such a ship would build France's morale, in part compensating for the loss of its colony Algeria. And so this massive, white-atop-black structure, longer than three football fields, with two striking red smokestacks and a distinctive whale-back bow, was built in Saint-Nazaire and was the longest ship ever built until the *Queen Mary 2*. When it sailed into New York harbor on its maiden voyage, it was welcomed with a small armada of tug- and fireboats spewing waterfalls and helicopters and airplanes swooping and circling overhead in celebration. The *France* was enormously popular right from the start, attracting the famous and selling out on many of its cruises.

But it never made a dime. Despite its popularity, fuel costs necessitated constant subsidy from the French government, and demand for transatlantic crossings dampened with the advent of the jet. In 1974, when oil prices jumped almost sevenfold, the government decided it should subsidize the future, not the past, and sank its money into the Concorde.

On the *France*, by custom, the women in first class wore fancy dress and the men tuxedos to dinner except on the first and last nights out, when, presumably, butlers were unpacking or packing their shipboard wardrobes. We were assigned tables, and I was not only the youngest at mine, I was the youngest in first class. The main dining room was large, domed, and formal: beautiful flowers at every table, burnished hotel silver at every setting, linens so white you needed sunglasses and starched so crisp they might have inspired Kevlar.

What happened next redirected my life: I sat down to eat.

Out came baskets of breads and butters and rolls in many shapes and with different herbs, followed by caviar and vodka. I drank the vodka, and dipped the little spoon into the caviar. Not sure about that one. This was followed by a thick mushroom soup—I didn't know till then that I even liked mushrooms, since opening a can of Broiled in Butter was the limit of my experience. But I liked *these* mushrooms! A fillet of turbot or sole stuffed with what seemed like a white winey lobster mousse appeared, then disappeared down my gullet, followed by a beautiful fillet of beef encrusted with herbs, then a plate of fat, fresh asparagus on a napkin. (I knew just enough about food to say "yes" to the hollandaise.) I passed on the salad and the cheese—I'd have to learn about them later. Several desserts were presented, and through either thrift or curiosity (certainly not hunger), I asked for two. One was the richest chocolate éclair I'd ever seen, bulging with crème Chantilly front and back like a parade inflatable; the other was a Nesselrode pudding with chestnuts. I finished everything. The whole experience took two and a half hours, longer than any meal I'd ever eaten. I took a breath. I smoked then, and could barely smoke. I certainly couldn't move. This was the loveliest way of spending an evening since the night outside the Denison field house with Diane X in the back of the hearse.

The people at the table were impressed at the quantity I'd put away. I wasn't; I was impressed by the quality. I'd never tasted food like this, never even seen pictures of this, never knew it existed. The only hint I'd had were those Eggs Sauternes back at Rick Boyer's house in Evanston.

Craig Claiborne considered the *France* the finest restaurant in the world. It may have been then; it wouldn't be now because of the sheer weight of the food and plethora of sauces. The kitchen reportedly took on 15 tons of meat, 30 tons of vegetables, 70,000 eggs, and 330 pounds of caviar for every round trip. Some 18,000 bottles of nonvintage and 4,500 of vintage wine were consumed along with 25,000 rolls and breads. There was one waiter for every six passengers, and the kitchen never made the same dish twice on a voyage unless specifically requested. You could order anything from your room at any time of day, from a *langoustes à la parisienne* to the chef's version of corned-beef hash—included in the price of the ticket. And the visual displays! Operatically elaborate ducks coated in sauces and surrounded by tiny chestnuts and salsify in a pool of the same sauce, like something from a topiarist on opium, glistening *oeufs en gelée* crisscrossed with perfect *fleurs-de-lis* of truffles from Dumas, sculptures of fish encased in shiny pastries. Each scale and gill and eyeball carved into the shell. It was my first total sensory immersion since the photographs of the pornographic novel at Lawrenceville.

The next day at breakfast, which most of the guests skipped, another astonishing array was presented. I didn't know you were allowed to eat broiled fish or smoked salmon or *omelettes aux fines herbes* or grilled pork loins with Bordelaise sauce . . . for *breakfast!* Worried I might not taste them all, I ordered them all, requesting American cheese in the omelette and could I please have some hollandaise on it? (A table companion emboldened me to try *béarnaise* by the third day out; didn't need much encouragement.) The waiter was unabashed; if I'd asked, I think he would have brought Eukanuba *périgueux* (truffles) without blinking. When the omelette arrived, I realized my assignment on this trip: It wasn't shuffleboard or gambling or drinking and dancing or trying to pick up girls or reading books or swimming in the two indoor pools on deck; it wasn't even about getting to London. It was to eat every piece of food on that boat, and I had only five days to do it!

I followed breakfast with an overpowering lunch, then a return bout, tuxedoed this time, for dinner.

I remember clearly that I ate every meal. I probably put on five pounds, or possibly twelve, which, after all the sloth at Denison, I didn't need. But this was such a novel experience. I grew to like caviar, the soft and blander cheeses (smelly would come later), and the wine. I didn't yet have the nerve to embrace the raw oyster (that came a few years later, in New Orleans), but I don't remember turning anything else away. I *must* have turned away some fish; no kid of twenty-three likes every kind of fish, but I don't remember. I knew I wanted food to be a major part of my life, and never again would I suffer a meal not acutely aware of what was on the plate. It didn't have to be *haute*, but it had to be deliberate.

I also knew I didn't want to be an actor.

There wasn't much to do on the ship between meals; in fact, I was beginning to wonder if there was anything in life *worth* doing between meals. Everyone was older. I tried going downstairs into second class and introducing myself around, but as I was to find out later in the bar scene of the seventies, that wasn't much fun and I wasn't very good at it.

The ship showed two movies a day, so I watched them. In the course of those screenings, I realized I wanted to make them, not be in them. I'd gone to movies and plays since early childhood, and often cut classes at that tutoring school to see a daytime double feature. I saw everything, knew every name filling every job. I was particularly interested in movies about teenagers because they showed me how I was supposed to be behaving—not just James Dean, but goody-goody Pat Boone (well, at least you could understand the words), demented Sal Mineo, and troubled, intense John Cassavetes. Without probing much, I concluded movies and plays were about actors; so I wanted to be an actor. My cousin Lee was rapidly becoming a star, and I loved the glamour of her life. When I'd taken acting lessons at the Cassavetes school in dark rehearsal rooms on West Forty-sixth Street, that, too, had been glamorous: We boys and men were all fashionably depressed, like Brando and Dean; the girls and women were all beautiful and sulky, like Natalie Wood, Joan Collins, and of course Kim Novak. Being an actor gave me an identity at Denison, and occasionally, it was enjoyable. Now I realized it simply wasn't a good fit.

My aunt Maymie had told me many years before that I would be a writer, and anyone who knew me felt the same way—I should be writing plays or movies or books or letters, they said. Something. And certainly my experience with the post office at Malcolm Gordon and Lawrenceville pointed in that direction. Maybe on the basis of the S.S. *France*, recipes. But it's always taken me forever to turn conclusion into action—profession, marriage, divorce, where to live. I assume that on my morphine drip, I'll discover I was always meant to be a cabinetmaker and live in Delaware.

When the *France* docked in Southampton, all I knew was that I had to find a place to live in a city I knew nothing about and get out of a school that was my reason for coming to that city but to which I no longer wanted to go. Not unlike the situation where my undying love for Pat Sutherland inadvertently ushered me into Denison, I was in swinging London, but for the wrong reasons.

I found the London School of Film Technique, and the principal was eager to have my American dollars spent there; but the LAMDA principal said with some impatience that I had been chosen as one of only eleven Americans, and that I had guaranteed them £2,400 that year. I would have to pay it whether I attended the school or not. Though marginally better off than other students because I could afford to live by myself, I couldn't risk all that money on my newfound professional goal—what if it turned out to be a lark, too?

TOURNEDOS ROSSINI AS SERVED ON THE S.S. *FRANCE*
(Filet Mignon with Foie Gras, Truffles, and Madeira)

(Adapted from Classic French Cooking *by Craig Claiborne, Pierre Franey, and the editors of Time-Life Books, Little, Brown, 1970) You may cut corners, but don't blame me if the ghosts of Claiborne, Franey, and the master chef of the S.S.* France, *Henri Le Huédé, haunt your dreams.*

¾ cup dry Madeira

2 tablespoons juice from a can or jar of truffles

1 cup *Fond Lié* (see page 79)

6–10 tablespoons clarified butter

4 slices homemade white bread, ¼ inch thick, cut into 2 ½-inch-diameter rounds

Four 6-ounce *tournedos*, about 1 ½ inches thick

Salt and pepper, to taste

4 round slices *foie gras en bloc*, 2 inches in diameter, room temperature

4 round slices black truffle, 1 inch in diameter, ¼ inch thick

2 tablespoons butter, chilled and cut into ½-inch bits

1. Reduce ½ cup of the Madeira and the truffle juice to ¼ cup in a small saucepan. Add *Fond Lié* and set aside.
2. In a heavy saucepan, warm 3 tablespoons of the clarified butter, then brown bread rounds until crisp. Drain on paper towels and set aside on a warm platter.

3. Add 3 more tablespoons of the clarified butter, raise the heat, and after drying the *tournedos* with a paper towel, sauté them in the butter 3 minutes on each side, until rare. Season with salt and pepper.

4. Place a *tournedo* on each crouton, top with round of foie gras, then a truffle slice.

5. Working quickly, pour off the fat from the skillet and add remaining ¼ cup Madeira. Deglaze and stir in the *Fond Lié* mixture. Stir and heat the mixture through.

6. Strain the sauce through a fine sieve into a small saucepan, swirl in the butter bits, pour over the *tournedos,* and serve at once.

YIELD: 4 servings

That was simple enough. Now for the heavy lifting:

Fond Lié
1 quart *Fond Brun de Veau* (see page 80)
½ cup chopped mushrooms
3 sprigs fresh parsley
5 tablespoons arrowroot
⅓ cup cold water
¼ teaspoon Caramel Food Coloring (see page 81)

---

1. In a 2-quart saucepan, bring *Fond Brun de Veau*, mushrooms, and parsley to a simmer over moderate heat. Reduce heat and cook uncovered for about 15 minutes.

2. Dissolve arrowroot in water in a bowl, then whisk mixture into stock. Add Caramel Food Coloring, a few drops at a time, until the stock is a rich brown color.

3. Simmer the sauce until it thickens somewhat, about 15 minutes.

YIELD: 1 quart, which may be refrigerated for a week or frozen for three months.

Fond Brun de Veau

5 pounds meaty veal shanks sawed into 2-inch lengths

2 pounds meaty veal shinbones, sawed into 2-inch lengths

1 pound veal marrowbones

2 pounds chicken parts: necks, wings, backs

2 tablespoons clarified butter

2 medium onions, peeled and quartered

2 medium carrots, scraped and cut into 1-inch rounds

5–6 quarts cold water

2 medium celery stalks, including leaves, cut into 1-inch lengths

2 medium leeks, washed and quartered lengthwise (white parts and two
   inches of green only)

10 sprigs of parsley

2 fresh thyme sprigs, or ½ teaspoon dried thyme

1 large bay leaf

1 large unpeeled garlic clove, smashed

1 teaspoon salt

½ teaspoon whole black peppercorns

2 medium tomatoes, quartered

½ cup canned tomato purée (unflavored)

----

1. In a heavy 12-inch skillet, in batches, brown the shanks, shins, marrow,
   and chicken parts in clarified butter, turning frequently with tongs. Don't
   let them burn! Transfer to a 12-quart stockpot.

2. Brown onions and carrots in skillet, stirring, and add to stockpot. Pour 1
   quart of water into skillet, boil, and deglaze. Add to stockpot with remaining 4–5 quarts of water (as much as you need to cover the bones).

3. Bring to a simmer slowly, skimming off foam and discarding it and scum.
   Don't let it boil, or stock will become cloudy. Add remaining vegetables
   and herbs, garlic, salt, and pepper.

4. Simmer stock for 7 hours.

5. Pick out meat and bones and vegetables and discard. Strain into a large
   bowl and let cool to room temperature. Refrigerate for up to 4 days, or

freeze for months. Before using, remove layer of fat that has accumulated
at the top.

YIELD: about 2 quarts.

Thought you were done? Hey, this was the *France*!

Caramel Food Coloring
1 medium onion, peeled and cut into ¼-inch slices
1 cup water
1 ½ cups sugar

1. In a heavy saucepan over moderate heat, stir onions *without fat* until they're
   almost mahogany-black. Add ½ cup of the water and the sugar and cook
   until mixture foams up and rises in the pan. Stir in the remaining water
   and don't be alarmed if the caramel hardens at this point.
2. Still stirring, continue to cook until hardened caramel melts and syrup is
   smooth. Strain through a fine sieve into a heatproof jar. Cover with a lid.
3. Use to color food. It will keep almost indefinitely.

YIELD: 1 ½ cups.

Rules of the Game

~~~~~~~~

S O A MONTH AFTER my night in jail, I began LAMDA classes. I wasn't the star I'd been at Denison—nobody was the star they'd been at college—and the atmosphere was competitive. We had classes in movement, breathing, dance, speech, and history, and we rehearsed scenes from Shakespeare, Molière, and Chekhov. I shivered through the fall in a studio flat near the (then) very down-market Notting Hill Gate and had to put pennies into a hallway meter several times in the course of a bath to keep the hot water four inches high in the tub. (Don't picture this.) I got on better with the English, for whom this was college, not grad school, and who were less combative than us Americans. I remember that a favorite riff with a British schoolmate named Roger Dunwell was our imitating Peter O'Toole's T. E. Lawrence after he'd trekked across the desert for days with an Arab lad and demanded of an astonished officers-only club, "We want . . . two . . . glahsses . . . of . . . le . . . mon . . . ade," and threatened to implode (as usual).

But most of all, there was the city itself, exploding with life and protest. Olivier, Gielgud, Finney, Richardson, Robert Stephens, Maggie Smith, Joyce Redmond, the Redgrave sisters—all were at the National Theatre in rep, night after night; Ian Holm, Glenda Jackson, and Janet Suzman were at the Royal Shakespeare Company. Noël Coward was live in the West End and Alec Guinness and Simone Signoret were in a dreadful but riveting *Macbeth* (performed in sweat suits) at the Royal Court. There were new plays by Pinter and Osborne, Peter Brook staged *The Persecution and Assassination of Jean-Paul Marat as Performed by the Inmates of the Asylum of Charenton Under the Direction of the*

Marquis de Sade, and nobody had ever seen anything like it. The RSC also mounted something called *US*, a shocking protest against America's involvement in Vietnam. It was all unbelievable! Everybody but Will Kemp and Aeschylus were in town and onstage. I think I spent about one night a month *not* in a theatre or cinema. You could *despise* the theatre and still see that it was making the earth shake in London. And there was always a race to the pubs afterward because they closed at eleven.

But, boy, was the food bad. On a student's budget, meals outside of beer consisted of sausages filled with highly questionable grains, soggy-crusted pub grub served at room temp, thin and runny custards poured over sweet "puddings," and something called a Wimpy, which was, if you can believe it, a really bad version of a McDonald's burger. After three months of this, for a reason I now forget, I ventured solo into Simpson's-in-the-Strand, a clubby British beef parlor with paneled walls, waiters in tails, and a serious air of condescension. I'm fairly sure I had the thinly sliced, red-juiced beef from the silver-domed carving trolley, brussels sprouts in cream, and something at the finish that was sticky with either golden syrup or treacle. At last, something one could eat in Britain—but not exactly the S.S. *France*.

What I remember most was watching a jolly fellow with a thickly veined nose and cheeks, ruddied from years of alcohol, dig two silver spoons into a ceramic tub of Stilton, which he then chased with a glass of port. He seemed sent for my delight from the casting department over at Ealing Studios, a Falstaffian Churchillian deliriously happy in his own, mostly unintelligible fog. After he left even jollier than when he arrived, I ordered the tub of cheese and a chaser of port—and found my own version of O'Toole's lemonade in this culinary desert: Stilton and port remains one of the great marriages in gastronomy.

None of us could afford that more than once or twice a year then—we were all 'umble hactors. LAMDA had eighty or so students, with our "advanced" class of twelve, who weren't English—eleven Americans and an Indian. I didn't think we were particularly advanced, just older, and had been to college. The English had grown up with Shakespeare in their bones and sausages, and we were doing our best to imitate them. They were amused by us Americans but had no respect for our playwrights; their reverence for

O'Neill, Miller, Williams, Mamet, and Neil Simon came much later. They did generally admire Brando and Robert Mitchum and Bette Davis, though.

The birds at LAMDA were elusive—Americans neurotic, English distant—and it was several months before I met Anna. She was on the rebound from Matthew Guinness, Sir Alec's son, and I was on the rebound from the world. The match only lasted a few months and was fairly fraught with minor disagreements—who got the extra pillow, and who paid for the bad sandwiches. I was nervous spending whole nights with girls. Not sure what to do. And all the beds were narrow. We visited Stonehenge and Salisbury and a dozen little inns (Six pounds a night! With breakfast!) and villages in a stickshift, right-hand-drive Morris Minor I'd bought for twenty-five pounds. We ate frugally, talked about the theatre, and were clumsy lovers. The relationship ran out of fizz rather than exploding, though we remained friends. When I saw her twenty-five years later at a memorial for one of the students, she was just as lovely as she had been at age twenty.

But we did spend a week in Paris, and its reputation as the most romantic of cities asserted itself in contradictory ways on my first visit there, because Dad hit on her.

I didn't really blame him. Anna was blond and very bird-of-the-period, wonderfully well spoken, being British and an actress (sort of a Brit squared), and as brilliantly intimidating as women with English accents continue to be to American men. And Dad was bored.

She and I were on a spring break from LAMDA. We found floor space in someone's cluttered apartment near the Bois de Boulogne. We tussled with the metro, braved the open-air elevator on the Eiffel Tower, clinging to each other in terror (never again), and took pleasure in discovering the very thin slice of ham inside the thick, buttered baguette from the corner brasserie, which exemplified for me the difference between French and American sensibilities: at home, the sandwich would have been reversed—pounds of meat and mayo, overstuffed between sweet, spongy slices of Wonder bread.

After two days, Dad phoned. I don't remember how he found me—or why, since in the twenty-four years following my birth I hadn't seen him for more than a total of fifteen days. Perhaps he wanted to see if my experience on the S.S. *France* had improved me. He was impressed that I was going to school in London, though I don't think he focused much on the kind of school it was.

When I saw him in Paris, the movie *Goldfinger* was a recent rage, and between visiting a handful of newsprint suppliers to satisfy the IRS, he spent a few days in London picking up an Aston Martin. Never mind that, short, fat, middle-aged, and 94% bald, he looked more like Khrushchev than James Bond, Dad wanted that Aston Martin. He was driving it around Europe accumulating the 1,500 miles or so required to beat the import duty back into the States, even though tooling and hoteling around Europe was way more expensive than just paying the tariff. But since the tooling and hoteling was also deductible (in pursuit of business), the case could be made that the government was actually paying for him to buy the Aston Martin. Dad loved America, and nothing gave him more pleasure than working it for all its worth.

His lifelong M.O. was to interweave pleasure so thoroughly with business that the government couldn't distinguish between the two, and he deducted just about everything he did. He wasn't the first person to come up with this scheme, but possibly he was the boldest and certainly the most thorough, and conceivably could have been the reason for the alternative minimum tax. He bought houses concealed as offices, Mercedes that somehow became company cars, first-class plane tickets (and eventually first-class planes) and cruises to Hawaii that were "essential" for doing business. (Well, he *did* have newspapers and a shopping center in Hawaii, and he *did* talk business aboard those ocean liners.) For years he claimed the small house he bought on the G.I. Bill in Las Vegas was his legal residence so that the mansion he built across town would be considered an office.

He was a flamboyantly excessive devourer of failing newspapers, radio and T.V. stations, highway billboards, real estate, food, booze, women, the air we breathe—and the latest, trendiest possession.

"Where'd you like to have dinner?" he growled into the phone. Since I had seen not only *Goldfinger* but the movie *Gigi*, I suggested Maxim's, the wildly expensive museum of *haute cuisine* featured in the film. Because I didn't know he was always happy to be generous when it was his call, I expected him to counter with a neighborhood café featuring hard-boiled eggs and unlabeled wine on the table. He quickly turned me around: "Fine—see you at nine."

Anna and I got as gussied up as grad students could and swanned into Maxim's and *la belle époque*. It was like dining in an opera, surrounded as we were by dozens of Colettes and Chevaliers, and over there in the corner a couple of Leslie Carons. I remember ordering *duck á l'orange* because it was the only thing I'd heard of except for *crêpes Suzette*, which I also ordered, not realizing both were laced with o.j. Dad had something with beef in it, Anna a lobster thermidor with a sauce so viscous that two George Foremans couldn't have finished it. It reminded me of the *France*. There was sauce on everything, all inspissated with butters, flours, crème fraîches. To me, it was all the *haute*st of *haute*, and delicious—though also somewhat oppressive. *Nouvelle cuisine* and its nasty little cousin *minceur* were a decade away. Dad was charming and funny, filled with war stories from his rambunctious life. He cheerfully announced that Scottish beef—not French—was the finest in the world, just to see the waiters blanch and make Anna laugh. She was pretty laughing.

The summer before, prior to my night in jail, I'd visited him for a week at his thirteen-acre lakefront property on the Nevada side of Lake Tahoe. He had two king-size beds right next to each other in his bedroom. It looked like a football field of mattresses. I couldn't figure out whether that was to fit more women in there with him or so he could sleep farther away from the one who was there. The guest quarters were considerably more spartan—he clearly didn't want to encourage anyone to stay for more than a few days. In keeping with his tax concerns, he'd built a dormitory filled with bunk beds and one bathroom, so that twice a year his executives would traipse up the mountain, climb into the bunk beds like little boys, and pee in a communal bathroom, and he could call it a business expense. It was also a none-too-subtle way of showing them the enormous gulf between employer and employee. I'd been thrilled and amazed to be with someone who seemed to have a complete handle on the way the world worked.

At one of the Tahoe dinners, he'd regaled his girlfriend *du jour*, a six-foot strawberry blonde named Jayne, my soon-to-be fellow convict Weed, and me with the story of his strike-breaking days in Las Vegas, and now he reembellished it for Anna at Maxim's. Anna was a socialist and both amused by the audacity of Dad's business manipulations and aghast at his selfishness.

"What are your labor contracts like?" she said.

"What labor contracts? Don't have any. Don't have any unions," Dad said proudly.

"However did you manage that?"

"A few years ago in Las Vegas my deliverers went out on strike. So I took one of the trucks out myself, delivered the newspapers all over town. When I got back, one of the strikers threw himself down in the driveway of the plant."

"Goodness, what did you do?"

"I drove right over him."

Anna inhaled sharply.

"Broke his back," he said cheerfully. He paused to let the shock register, then added, "But I broke the strike, too!" He grinned so hard his clenched teeth were almost crying.

Anna was speechless, and Dad loved it. He told the story with such joy, not cruelty, that if you hadn't heard the content, you'd swear he'd just related a story about curing a major disease or climbing a serious mountain.

I was completely enthralled. His action was bold and swashbuckling and in defense of everything he held most dear: his business, his art. He had made a pre-emptive strike—and a successful one—against thugs attempting to rape his family, destroy his religion, overthrow his country. It didn't occur to me then to empathize with the striker: He and his fellow thugs had tried to violate the religious sanctity of Dad's essence; they hadn't created this company, hadn't taken risks to preserve it, hadn't stayed up days on end to make it grow, hadn't *created* a single thing—*he* had. And now they felt entitled to a piece—an enormous piece—of his work of art. I felt nearly as triumphalist as he did: Those jobs wouldn't exist if it hadn't been for him, and now they were going to cripple him? Not without a fight! It felt like narration from a novel that I could comprehend but not grasp. I couldn't sympathize with the striker's broken back because I'd never experienced drama and violence like that.

And he was my father.

Over the years, Dad told the story repeatedly, and it was never clear how much of it—if any—was true. The threat of his rage made him too frightening to challenge with questions about its authenticity. But I'm sure the kernel was accurate. As far as I know, he broke every strike thrown at him till he ran into the unions of Hawaii; and if he didn't run over that picketer's back, surely the strikers thought he could and would.

"Only have to do something like that once, dear," he told Anna. "Word gets around."

"But . . . but . . . didn't the police arrest you or something?" she said.

"Why should they? It's my driveway. You don't expect somebody to be lying down in your own driveway, do you?" He glowed and glowed. He had defeated the Hun, the Japs, the slants, the towelheads. I envied him his joy—such was my moral compass at the time. Anna was taken aback as much by his shamelessness as by the deed itself.

When the dust settled, I tried to talk to him about my graduate program, but it bored him. "Graduate school's just another word for welfare!" he thundered. "Besides, didn't Jimmy Stewart just walk on the lot?"

I told him how much I'd like to have a house like his at Tahoe someday.

"Sure, son, everybody'd like to take a pill and be rich."

"Well, you've certainly been lucky."

That got him particularly peeved. "Lucky? Hell, my life didn't just *happen!*" he snapped.

All that o.j. kicked in, and I headed for the loo. When I returned a few minutes later, Anna had a startled look on her face. Dad must have told her about the nights he'd spent with Nat King Cole and General Eisenhower at the Dorchester during the blitz, or how he'd wound up as one of Nat King Cole's pallbearers, which may have been true.

He wanted to go, so we went outside and looked up at the Paris sky. It was a beautiful moonlit night. Suddenly a shooting star went by and, without missing a beat, he pointed to the star and wished on it. "Moneymoneymoney-moneymoneymoney!" he said exuberantly. Then he went off to the Elysée Palace, or wherever he was staying.

On the long, raggedy metro ride back to the Bois de Boulogne, I found out why Anna had looked so stunned.

"Your father asked me to go back to Las Vegas with him," she said.

"What?" I didn't know whether to be shocked or angered or flattered. After all, I finally had something he approved of so strongly that he wanted it for himself. My girlfriend! "What did you say?"

"I said, 'No, Mr. Reynolds, I don't think that would be proper. I'm in love with your son.' That stopped him, and he behaved like a perfect gentleman. 'Of course, dear, of course,' he said, and asked me about my parents and the war."

It stopped me, too, because Anna also hadn't told *me* she was in love with me. I wondered if she meant it or if she'd said it just to counter Dad's proposition. In any case, Paris had suddenly become surprisingly romantic for all three of us.

"Are all you Yanks like that?" she asked, amused.

"Yes! Come back to Las Vegas with me!" I said. She laughed, and we climbed the steps to our high-rise. Two or three months later we broke up—we couldn't seriously penetrate each other's self-protection—and I heard many years later that she had been married once or twice.

On my most recent visit to Paris a couple of years ago, I found no *duck á l'orange* on any menus. Instead, I found a delectable—and, needless to say, lighter—*pissaladière*, a thin pastry lightly brushed with crème fraîche, caraway, and shredded duck at the heavily luxe Plaza Athénée, where Alain Ducasse recently set up shop. I went with Red, whose birth-certificate name is Heidi Ettinger and whom I'd been seeing for a few months, and there was much laughter, which I'm sure will become a memory for future visits. But not like the first.

I don't plan to take my sons to Maxim's anytime soon, with or without their girlfriends, just in case this sort of thing is genetic. On the other hand, maybe I will, because in some areas, at least, I behave a lot better than my father did.

But every time I've been in Paris, and at just about every meal, the image of my old man making a pass at my girlfriend refreshes itself in my memory. And despite his ruthlessness and lechery, I picture him adventurous, optimistic, unbridled, squoze behind the wheel of what was at the time the hottest (and possibly smallest) car in the world, grinning madly, mindless of his appearance and what rules he broke, zipping around Europe courtesy of the IRS.

Could he do this and still not get a crown?
Tuuuuuut, were it further off, he'd pluck it down!

PISSALADIÈRE AU CONFIT DE CANARD

You may make this dish, adapted from Le Relais Plaza at the Plaza Athénée, with pre-pared duck confit and any thinly rolled pizza dough. Dad would have loved it—as long as someone else put it together for him. You may make your own crème fraîche by mix-ing 2 tablespoons of buttermilk with 2 cups of heavy cream and letting it stand until thickened—a few hours or overnight, usually. Fromage blanc is very much like sour cream, and yogurt makes an excellent substitute.

For the confit
4 whole duck legs
½ cup kosher salt
1½ teaspoons whole peppercorns
3 garlic cloves, peeled and crushed
3 sprigs fresh thyme
1½–2 cups duck fat

For the short-crust pastry
2 cups all-purpose flour
½ teaspoon salt
2 sticks unsalted butter, cut into ½-inch cubes
1 large egg
3–5 tablespoons cold water

For the toppings
8 ounces fromage blanc
½ cup crème fraîche
¼ teaspoon freshly grated nutmeg
¼ teaspoon kosher salt
¼ teaspoon freshly ground black pepper
2 Vidalia or other sweet onions, peeled and sliced into paper-thin rings

1 teaspoon caraway seeds
18 walnut halves

---

1. *To make the confit:* Seal the duck, salt, peppercorns, garlic, and thyme in a zip-top plastic bag. Refrigerate for 12 hours. Preheat the oven to 200 degrees. Remove and reserve the peppercorns, garlic, and thyme. Rinse the salt off the duck. Place the reserved seasonings and the duck in a deep casserole so that the legs fit together nicely. Cover with duck fat. Bake until a skewer inserted in the leg slides in and out easily, about 3 hours. Cool the casserole on a rack to room temperature. Refrigerate until needed, up to 1 week.

2. *To make the pastry:* In a large bowl, combine the flour and salt and mix well. Add the butter and cut in with a pastry blender or your fingers until crumbly. In a small bowl, beat the egg with 3 tablespoons of the water and sprinkle over the flour mixture. Toss with a fork until moistened. Drizzle in remaining water, 1 tablespoon at a time, if needed, until the mixture holds together. Divide the dough into 6 equal portions and shape each into a disk. Wrap in plastic and refrigerate for at least 2 hours.

3. *To make the* pissaladière: Preheat a pizza stone in a 500-degree oven. Drain the fromage blanc in a cheesecloth-lined sieve for at least 2 hours, squeezing out the liquid; place in a bowl with the crème fraîche, nutmeg, salt, and pepper and mix well. Remove the duck from the fat and pull the meat into thin shreds. On a floured surface, roll each disk of pastry into a thin round and trim the edges, using a plate as a guide. Spread with the cheese mixture, dividing it evenly. Top with the onions, caraway seeds, and duck, dividing them evenly. Crumble 3 walnut halves over each round and bake 3 at a time until crisp on the bottom, 3–5 minutes.

YIELD: 6 servings.

I remember trying to figure out then, and I often wonder now, What exactly is British food? Roast beef? The famously inedible Bovril and Marmite? Oh, I know: that comfort food with preschool names like bubble and squeak, toad-in-the-hole, and spotted dick. Well, every country has roast beef, and the other caricatures sound like *Tonight Show* rim shots. But certainly British food has the worst PR of any cuisine in the world, even today. Its sternest detractors (not just the French) claim it's causing the hole in the ozone layer. Although friends of mine say foreign food in Britain—French, Italian, Chinese, and Indian, in particular—is often better than in its native land, the popular belief is that the Brits still haven't figured out how to cook their own, despite its renaissance of celeb chefs like Gordon Ramsay and Heston Blumenthal. And it's not embraced by many outside the U.K.: There are probably more Chinese, Thai, and Papawaiian restaurants on any one block of New York than there are British restaurants in the entire city.

"Our country lost its way after World War Two with rationing and scarce money," David Chambers told me. Chambers is chef at Rules, the 207-year-old institution in Covent Garden that is the Englishest of all English restaurants. For years, I thought roast beef, Stilton, and port were about all there was to recommend English food. But I realized that, as with Hemingway and Beckett, it's merely easy to imitate badly. Just try the steak-and-kidney pie at Tea & Sympathy in New York. Or read a little Mamet.

A favorite stomping ground of Dickens, Edward VII, and Graham Greene (much of whose *End of the Affair* took place here), Rules boasts a private room that was the setting for a celebrated dinner for Margaret Thatcher and her cabinet—at which she, upon being asked by a waiter, "And, Madame Prime Minister, what about the veg?" purportedly said, "They'll have what I'm having."

In a country that actually applauds eccentricity rather than simply paying it lip service (John Ashcroft, call British Airways), Rules is probably the most eccentric—and therefore most British—restaurant in London. Its interior would give a case of shingles to any modern decorator outside of Las Vegas. There on a wall of one of its three chandeliered rooms, cheek-by-jowl with a huge gilt-framed oil of Hamlet holding Yorick's skull, hang black-and-white cartoons and watercolored *Vanity Fair* portraits of the once-famous, and a couple of mounted ibex heads; over there, a quartet of women's busts in marble; above is a stained-glass faux skylight in the Cubist style; and right *there*, painted on a curved section of wall, is a full-color mural of Lady Thatcher— Lady Thatcher's hair, mostly—revealing garters on one thigh and all armored up as St. George, the Falklands in the background. In her hand she proudly proffers a staff whose pennant is emblazoned, RULES. If, as Russell Baker once wrote, the white race is not really white but pink, surely the Brits are the pinkest of all, and the clientele at Rules the pinkest of the pink.

Aside from the more common (and milder) pheasant, venison, and grouse, at various times of year you can also get what might be called Extreme Game—animals I was sure only existed in *Alice's Adventures in Wonderland*: blackgame, pochard, snipe, teal, ptarmigan, and wigeon. Extreme Game is an acquired taste, often very liver-y. If you're not used to it, it can be a shock (and if you're squeamish, best not ask exactly what jugged hare is; for the stout-hearted, I've provided the definition on page 98). The smell of wigeon we had on one visit practically blew us out of the room.

But what I find most enjoyable about Rules is its singularly British fare—a slice of the most sensual goose liver cut with slivettes of wild duck, amazingly creamy and light at the same time; the lush and salty Stilton-broccoli-and-almond soup (or the Stilton-and-walnut quiche with a spiky pear chutney); the many fresh vegetables; or the steak-and-kidney pie (also called pudding) made with a suet crust and served with a baked oyster on top (if you don't like the bitter taste of kidney, don't eat it; it's delicious without, though better with). The desserts, particularly the Sticky Toffee Pudding with Butterscotch and Vanilla Custard and the Sauterne Crème Caramel and Armagnac Prunes will time-travel you back to a most urbane kindergarten.

A NIGHT AT RULES

STILTON-AND-BROCCOLI SOUP

2 tablespoons olive oil

2 ½ cups leeks (1 Holland leek or 2 medium leeks), tough outer green leaves removed and thinly sliced

1 cup chopped onions

½ cup finely chopped celery

2 ¾ pounds broccoli, the stalks peeled and diced, the tops separated into florets

7 cups chicken stock
1 cup heavy cream
¾ pound Stilton, coarsely grated
Freshly ground black pepper
Salt
1 cup thinly sliced almonds

---

1. Heat the oil over medium-low heat in a large stockpot. Sweat but don't brown the leeks, onions, and celery, about 20 minutes. Add the broccoli and sweat for 10 minutes more. Add stock.
2. Bring to a rolling boil over medium-high heat, then lower the heat and simmer till the vegetables are just tender, no more than 10 minutes.
3. Purée the vegetables and return them to the pan. (You're just about done.)
4. Ten minutes before serving, stir in cream, then grated Stilton. Once the cheese has melted, taste (Stilton is salty). Add pepper and, if necessary, salt.
5. Serve immediately, passing the almonds separately. Don't be afraid to scoop big spoonfuls of almonds into the soup—they give wonderful textural contrast.

YIELD: 12 cups.

ULTIMATE STEAK-AND-KIDNEY PUDDING

2 ½ pounds beef chuck, cut into 1-inch cubes
1 ½ teaspoons salt
¾ teaspoon freshly ground black pepper
3 tablespoons lard (way preferred) or (ho-hum) mildly flavored olive oil
⅓ cup finely chopped onions
⅓ cup finely chopped carrots
¾ pound veal kidney, cut into 1-inch pieces
⅔ cup all-purpose flour
8 cups hot beef stock
3 cups quartered mushrooms

5 tablespoons Worcestershire sauce
Savoury Suet Pastry (see page 96)
At least 6 oysters, but as many as you want, shucked

EQUIPMENT NOTE: You'll need enough pots and pans and racks to hold 6 pudding basins.

1. In a large pan, sprinkle the beef with salt and pepper, then brown in melted lard. Add onions and carrots and sauté 10 minutes more, then add the kidney and continue sautéing another 15 minutes.
2. Mix in the flour and cook another 10 minutes. Add stock, mushrooms, and Worcestershire sauce, scraping up whatever's stuck to the bottom. Simmer for 45 minutes, stirring occasionally. Taste for seasoning.
3. Cut off ⅓ of each pastry disk and roll the remaining pastry into circles about 10 ½ inches in diameter and ¹⁄₁₆-inch thick.
4. Line six 18- to 20-ounce pudding basins or 5-inch ramekins with the pastry, pressing dough evenly around the sides. Fill with steak-and-kidney mixture. Roll out the reserved pastry and cover each pudding, crimping the edges closed.
5. Here's the weird part: Wrap each basin *entirely* in plastic wrap (this makes it a steamed pudding rather than a browned pie—in fact, don't be alarmed when the pastry doesn't color much). Tie string around the basin, securing plastic wrap, and place the puddings on racks in pans of simmering water, covered, for 2 hours, making sure the water stays two thirds of the way up the sides of the basins.
6. Remove the puddings from the water bath and remove the plastic wrap. Just before serving, cut a small hole in top of each and insert as many oysters as you like (at Rules they put one oyster inside the pudding and another on the side in its shell).

YIELD: 6 puddings.

NOTE: These are best when the fillings are made a day ahead and refrigerated overnight—either in the pastry or not—and then steamed before serving. They can be kept for 3 days, cooked or uncooked, in the refrigerator. Reheat in a 375-degree oven until hot, about 30 minutes.

SAVOURY SUET PASTRY

3 cups all-purpose flour
1 cup, or 8 ounces, beef suet, coarsely chopped (preferred), or slightly less exciting unsalted butter placed in the freezer overnight, and cut into small chunks
About ⅔ cup hot water (½ cup cold water if using butter)
4 tablespoons finely chopped chives

1. In the bowl of a food processor pulse the flour and suet (or butter) until the fat is incorporated, about 9 times. Continue pulsing and add the water slowly, till the dough forms clumps and leaves the side of the bowl.
2. Knead the dough on a floured board till soft, incorporating chives. Make a thick disk about 6 inches in diameter.
3. Cut the dough into 6 equal portions, form smaller disks, wrap in plastic, and chill for at least two hours before using.

YIELD: pastry for 6 puddings, 18–20 ounces each.

STICKY TOFFEE PUDDING

4 tablespoons unsalted butter
⅔ cup firmly packed brown sugar
2 large eggs
1 cup self-rising flour
1⅓ cups pitted dates, coarsely chopped
1 cup water
6 tablespoons golden syrup
Butterscotch Sauce (see next page)

1. Preheat oven to 300 degrees.
2. In a mixing bowl, cream the butter with the brown sugar, then beat in the eggs and fold in the flour.
3. Purée dates with water and add to batter.
4. Film six 7-ounce custard cups with golden syrup, then fill with batter and bake in the oven 40–45 minutes or until a knife inserted at the edge comes out clean.
5. Immediately run a knife around the sides of the puddings and invert onto individual serving plates. Pour warm butterscotch sauce over each and serve.

YIELD: 6 puddings.

BUTTERSCOTCH SAUCE

1 cup heavy cream
½ cup brown sugar
½ cup white sugar

1. In a small heavy-bottomed saucepan mix all the ingredients and bring to a boil over medium heat. Cook, stirring almost constantly, until reduced and thickened, about 20 minutes. This is delicious not only on this pudding but on just about everything except steak.

YIELD: 1 cup.

If all this sounds heavy (and much of it is), be reminded that in addition to the delicate grilled Dover sole and the poached finnan haddock, game is practically fat free. To my mind, a perfect evening in London is spent eating the preceding menu at Rules, then walking a few blocks east, past Simpson's-in-the-Strand, crossing the night-black Thames on Waterloo Bridge—St. Paul's glowing on your left, Parliament alight on your right—and catching a play at the National; and then crossing Waterloo Bridge back—St. Paul's on your right now, Parliament on your left—and if you've got room, stopping back at Rules (or Simpson's) for a little Stilton, port, and highly civilized condescension.

Oh, and as promised, here is the definition of jugged hare (though in deference to the faint of heart, it can be read only in a mirror):

ЈUGGED HARE IS A RABBIT WHOSE THROAT HAS BEEN SLIT
AND IS THEN COOKED IN ITS OWN BLOOD.

How a Fat Apple Pancake Saved Christmas

~~~~~~~

E ATING CHRISTMAS DINNER alone for reasons tragic or trivial can be brutal. I've done it too many times—never voluntarily, but fortunately thus far for reasons fairly trivial.

When I was on Christmas vacation from grad school in London in '65, I missed the train for a tour of Moscow a bunch of us had signed up for—and when you miss the train for Moscow, you miss *the* train for Moscow; the next one was a week later. Not only does everything, absolutely everything, close for Christmas in London—restaurants, movie theatres, even the Turkish baths—but then the following day is Boxing Day, when even *more* establishments close. Every single friend was out of town, and I remember walking around for nearly two hours before finding an empty Indian restaurant serving a kebab so dry it crumbled in my mouth. The following year, a bunch of us spent Christmas day in East Berlin, the unmerriest city not named Wheeling in history. But it was like Fezziwig's office party compared with that holiday in London.

My most memorable holiday spent alone was the Christmas Mother threw me out of the house because I'd grown a beard.

My junior year in college, when I phoned her to say that I was coming home and had grown a beard for a role I'd be playing—Dogberry in *Much Ado About Nothing*—I was greeted with the pleasant amusement I'd come to know as a warning: "Oh, you have, have you?" Somewhere in the back of my head a little light about the size of the sun went on. I think by that time I'd already told her

I'd bought a hearse to drive around in—though I didn't tell her it was because the women's dorm hours were so limited.

Of course, context is everything. Our Seventy-second Street apartment was white-gloved and heavily doormanned, and I often felt it was unseemly to step into the elevator without a necktie. The first night home went smoothly enough, complete with my telling her how much smarter I'd become since the summer and her nodding pleasantly. She did mention that parking the hearse was my responsibility, not hers. "And you'll have to park it around the corner so the doormen don't get depressed."

The second night she mentioned sweetly over the well-done lamb chops with mint jelly *à la Ukraine*, "I don't know that I really like the beard, dear," which is basically New England–speak for "Get rid of that thing before I burn it off with a blowtorch." By the third or fourth day, she had become increasingly agitated. I had the sense she wasn't sleeping. Finally she told me over more well-done lamb chops: "You'll have to shave that beard. The doormen are laughing at you behind your back and calling you 'Fidel.' " Pause, pause, beat, beat. "And I hate that hearse!"

How could she? I thought the hearse regal and was insulted by the comparison to Castro, who had taken over Cuba four years earlier but was still fresh news.

"Mother, he can't even grow a beard—he's got bald spots all over his face."

"Shave it! I can't sleep!"

"No!"

"Shave it and move that hearse!"

"No, it's my right to grow a beard and drive a hearse"—or some such semi-Constitutional defense.

"Shave it or get out!"

"I'll get out!"

"You'll be out for Christmas unless you shave that beard!"

"I don't care!"

"Get out now!"

Was she kidding? Did she think I'd yield my masculinity, self-respect, and newly acquired devotion to the First and Second Amendments (if you consider either a beard or a hearse a firearm)? I wouldn't budge, and neither would she, and she had all the money. Not exactly William Inge, but it went something like that.

I was given a few bucks and checked into a flophouse over some railroad tracks way west on Forty-second Street, where Mayor Bloomberg later hoped to build a stadium for the Jets. I'd heard it was cheap, and it was. Either the room was clean and safe or I was in my immortal phase. I phoned a couple of friends, and they were mighty impressed by what they considered my strength of character. We bombed around the city, reveling in our freedom. Nancy phoned in tears. "How can you be away for Christmas? She can't do this!" But she could. And so could I.

Christmas day rolled around, and my friends became unavailable—all, I imagined, surrounded by loving families in plaid bathrobes, warm noggy drinks, fireplaces, gift certificates for Jaguars, and mountains of gift wrap. Christmases had always been happy high points for us. There was no arguing, Maymie and sometimes Grammie would visit, and we'd go to the theatre in the afternoon. But the sweetest and saddest aspect of Christmas was that Mother allowed herself to give us all presents without suffering the guilt she would have felt the rest of the year—and found she enjoyed it. She felt more constricted at birthdays, and presents were out of the question at any other time of year. Once or twice at Christmas, she hit home runs: After my first term at Malcolm Gordon—just before the letter-writing—she was so pleased by my change in personality that she gave me a reel-to-reel tape recorder, the only thing I really wanted. Usually, she'd ask us for a Christmas list, and then would automatically ignore whatever was at the top. I once told Nancy, "I know the trick of this. I'll put 'lump of coal' as my first choice and 'Triumph TR3' as my second, and I'll get a car." But her generous nature slipped out at Christmas. She'd deliver on the rest of our list and throw in some cute trinkets in addition.

But the climax generally came when Dad's presents were unwrapped. As far as I can remember, Nancy and I never asked him for anything because it wouldn't be big enough, and he had a better imagination. We also knew that if we asked him for something, he would conclude we were just after his money and wouldn't give it; but if the inspiration was up to him, he would astound us. The giving of gifts is so revelatory of character: Certainly it communicates how the giver feels about the givee financially; but it also reveals the taste and creativity of the giver as well as the time and thought devoted to the gift and the aptness for the recipient. Dad was the most visionary gift-giver ever, opening my eyes to the material world outside and extending the hope that someday I, too, could come up with inventions like these, or accomplishments that would allow me to attain these things, or the curiosity and nerve to leave my surroundings and explore the universe. They were challenges. He gave me a full Lionel train set when I was four, before I knew such a thing existed; at eight, the first Polaroid camera—a big clunky thing by today's standards, but magical (black-and-white pictures in sixty seconds!)—the first digital watch, also magical; and years later, a microwave oven before anyone except the Department of Defense knew what one was. He sent Nancy dolls and clothing wrapped in spectacular colors and gadgetry from Neiman Marcus. In his presents, he treated us like a doting, protective dad.

I don't remember feeling unhappy the Christmas I got thrown out. I remember feeling self-righteous—at least till about 11 A.M., when the self-pity kicked in. It was about that time that I remembered Reuben's.

The restaurant was cavernous—three immense floors at 6 East 58th Street, filled with the smartest of the smart. And most important, it was open Christmas day. My friend Ronnie had joined the army when his grandfather, the patriarch of the family, refused to pay for college because he himself had never been. He hoped Ronnie would one day take over the restaurant, so he worked him mercilessly, ten- to sixteen-hour days—because that's how he had worked. Ronnie's skin grew pasty, his heart despondent. Unable to afford tuition, he enlisted. So he wasn't in town.

Reuben's had no smart set on Christmas day. It did have forty-four combinations of sandwiches, most of them named after Sophie Tucker, and what might be considered early fusion—a haphazard marriage of deli and continental. It also had the sweetest, hottest, hugest German apple pancake in pancake history. When I'd gone to the restaurant with Ronnie and friends, we would order one of these monsters—about the size of a pizza—for three or four of us. But this Christmas, I decided I wanted a whole one for myself. No turkey, no sweet potatoes, no pies. Just that pancake.

The crust was thin, not puffed, with apples all through it, in, under, on top;

I never could figure out how those apples got interwoven in there. And on the very top, a blizzard of sugar. God, it was sweet. And hot—you had to let it cool for ten minutes or if you put the roof of your mouth near an Esso pump you'd start a fire. I ate it mouthful by piggy mouthful, way beyond the point of satiety. Take that, Mother! I'm having a great Christmas! I don't care if my face breaks out and I put on five pounds! And she did and I was and it did and I did. It was about the most delicious thing I'd eaten in my life. I loved it, and in the process learned how to cope not only with self-pity but with sorrow: hedonism!

Food supposedly stands for so many meaningful things other than food— love, sex, happy and unhappy childhoods, family, excitement, wealth. And sometimes, occasionally, discreetly, and admittedly for a short time, stuffing yourself delivers them all.

REUBEN'S APPLE PANCAKE

There are many recipes for this pancake, all claiming to be authentic. After trying several and scrunching up my nose with dissatisfaction, I got in touch with Ronnie, now Ron, living in Los Angeles and in the export business, and he verified this one as the real thing.

The Granny Smith's tartness gives a little contrast to all the sugar in the recipe, and it's crisp enough to hold its shape despite all the heat.

1 large Granny Smith apple
Scant ½ cup sugar plus 1 ½ tablespoons sugar
½ teaspoon ground cinnamon
3 large eggs
½ cup milk
½ cup all-purpose flour
⅛ teaspoon vanilla extract
8 tablespoons unsalted butter

1. Peel and core apple and slice into moon-shaped pieces, ¼-inch thick. Place in a bowl and toss with 1 ½ tablespoons sugar and the cinnamon. Cover and refrigerate for at least 24 hours, stirring occasionally.

2. When ready, preheat oven to 400 degrees. Whisk eggs and milk in a bowl until blended. Whisk in flour and vanilla until smooth.

3. Heat 2 tablespoons of the butter over medium heat in a shallow 12-inch nonstick ovenproof skillet until it sizzles. Drain apples and add to the pan. Cook, stirring, until apples soften, about 5 minutes.

4. Melt 2 more tablespoons of the butter in pan. Pour in batter and quickly arrange apples evenly before batter sets. Increase heat to medium-high and pull edges away from pan to allow batter to flow underneath and cook, sliding a wooden spatula under pancake to keep it from sticking.

5. When batter is set but still wet, sprinkle with 2 tablespoons of the sugar. Place a cookie sheet over pan and invert the pancake onto it. Return pan to heat and add 2 more tablespoons of butter, swirling to coat. Slide pancake back into the pan to cook other side. Reduce heat to medium. Sprinkle top with 2 more tablespoons of the sugar. Cook until sugar on bottom side is caramelized, about 2 minutes.

6. Using a cookie sheet, flip pancake out again. Slide pancake back into pan 2 more times, adding 2 tablespoons of butter to pan and sprinkling with 2 tablespoons of sugar each time. Adjust heat so that the sugar caramelizes but pancake doesn't burn.

7. Bake in pan until brown and crisp, about 20 minutes. Slide onto a platter and serve hot.

YIELD: 2 servings.

Exit, Pursued by a Bear

I THOUGHT I'D BE an actor ever since those Cassavetes classes at fourteen, through those five years at Denison and summer stock, and fifteen months at LAMDA. As mentioned, I began to dislike the art shortly before LAMDA, and once I actually joined the profession, I was more convinced than ever it wasn't for me. For months in London I assumed I would spend most of my life in Europe; but when Mother died suddenly in January of '67, during my second year, I sped back to the States for her funeral and decided I was sick of schools and needed to enter the real world—even the not-very-real world of the theatre. It was all I knew. And swinging as London had been and would be for a few more months, America was where the world now focused.

A year looking for work convinced me what a horrid profession acting is, unless you love it. I was lucky and was mostly employed that year, but I hated being under the thumb of casting agents and directors with bright ideas, and, once ensconced in a long run of Tom Stoppard's *Rosencrantz & Guildenstern Are Dead*, couldn't stand the repetition. More than anything, I disliked being on call to be somebody else at 8 P.M. After all those years performing Shakespeare and Chekhov and Shaw in the comfort of academe, I was also pretty much appalled by the literature I was going to have to deal with as a pro (though the Stoppard play certainly sang beautifully).

Unless you're one of about twelve superstars, you're powerless as an actor—anyone in the business can tell you what to do. And I found people generally dislike talking to actors because everything eventually returns to their chief source of reference, themselves. I'd turned into that. Acting (and the shrinks) had made me so self-conscious that I'd observe myself doing everything from shaking hands to drinking coffee to kissing a girlfriend's inner thigh. There wasn't a spontaneous, un-microscoped bone in my body.

The audition process made me feel an inch tall, even when I landed the part. Auditioning is based on acceptance and rejection for the most intimate, personal reasons—and the ratio of acceptance to rejection is about 1:11, or in some cases 1:11,000. It's never enjoyable to be turned down for a job, but to be turned down three or four times a week solely on the basis of your personality is psychological demolition. Picture asking thirty-five or forty girls to dance on one night and not one of them saying yes. No matter what reasons they give—I'm in love, I'm busy, I have a headache, I don't know this dance— eventually you take it personally. As an actor you're told you're the wrong height, weight, color, shape, type; but in the end it's always interpreted as personal deficiency. Actors who steel themselves against this sort of assault (and every successful actor must) lose part of the very emotional life they need to mine: So much effort is spent building a fortress around the soul to ward off the rejection, they can't access this essential chunk of their animus. Those who manage to preserve the secret tunnel to their inner lives usually succeed when young and before the tunnel walls have been bashed down.

By 1967 I actively hated the profession, but having no Plan B, plodded on, stoking a fire somewhere in the back of my head. That summer, I had landed plum roles in the three Shakespeare plays being produced in Central Park, part of Joseph Papp's Shakespeare in the Park company that included Raul Julia, Charlie Durning, Olympia Dukakis, David Birney, and Harris Yulin, among others. For starters, I was to play Antipholus of Syracuse, one of a set of twins that were the leading roles in *The Comedy of Errors*. But before rehearsals began, the director had the bright idea to recast the twins with a single actor, resulting, I assume, from a "high concept" he'd dreamed up one night when feeling, as too many directors do, that he had to put his own stamp on Shakespeare. Peter Brook should be allowed this liberty . . . and *no one else*. Unfortunately, Gerry Freedman, an extremely enjoyable man and capable director, who now runs the North Carolina School of the Arts theatre program, was not Peter Brook. It became clear in early previews that the audience couldn't tell which twin the single actor was supposed to be. I had been reduced to a few lines as Solinus, the duke, which I played with a Cockney dialect, an equally pointless high concept of my own. Freedman saw the errors of his own comedy and recast the recast two nights before the first performance, but because I looked nothing like the single actor, I wasn't part of the recast.

But that was nothing compared to *King John*, in which I had only a few lines and from which I was fired by the legendary impresario Joseph Papp himself. Joe was one of the great producers and entrepreneurs in the history of the New York theatre, possibly *the* greatest, and a larger-than-life, professionally testy, street-savvy character; but he was a terrible director. Nothing he ever directed was well received, by either audiences or critics or, most important, by me. *True West*—possibly Sam Shepard's best and certainly funniest play—was initially considered one of his worst because it had been directed by Joe in 1980; only after the Steppenwolf company got hold of it five years later was the play viewed as the masterwork it is. So it was hard to know intellectually whether being fired by Joe Papp was a crushing setback or a badge of honor, but it was certainly a blow to my pride. I'd just returned from LAMDA and am sure I irritated him with my pompous English affectations; he preferred hiring cabdrivers and ex-cons and letting them run around the stage nude and improvising.

But he *was* a great theatrical force. He reassigned me to Third Spear Carrier status, and I think I earned a modicum of respect by telling him that no, I quit, forfeiting the salary. This stopped him. "Yeah?" he said with his street-tough accent. "You wanna do that? Okay. Okay. I'll get you unemployment." He liked people who stood up to him, even those with British pretensions. By the time the third play of the summer rolled around—what turned out to be a ludicrous production of *Titus Andronicus*, also directed by Gerry Freedman, in which everyone wore identical masks and costumes, which, coupled with the lunatic P.A. system in the park, made it impossible to tell who the hell was talking. I prayed nightly for rain.

Being cast as an understudy in *Rosencrantz*, the hot play of the year, was a coup. But despite all my training and experience, it turned out to be the runway off which I jettisoned out of the business. I was psychologically ill equipped for the job as understudy, since panic isn't what's needed in someone given thirty minutes' notice to confidently tackle an immense role. And to give you an idea of my importance to the play, I was also cast as a member of Claudius's court (as was Elizabeth Franz).

I was well rehearsed during the out-of-town in Washington, and in the previews in New York, but the night the real Rosencrantz—Brian Murray, youthful and hilarious—showed up flu-ish was terrifying. Brian was a naughty boy in those days and burned not only both ends of the candle but the middle of the wick. That winter night he appeared at half hour logy and flushed. Because of union rules, my Guildenstern understudy and I weren't ever allowed to rehearse on the set or in costume or with props or with lights.

The real Guildenstern—the superb and impossibly imperious John Wood—quickly ran the first few lines of the play with me. We'd barely met, let alone rehearsed, and I raced through the part. "You don't need to go so . . . *fast*, you know," he said, barely suppressing panic and rage and reminding me of O'Toole on the two glasses of lemonade. When we took another go at it, I suddenly couldn't remember many of the lines, and Wood's eyes saucered as if blinded by the headlights of an oncoming train. But I'd played all those classical roles, and old men and young pups, and gone on with only two and three days' rehearsal! I should be able to do this! And what about the two shows I'd just done in the park that I *didn't* get fired from?

But my heart beat as if someone had told me to wingwalk. I slipped into Brian's doublet only to find my love handles larger than his, and a costume assailing the source of my future sons' very existence like a jockstrap designed by the inventor of Brillo. Wood huddled with the stage manager and a representative from producer David Merrick's office; they all looked over at me across the stage in my too-tight Elizabethan garb and then plunged into heated discussion, stopped, looked at me, plunged in again. A phone call was made. Within minutes, a little man with a black doctor's bag appeared and marched into Brian's dressing room. A few minutes after that, Brian emerged whistling and ready for the decathlon.

The stage manager ambled over and said casually, "Brian's feeling better. You won't have to go on." Any other actor would have thrown his grandmother under a train to go on for Brian that night, but I nearly fainted with relief. When the blood returned to my loins, I determined to get the hell out of show business.

That wasn't the only reason to get out, but it was the reason to get out NOW.

It was also January 1968.

When I was in London, three of the more socially conscious Americans at LAMDA gave me a crash course in current events. Denison was a small, mostly Republican school delightfully—but provincially—removed from the outside world. Though my head was constantly aflame with schemes to avoid the draft, I paid little attention to politics then and so followed everyone in patriotically paying lip service to the war in Vietnam. But the Americans in London had been to Harvard and UC Berkeley and saw a fresh lamb chop in me. They opened my eyes to the horrors of the United States invasion, and though my eyes have re-opened since (the Vietnamese did invade Cambodia as predicted after we left), our involvement was butchery, catastrophic, and ill conceived (and probably led to the subsequent atrocities). That my generation was ordered to participate in this wretched destruction was not just galling, it was worth sacrifice, struggle, and activism. The world was on fire, and well before the understudy crisis, I would stew in the *Rosencrantz* dressing room night after night while waiting to go on in yet another pointless crowd scene: Life was happening everywhere around me, and all I was doing was this infuriating and insulting play. And it was one of the good ones!

I'd done my patriotic share earlier that year by dodging the draft, thanks to not one but two letters from psychiatrists, each claiming I was so troubled that neither would be held responsible if I were drafted—by implication putting the army on notice that I might pull a *Full Metal Jacket* on some barracks or go nuts in the motor pool or sue the United States government. The draft officers on Whitehall Street had seen every conceivable performance and excuse—burly heteros limply lisping with their hair dyed pink to pass for queer, guys with blood pressure of 800 over 90 from a week of sleeplessness and drugs, others whose urine was neon—but as far as I know, not a believable depressive with *two* letters claiming instability.

DRAFT OFFICER
(Reading psychiatrists' letters)
Do you often feel depressed?

ME

(Looking depressed, shoulders sagging)

Yes.

DRAFT OFFICER

Are you depressed now?

ME

(Hugging my clothes to my chest)

Yes.

DRAFT OFFICER

(Scribbling notes, stamping forms)

You're excused.

It was a much better performance than I was giving in *R&G Are D*. I was classified 4F, which meant I couldn't serve in the military unless all the buildings in America were on fire and a nuclear explosive in transit fifty yards overhead.

I knew this was a rich kid's dodge and wanted to be patriotic by fighting against the war, not fighting in it. In retrospect, the tiny dollop of John Wayne in me wishes I'd gone and fought—but that's a tiny dollop indeed, and in any case, my 20/600 eyesight probably would have resulted in my being assigned to typing in D.C. or to Whitehall Street to judge draft-evasion performances.

There were millions of us anti-warriors in those heady days, as spirited in our objection to American participation in our war as the soldiers for World War II must have been in prosecution of theirs. There was nothing shameful about it; we were proud of it. And it has surprised me since that the very people—my friends—who were so against the war turned out thirty-six years later to champion John Kerry for his service but were mum on the subject of his subsequent repudiation of it, the exact reverse of the positions they'd held during the actual conflict. Actually, both were brave positions—probably opportunistic, but brave nonetheless. And initially, I admired Bill Clinton for evading service and expected him to be proud of it. It was infuriating when he attempted to weasel his way out of it (though darkly amusing when he intricately re-revised his own revisionism during the Kerry campaign and said he should have joined up after all!). I don't mind when politicians risk accusations of flip-floppery and change their minds. It indicates they recognize doubt and can lead to growth. I plan to change my politics twenty or thirty times. But I don't see Clinton's double reversal as psychological growth, just a politix a little too conveniently flexible.

In any event, the theatre had nothing to say to me or to the country or to the world then, and I fled the stage of the Alvin for a week to see an old girlfriend in Milwaukee and, when that became uncomfortable, joined Eugene McCarthy's presidential campaign. I stayed with the campaign for seven months, through the convention in Chicago. My back was so completely turned on the theatre that I felt like a reformed whore: Even seeing a play made me uncomfortable, and the nightmares I had of acting again constituted excellent aversion therapy. It wasn't until seven years later, in 1975, when I finished my first play, that I thought the theatre anything but worthless.

The Fastest Food

~~~~~~~~~~

A FEW MONTHS BEFORE I left *Rosencrantz*, I signed a contract with the Tyrone Guthrie Theater in Minneapolis and regretted it almost immediately. The Guthrie and the ACT in San Francisco were the leading regional theatre companies in the country, and I had landed two strong roles in their season, and if I'd just graduated Denison, I'd have been thrilled. But I didn't really need any more experience (or if I did at this point, I was hopeless) and suffered instant signer's remorse: How would this differ from being back in school, really? Just more performances in classic plays; I certainly wouldn't find career advancement in the Midwest. Besides which, I continually forgot, I didn't like being onstage!.

There wasn't much romance in my life, though I certainly pursued it frantically. If anything more than a one- or two-night involvement threatened, I panicked and found a reason to break it off—or better, for her to break it off. I was eager but clumsy sexually and was really only good at pleasing myself. I realized it, and it was infuriating. I simply didn't know what to do. Most distressing, I didn't enjoy sleeping with anyone—the actual going-to-sleep part—and would be up all night scared the person was moving in on me in some metaphysical way. If I wasn't already there, I was well on my way to becoming a choice New York neurotic male.

Then I met Etoile.

Marian Watson, who at the time was referred to as a Negro, was a translator at the U.N. and preferred the name "Etoile" because it was glam. She wore the shortest skirts, most beautiful silk turbans, and best underwear of anyone

I'd ever known. Though not as tall as Iman, Etoile had the same conversation-interrupting impact on a room when she entered it. People were generally speechless for a moment, then suddenly in a swarm around her, magnetized and helpless.

Uncle Bus and Margaret met her with me one night at Sardi's, and for just about the only time in his life, my uncle started stammering. I hadn't thought to "warn" him, though it was much rarer to see an interracial couple in 1968 than it is today, even in New York. My sister, Nancy, had recently married a man of Korean descent, and his ethnicity seemed completely irrelevant. Why should this be any different? But, of course, it was.

Etoile had some explaining to do with some of her black friends about me, but it didn't seem to faze her, and I never sensed even a raised eyebrow from anyone I knew—though I was well aware that Dad would have thrown me out of the universe if he'd found out. Fortunately, he wasn't in the habit of asking about my personal life.

Etoile and I agreed on everything, and I don't remember a single argument for the first eight months of our nine-month relationship—except about political candidates. She and all her friends were for Bobby Kennedy the moment he announced, and I was a Eugene McCarthy supporter the moment the New Hampshire primary heated up. I thought Kennedy a coward for not standing up to LBJ in New Hampshire despite being asked several million times. Only after McCarthy had risked everything and won a surprising 42% of the vote in New Hampshire did Bobby opportunistically throw his hat in the ring. But then, I had procrastinated, too, stewing with discontent in the *Rosencrantz* dressing room and wishing I were in New Hampshire to fight the quixotic battle but only taking action once McCarthy had done so well (or Johnson so poorly).

A week out of the play, I flew to Milwaukee and joined the campaign as a canvasser, and after a couple of days in the snow was brought inside to help run things. I didn't eat a home-cooked meal for the next seven months and came to value the paper bag's versatility as a portable dining table.

And what happened in the next two weeks reversed the direction of the Earth's spin. On March 31, after thousands of us had spent many sleepless and well-shaved weeks doing whatever we could to be Clean for Gene, President

Johnson announced that he wasn't running for re-election. The McCarthy headquarters in downtown Milwaukee, where I'd been sleeping vertically, went berserk: We were sure *we* had made him resign; I, in fact, was sure I *personally* had made him resign. We had unseated a president! We were going to elect another one! Us kids! The power we felt was heady, made headier still when our man won the Wisconsin primary with 56% of the vote.

I flew back to New York and Etoile drunk on power, envisioning a life of politics, revolutionary campaigns, primary nights more exciting than theatrical opening nights.

Two days after this dizzying turn of events, Etoile and I were walking the streets at dusk, amiably arguing the virtues and demerits of Kennedy and McCarthy, when I glanced at an extra on the newsstand: the Reverend Martin Luther King, Jr., had been shot and killed in Memphis. Etoile crumpled and burst into tears. "Why are they doing this to us?" she cried. "Why Martin?"

We were near the apartment of a new friend whom I'd met in Milwaukee on the campaign. He was white and it turned out was married to a black woman, and it was the best place for Etoile and me to spend the evening while the rest of the country went mad, as it damn well should have.

She was inconsolable for days. Bobby Kennedy had made a heroic speech the night of King's assassination; McCarthy had barely noted it. Etoile and I re-rated our candidates: Mine had certainly dropped the ball. Or had he? He hated the notion of stirring a crowd for any reason. Meanwhile, the campaign and its fast-food bag lunches steamed uncontrollably along with no time to pause.

I was asked to set up a storefront for McCarthy in Indianapolis's inner city, and spent the next few weeks flying by the seat of my pants till the Indiana primary. Every minute was a new experience. Paul Newman and the senator held a rally opening the storefront but it attracted little attention: Kennedy was the favorite and the media darling. McCarthy seethed.

I talked to Etoile on the phone and rubbed my eyes red, longing for her endless, comforting body to sleep next to, which she'd taught me to enjoy and with which she calmed my sexual agitation. And then suddenly, she was there! Without warning, a few days before the primary, she showed up in Indianapolis, short skirt, heels, and silk turban, her chic a notch higher than anyone else's (as always), and canvassed the astonished neighborhoods . . . for McCarthy! No one had ever seen anyone like her.

In spite of her, Kennedy won the Indiana primary—the first in direct combat with McCarthy—in early May, and I was hustled off to Nebraska, where the next primary would take place. Etoile returned to New York. I didn't know how I felt about her now—she'd made such an extraordinary sacrifice by switching political allegiances, which I was sure she'd done just for me. But we had many disagreements, and I found she hadn't been completely candid about the work she was doing at the U.N. She would never let me visit her there, and it turned out she was a secretary, not a translator, which wouldn't have bothered me had she told me. But she was anxious just being Marian.

In Nebraska, I became an advance man for the senator, which meant preceding him to events and more or less producing them: arranging light and sound cues, deciding which hot dogs he'd eat and which babies he'd kiss. It also meant spending time with him, which was a treat: Courtly, witty, philosophical, understated, Gene McCarthy was an intellectual and a sincere Catholic who worried that his candidacy might seem vain and overreaching to his God. He was always interested in those of us who supported his campaign, and always respectful. It was no wonder Bobby Kennedy complained, "Why does McCarthy get all the A students and I get the B's?" (I was the exception.)

"An actor, huh?" McCarthy said to me as we drove to a speech he was making in Omaha. The poet Robert Lowell was in the backseat with him. "Which playwrights do you like?" the senator asked.

"Shaw and Chekhov and Beckett and Tennessee Williams and of course Shakespeare," I said, without much originality. "I'm going to the Guthrie in the summer." I'd turned my back on the theatre but thus far hadn't found a way to get out of my contract.

"I've been there," the senator from Minnesota said. He looked more interested. I told him and Lowell about *Rosencrantz*, which was a prestigious credit, and they nodded in recognition.

I then told the senator how my advance partner, Peter Ellyard, and I planned his entrance. It was a gymnasium, I think, and Allard Lowenstein would warm up the audience, then the lights would dim, the local band would blare. McCarthy would enter from a corner, the spotlight would pick him up. Cheers from the crowd would build, he'd climb a few stairs to the podium, shaking hands along the way, and as the laudation crescendoed, the band would die down and there would be a minute or so of pure, blissful, insane ovation. It would be a sensational entrance, a brilliant event.

Except for one problem.

Eugene McCarthy was a cerebral public speaker, not a rabble-rouser, and Allard Lowenstein, who regularly introduced him at rallies and later went on to become a one-term congressman from New York, was an incendiary one. Lowenstein could whip the cremated into an emotional frenzy, with the result that the audience was usually disappointed by the senator's professorial delivery, regardless of the brilliant content. If Lowenstein had intro'd the charismatic Kennedy at a rally, Bobby probably would have been crowned king well before the election. We learned to accommodate, which sadly meant asking Lowenstein to step aside.

Kennedy won in Nebraska, too, and in D.C. Just as our ship seemed ready to go under, we rallied in Oregon and handed the Kennedy family the first election defeat in its history.

Etoile flew out to Los Angeles for the California primary a week later, taking time off from the U.N., again supporting McCarthy. She arrived shortly before Kennedy won, which was shortly before he, too, was murdered. I was working at the Beverly Hilton that night and found her. We couldn't believe this had happened: first King, now RFK, all against the background of a raging war and even more raging war protest. We held each other for the rest of the night.

Despite the closeness we'd felt and the tragic events we'd shared, or perhaps because of them, or perhaps the divisions between us were as irreparable as were the country's, or perhaps because I was simply too immature to appreciate the possibilities of this relationship, we had grown apart in serious ways. We returned to New York—she to her job, I for the New York primary—and split up.

I ADVANCED MCCARTHY at his first event after the Robert Kennedy assassination. It was a speech at the Waldorf-Astoria in New York, and it was grim: He was pale, terrified by what had happened (not for himself, but of the maniacs the divisive campaign had unleashed).

We went up in the elevator together. He knew he knew me . . . just not exactly who I was. I introduced myself, then said, "Actor."

"Oh, yes," he said, brightening for a moment. "The Guthrie." He was immediately sober. "How many people?"

"Four hundred, maybe five. They're really looking forward to hearing what you have to say." I was trying to pump him up but succeeded only in adding a line or two to his face and fifty pounds to his shoulders. He didn't want the responsibility of leading anyone anywhere.

Instead of the inspirational, upbeat speech both his and RFK's supporters yearned to hear, he gave a plodding and unexciting one. It was then that those opposed to Lyndon Johnson and Hubert Humphrey decided they needed an additional candidate to pick up the fallen Kennedy banner, and recruited George McGovern.

DAD WAS A BIG DEAL in Las Vegas, and my experience with that city is so loaded that I don't know whether I love it or hate it, fear it or think it a jubilant expression of optimism and folly. The company of which he was sole shareholder, Donrey Media Group, owned the largest newspaper, the *Las Vegas Review-Journal*, many of the billboards (billboards . . . *in Las Vegas*), a radio station, a television station (for a while), real estate, and other businesses. At one point he owned more than sixty newspapers. He built an enormous office/home on its outskirts, and watched as the city expanded to his guard fence. When he wanted in to something, people jumped. While he was alive, I was welcome in any saloon, showroom, or main room in town, because I was his son. Someone made a phone call, and the elusive Siegfried and Roy tickets were suddenly available.

I had been almost whimsically put in charge of five western territories for Senator McCarthy. The regional directorship was something most campaign strategists would consider way over my head; but the McCarthy campaign was run almost entirely by college kids, and as I was almost one of them— and one of the more enthusiastic ones at that—a man named Curtis Gans decided, what the hell—let's put him in charge of Arizona, California, Nevada,

Hawaii, and Guam. Maybe he can swing a delegate or two away from Hubert Humphrey or George McGovern. Strategically, McCarthy should have picked up the fallen baton of the assassinated Robert Kennedy and been Humphrey's only opposition, but Kennedy and McCarthy had become such bitter rivals, and the supporters of each such enemies that they could not join forces.

And thus I was assigned to rally what few troops there were in the western states. Nevada and Arizona Democrats were seriously Establishment, and there was no chance of wresting a vote from them at the convention; California was slightly more in play. But I started with Nevada.

Because I'd seen Dad for only three weeks or so in my life, and this particular kingdom was so far away from New York, I was unaware at this time of his importance in Las Vegas. He was certainly the subject of much discussion in the family, but whose father isn't? To me, Las Vegas big deals were Howard Hughes, Frank Sinatra, and Bugsy Siegel.

I made an appointment with Senator Alan Bible, an ultraconservative Democrat who today would be an ultraconservative Republican. My task was to ask his support for Senator McCarthy—tantamount today to asking Pat Buchanan to support Barney Frank for president. The appointment was granted immediately.

Dad, too, was a well-known conservative who, when asked to which candidate he gave a contribution, replied, "The winner." His first concern was business, and he regularly gave to both parties. He always seemed interested in my political opinions, without necessarily agreeing with them, but had recently come to realize the war in Vietnam was hopeless, costly, and stupid. But when I'd asked him what he'd think if I dodged the draft, he'd said, "I'd think you were a shirker."

After LBJ dangled an ambassadorship to Australia in exchange for money and Donrey newspaper support in 1964 and then reneged, Dad turned on him with rancor. He was already philosophically far to the president's right.

After we had exchanged pleasantries, Senator Bible said, "Let me get this straight. You're Don Reynolds's son . . . and you're working for Senator McCarthy?"

"Yes, sir," I said.

"And your father is backing him, too?"

"I'm not sure, but he has an open mind." He didn't, of course, but I didn't know that. For a few minutes, Senator Bible's world was upside down.

Later that day, I went to the *Review-Journal*—to ask its support for McCarthy, a quest that would have pleased Don Quixote. It was part of the routine we campaign workers were instructed to attempt. The editor, a pleasant man named Ralph something, said, "You're Mr. Reynolds's son and you're supporting Senator McCarthy?"

"Yes, sir."

"And your father knows you're here?"

I'd written Dad I was coming out. "Yes, sir." In retrospect, I think of myself as Candide, only less aware. Ralph, who as editor regularly pirouetted around many elements of the civilized underworld, as well as Kirk Kerkorian and Howard Hughes, without ever authorizing an investigative report in the newspaper, had met his match. So he rolled up his sleeves and joined in.

"Any chance of Senator McCarthy coming here?"

"I certainly think he should," I said firmly. Well, he should have—if the campaign had twenty or thirty months to go. He could have warmed up for Bobby Darin—that's how seriously he would have been taken in Nevada.

The next day, a photograph of me shaking hands with Ralph spread across the front page of the *Review-Journal* with the headline MCCARTHY MAY VISIT LAS VEGAS. I was impressed with my salesmanship and importance. Incredible as it may seem, it didn't occur to me that I'd been welcomed into Senator Bible's chambers and headlined by this paper not because of the newsworthiness of my candidate or the persuasive oratory of my silver tongue but solely and simply because of whose son I was.

That day, Dad phoned. "I see you got yourself on the front page of the paper," he said, quite amused by what he thought was my brazenness but which, alas, turned out to be naïveté. Why shouldn't he be amused? He had 364 other days that year to put what he wanted on the front page. Poor Ralph probably thought he was buttering up The Old Man. Whenever I reflect on those days, I turn beet red, and the image of the Tim Holt character in the film of *The Magnificent Ambersons* rears: Holt played the dim and narcissistic son of an influential midwestern family who's unable to grasp reality, and to the end believes the world revolves around him. Makes me laugh and wince to this day.

The Democratic convention in Chicago was a theatrical event unparalleled either in London or New York, complete with a circus at its center and the lion eating its lion tamer as a climax. Brilliantly and sometimes hilariously whipped to a frenzy by the comic activist Abbie Hoffman (and the considerably more insidious Jerry Rubin) and opposed by the equally hilarious *and* insidious Mayor Richard Daley (father of the city's current mayor), we McCarthy supporters tried to discredit the convention by staging nightly demonstrations and pulling pranks on the television journalists, the police, and the Establishment, as represented by the unfortunate Hubert Humphrey.

On the final night of the convention, the police and the mayor decided they'd had enough of their chains being pulled. I was in the streets and missed by a whisker their attack on the McCarthy and McGovern headquarters at the Hilton Hotel (with the complicity of the hotel management, whom I subsequently cursed by vowing never to stay at another Hilton for the rest of my life; because there are other hotels in the world more comfortable and inviting than those in the Hilton chain, it hasn't been much of a sacrifice). On the pretext that bottles were being dropped from hotel windows, the police invaded the offices and sleeping quarters of the campaign workers and beat many of their occupants brutally and bloodily.

Fully depressed by the nomination of Humphrey, whom we now despised more than Nixon even though about five minutes ago he'd been a champion of liberal causes, most notably in the area of civil rights, I joined a friend, Walter Dallenbach, in Santa Barbara to campaign for Stanley Sheinbaum, an academic and an economist who had married one of the daughters of one of the Warner brothers and was now running for Congress. Stan was the first of many interesting contradictions I would encounter on the Left: A rich Marxist, he married a millionairess and turned her considerable fortune into an even more considerable fortune by cleverly trading foreign currencies. He was staunchly against the war and intelligently reformist in social matters but was running against the popular, conservative lemon rancher Charles Teague, who had been elected to Congress seven times, soon to be eight.

One of the Left's whipping boys in California in '68 was the statewide superintendent of schools, Max Rafferty, usually referred to by us as "Fascist Max Rafferty," a sobriquet ascribed to just about anyone who didn't agree with us. When Teague came out in support of Rafferty, we plastered the voting district with ads that said TEAGUE ENDORSES RAFFERTY! This was tantamount to the Kerry campaign taking out an ad in Alabama that said BUSH 43 PRONOUNCES IT NOO-KYUH-LER! We might as well have given the good lemonist a campaign contribution: Not only did he defeat Sheinbaum two-to-one, but the district also voted heavily for Rafferty! But of course Stan never had a prayer in that part of the world then: He was a Jew, a beyond-Left liberal, and a public speaker who combined the many spoken ellipses of Bill Bradley with the drone of an uncomic Jackie Mason, and all the folksy lemon rancher had to do was put out a quaint singing commercial to trounce us. Stan went on to become a political force in Los Angeles, at one time serving as president of the police commission, but he never ran for office again.

In the bigger picture of 1968, the devil had been elected president. We were all sure it was the end of America. I wrote in McCarthy's name, though voting for the comedian Dick Gregory was the fad, and returned to New York to see what the rest of my life was going to be like.

Walt (a screenwriter) and his earth-mother wife, Em (now a therapist), and I hashed and rehashed the plight of the Left over joints of fine, but by today's standards mild, grass. In some sort of peculiar anti-Establishment protest, I gave up drinking and substituted pot for about a year, giving it up minutes before it made me terminally paranoid.

What worried the Dallenbachs and me about the campaigns we'd worked on—and the politics of the Left in general for the next fifteen years—was the comfort everyone seemed to take in failure. We were on God's side, fer sher . . . but we weren't actually supposed to win anything because that would mean we had copped out and betrayed all the victimization movements we championed—the persecuted Vietnamese, Americans of color, women, the incipient gay revolution. We were to continue to field noble kamikazes like McCarthy and McGovern and even Bobby Kennedy, and later on, Fritz Mondale, but they weren't actually supposed to *win*, were they? Martyrdom felt familiar and welcoming to me, at least partially because it echoed Mother's. So we'd do it through the back door: on campus.

A startling reinforcement had come from Hollywood the year before. The iconic movie of the era, *Bonnie and Clyde*, exemplified the notion of the noble loser. Hard to believe now, but post-WW2 Hollywood, despite toe-dipping into the rebellious worlds of Brando and Dean, overwhelmingly reinforced the status quo. *Bonnie and Clyde*, a love story with guns, changed all that, pitting a band of idealists, all emotionally wounded in one way or another, against an uncaring, and eventually overpowering, Authority. The writers Robert Benton and David Newman and the director Arthur Penn made the movie so representative of the era and so powerful, emotionally and aesthetically, by victimizing its glamorous characters. Its sexually magnetic lovers were criminals who robbed banks and killed people—a complete reversal of the usual Hollywood formula. It was also horrifyingly violent (for the period) and scary—I spent nights awake, brooding over the shoot-out at the motel, with Estelle Parsons and Gene Hackman at their absolute best. But I never found anyone my age who didn't side with the killers, though they couldn't have been more morally reprehensible. I was completely on their side, too. Played by Warren Beatty and Faye Dunaway, and valiant but defeated, they were our heroes. And they would have lost all validity if they hadn't been defeated.

I wrote Dad that I was looking around for a job, and he wrote back offering me one as a cub reporter on the *Review-Journal*. I accepted quickly, relishing the idea of contact with him and a chance to learn something about journalism. As the fateful day to board the plane to Las Vegas approached, however, I got cold feet. Stories Mother had told me about Dad's treatment of his associates—and most particularly, his son Don Junior—had me tossing with worry. Even given her bias, the stories had the ring of truth; it seemed the closer you were to Dad, the more he pushed you away, and not gently, but with a nightstick. And if it was a work situation, you became the class victim. A lawyer Dad retained in New York confirmed these concerns.

After days spent fretting whether to work for him, I decided not to. I regret it enormously and at the same time am relieved at the bullet I dodged. One of his longtime associates, Fred Smith, subsequently told me, "It was the smartest thing you ever did. Your father ruined Don Junior's life."

Not only did I dodge a bullet, I fell into a tub of butter. Closing the door on that career path immediately opened one on another. Dave Garth, who had been one of McCarthy's media advisers and was also New York mayor John Lindsay's, took a liking to me during the campaign. He phoned to ask if I'd like to be the mayor's assistant press secretary. I jumped. "I can be there in twelve minutes," I told him. He laughed, but he also knew what a great experience it would be. Lindsay was one of half-a-handful of great white hopes the American Left had, certain to run for the presidency—if only he could get reelected as mayor of New York. Though nominally a Republican in the most Democratically bureaucratic city west of Beijing, there was little doubt he sought the mantle of JFK, to whom he was constantly compared. And this was now 1969, an election year for the mayoralty in New York. I didn't ask about salary or responsibilities; I was now a career politician!

Except that the following day, Garth phoned to say, "Sorry—that job is filled. How'd you like to go work for David Frost?" I was heartbroken and unheartbroken in about thirty seconds, and in about sixty switched from career politician to career TV producer.

Frost was an Englishman who had made a reputation in the United States as an acerbic wit on the weekly satiric show *That Was the Week That Was*. He was a star in England, a great TV interviewer, and a popular host.

The format of American TV talk shows was fairly uniform in 1969: They were generally ninety minutes long, and the host sat behind a desk interviewing guests who were primarily involved in show biz. Occasionally, an author or politico would appear at the end for ten minutes, but the overall tenor was one of frivolity and amusement. The champ, of course, was Johnny Carson on NBC, and the streets of the unemployed were littered with pretenders. Two popular daytime shows were hosted by Merv Griffin, who appeared five times a week for Westinghouse Broadcasting, and Mike Douglas. CBS decided to go toe-to-toe against Carson and hired Merv away from Westinghouse. So Westinghouse brought Frost over to fill that slot, and Frost brought with him two energetic former newspapermen, Peter Baker and Neil Shand. The three of them wanted to revolutionize American television, and for a while, they did.

Frost and his men couldn't stand pontificators and other guests who just prattled; they weren't interested in actors talking about acting or novelists talking about interpreting life; they wanted *visceral* TV, in which the guest would be dramatic—by either embarrassing himself or being embarrassed by someone or getting into an argument or crying or in some other way revealing himself in a way he never had.

There were two bookers for the singers and comics, and four of us who were responsible for everything else: the writer John Berendt, the wild Woodstocker and writer Alice Turner, the socialite Jeanne Vanderbilt, and me. It was up to us to make the show different from all the others. So when I was put in charge of Jane Fonda, I got her to talk about her mother's suicide, her relationship with her father, and politics, none of which she'd ever done before (hard to imagine Jane as a political virgin, but she was then). We booked Jacqueline Susann, fresh from her triumph with *Valley of the Dolls,* and ambushed her with Rex Reed, Nora Ephron, and John Simon in the audience. Rex and Nora rolled over, but John accused her of writing "trash"; she countered by angrily calling him a Nazi; he countered by saying he was Yugoslavian, not German; she accused him of not reading the entire book; he shot back, "You don't have to go through the entire can to know the whole thing is garbage." Mayhem! Cheers from the Frosties!

I booked a debate on the antiballistic missile system between Dean Acheson and Senator Charles Percy, which network news departments had been trying to do for months, and Frost was an excellent referee; I booked one of my childhood heroes, Elia Kazan, with a film-clip retrospective. He revealed, among other things, that despite his sensitive and noble screen image, James Dean was rotten and selfish. We initiated the first of the shows with only one guest for the entire ninety minutes, and I was lucky enough to get the assignment: Orson Welles.

David Frost didn't study much of the research we so thoroughly prepared for him because he had a photographic memory and could command most subjects in a matter of minutes, and whenever seriously confronted, he was the single best interviewer I've ever seen. He was so good on his feet that I never saw anyone get the better of him. Adam Clayton Powell once innuendoed that he knew who had *really* killed President Kennedy.

"Who?" said Frost.

"We know, we know . . . don't we," said Powell, winking conspiratorially at the audience. These were days of black power and all the ABO (Anybody But Oswald) Kennedy-assassination theories, and most interviewers wouldn't have challenged Powell, a rascal and a media darling.

"You can't come on national television and say that. If you know who killed

President Kennedy, you have to substantiate it. Otherwise you're just being irresponsible," Frost said sternly. Powell was shocked and eventually backed down.

Dean Acheson had haughtily confronted David backstage before the ABM debate.

"Mr. Frost, I am sorry I agreed to do this program. You are not a serious person, and I believe you are ill equipped to participate in this discussion," Acheson said imperiously. The Frosties loved the *Guinness Book of World Records,* and the previous show, which Acheson had seen, featured a man who could put thirty or fifty or seventy lighted cigars in his mouth at the same time.

"That is very disrespectful, Mr. Acheson," Frost said sternly. "You clearly have not seen any programs I've done in England, and I assure you you will be treated intelligently and with respect. And I am extremely well informed on the subject." He wasn't, until he subsequently photo-memmed my notes, but Acheson, used to being addressed only by those on bended knee, capitulated and was, in turn, respectful to Frost.

What David wasn't good at was a talk show's lifeblood, the second-tier celebrities; he imitated what he considered to be American show-biz insincerity and wound up doubly insincere; hence unknown singers and mediocre comedians would become "one of the greatest in the history of the business" show after show. He was also a terrible monologuist, and though the comedy writing was often funny, he would read his opening monologue from a clipboard, which was distinctly unfunny. But he had brass; at one taping, the monologue received such little laughter that he said, "All right, stop tape. We're going to do this again, and this time, everybody please laugh." Which they did.

Frost won an Emmy or two, and the television world sat up and took notice, but eventually he wore out his welcome. He couldn't get folksy like Johnny or Merv. We were imitated, and it got harder to be fresh. Others took on the ninety-minute and Kazan film-clip ideas and, worst of all, David simply wasn't a comic. Rule Number One was that this sort of show had to be funny, and if it wasn't, it didn't matter whether you could book Garbo, Howard Hughes, and Charles Lindbergh, the Three Unbookables. David was amiable, he was immensely good-spirited, optimistic, energetic, and an extraordinary businessman; but actually getting the audience at home or in the studio to laugh on a regular basis was beyond him.

The Frosties were demanding and exciting to work for, and they paid each of us four horsemen the grand sum of $250 a week. They were aware of the talk-show perks: Besides all the movie screenings, free plays and concerts, glam dinners, and other events, there was a social life. Whenever possible, I tried to improve mine, booking and attempting to romance as many women as I could. It was as close to rock stardom as I would ever get.

The Frosties experimented with hiring a mini–repertory company to perform comedy skits, and one of those chosen was an old friend from my acting days, Oliver Clark. We have remained the best of friends for nearly forty years.

Meat Loaf: The Musical

Unlike me, Oliver, not only actor but cook, magician, mechanical-bank collector, folk-art enthusiast featured in *Architectural Digest*, and one of the all-time ten-best dinner guests, has never stopped performing. When I saw him recently, he was pouring olive oil into a pan and tossing in half a head of garlic with the theatrical flourish that is one of his many trademarks. He was standing in Red's kitchen, whipping up meat loaf and rigatoni, and it reminded me of the time we once wrote a musical together.

"I got this pasta from Malcolm and Kelley McDowell, and you must put the garlic in the oil before the tomatoes, or the oil will never"—he relished the word—"in-fu-u-se." Oliver is the only person I know who does imitations not only of Gielgud, Ralph Richardson, and Albert Finney but also of Maya Angelou. The tomato-garlic homily was his Gielgud.

We met in 1965, shortly before I went west to get arrested with Weed. We were appearing in a production of *She Stoops to Conquer* at the Cincinnati Playhouse in the Park. Oliver played Tony Lumpkin, one of the leads, and I played both a butler and a footman, with a total of four lines.

Oliver achieved fame as one of the patients on *The Bob Newhart Show* and on his own short-lived sitcom. We started composing our musical after I moved from the Frost show to *The Dick Cavett Show* at ABC, selling my soul for network exposure and a raise to $400.

The show taped at 5:30 P.M., and when it was over at around 7, I'd frequently meet Oliver for dinner. He weighed 320 then and has battled weight most of his life, bungeeing all the way down to 170, only to fly up 100 pounds a few months later. Right now he's about 220 and, as always, on guard.

"When I die," he said once, "they'll come up with a pill that has your ideal weight on it. If you take a pill marked 178 in the morning, you can eat anything you want, and at day's end you'll weigh 178. But it won't happen in time for me to enjoy it."

Oliver's real name is Richard Mardirosian, which he changed for the stage before Barbra Streisand made using real names stylish. He chose Oliver because the musical *Oliver!* was running when he came to New York, and Clark because it went well with Oliver. He grew up working the grill in his dad's blue-collar restaurant in Buffalo, and so he likes direct food, like the meat loaf he was prepping at Red's. Back in our musical days, we'd usually have a prime rib and the tomato-onion-iceberg salad with blue cheese at Beefsteak Charlie's or some other midlevel red-meat palace, though occasionally we'd go on a bender (his acting career was flourishing, and in '71, $400 was handsome) at The Palm or Peter Luger, because, as Oliver intoned in his self-parodizing British baritone, "You can get many beeves, good Jonathan, all of them pri-i-ime." After dinner we'd often walk uptown, fooling ourselves into thinking that a post-prandial of forty blocks would neutralize the billion or so calories we'd just horsed down. Usually the freewheeling conversation revolved around the theatre, politics, food, and people we knew. On one of those strolls ("Let us walk against the elements, wearing good tweeds, hands clasped behind backs," was a customary invitation; he was in his Victorian period), I must have mentioned my interest in writing a musical, because that's what we did for several weeks.

Outside of kindergarten pageants, the first play I saw was the musical *Where's Charley?* at about age six and remember singing "Once in Love with Amy" for what must have seemed to others several months afterward. My second was *Guys and Dolls* at age eight. Both were by Frank Loesser. I saw *Damn Yankees* twice as an early teen, and fantasized about the woman in pajama-tops-only from *The Pajama Game*. I continue to love *My Fair Lady* and *Carousel*. My favorites, though, are everything that Gilbert and Sullivan ever wrote and *The Music Man*—particularly but not exclusively with Robert Preston. It has the most sophisticated lyrics disguised as bumpkin writing—a goal that

Oscar Hammerstein II so frequently sought and achieved and at which Meredith Willson excelled—of any show I know. Its story line is simple, but perfect (perhaps not needing quite so many references to Balzac), every single melody is memorable, and above all, it is unpretentious and true to itself in theme and style. To me, there is nothing more infuriating than pretension in the theatre, whether it be a musical or a straight play, nothing worse than the layering on of importance for its own sake. This doesn't mean a musical can't be serious. I'm a great admirer of *Gypsy* and *Cabaret* and *Sweeney Todd*, but only of *West Side Story*'s music, lyrics, and choreography, and not at all of *Company*, which tries desperately to say something "important" about marriage and is on the level of a kid looking in the window. And *Movin' Out*, in my opinion the best musical in the last decade or so, couldn't be more serious. It gives its subject profound meaning honestly, not glibly or facilely.

I've tried to write two—one about *American Bandstand* (at exactly the moment *Hairspray* was in the works) and one about the 1968 campaign. Neither saw the light of day. I also doctored the brief Broadway revival of *Whoopee!*, which Brendan Gill called "this rouged cadaver of a musical" in 1979. Not much success there. When musicals are good, and intelligent, they are everything the theatre should be: thrills, spectacle, artifice, intellect, emotion.

"I remember that musical," Oliver said now, whacking away at the lids of a couple of portobellos for the meat loaf. "You were completely bamboozled. Now listen to me: You must chop everything the same size so nothing stands out texturally." He brought out a green pepper and made same-size pieces of it. "I love me m'green pepper, but some people hate it. I'll leave it out if you want." No, I assured him—anything he put together would be excellent.

"Excellent!" We used to say this to each other all the time, it being a line from the musical *Ben Franklin in Paris*, in which he played Louis XVI. "Excellent! A copy of this news to his Britannic majesty in London!" is how I remember it. He loved the line because it was so silly. Acting is often silly—that's part of its joy. We shortened it simply to "Excellent!" and said it so often that to this day, forty-plus years later, it is still part of my phraseology; and because it's difficult to spend an hour with Oliver without starting to sound like him, I say it with his intonation.

When we started our musical, I was amazed at how adept he was at it. He came up with snippets of music that sounded Broadway-commercial. He even came up with a credible story line: A repressed Englishwoman falls in love with a rambunctious American, their parents are against it, she discovers herself. Not *Phantom of the Opera* exactly, but something to hang a few songs and dances on.

And his lyrics not only rhymed, they made sense. "If you're smart," he'd start singing, boomba-ing the percussion between lines, "do something crazy just for once."

> If you're sma-a-art
> (ba boomba boomba)
> Do something foolish just for once
> (ba boomba boomba)
> Lose your he-e-ad
> And you might find your
> he-a-art!

I couldn't improve on this but offered something rather feeble for another song. He mused on it, then haltingly began what we called the heroine's "I Want" number:

> The right finger of me left hand
> Is the loneliest place in town.

The improvisation materialized into a song over several weeks. After a few minutes of working at it, we'd run out of steam and start in on how to stuff pork chops.

Back at Meat-Loaf Central, Oliver added cream cheese to the other ingredients, then pawed at the mixture with two forks. "If you mix too much, the meat gets tough." He pushed the loaf into the oven. "Now all we have to do is boil the rigatoni. And that, as they say in France . . . is . . . *that*."

After a month or so of our strolling songwriting sessions, we had a complete story line and four or five plausible songs. With titles! "The Right Finger of Me Left Hand," "The Uncle Sam Rag," "I Feel Merely Marvelous." These sound like possible Broadway tunes, don't they? Not as good as *The Music Man*, maybe, but I found myself humming them at all hours.

I was having a clandestine relationship with a co-worker at the Cavett show, Bridget Potter. She was a former political activist who ran with Abbie Hoffman and had been part of the group that once dropped hundreds of dollar bills from the balcony of the New York Stock Exchange just to see if the brokers would scurry after them. (They did.) She was a lively British expat who wore skirts so short they were often referred to as wide belts, the tantalizing fashion of the day. Bridget had been married for a year to a widly radical radio personality who insisted they have sex once a day. After they divorced she found she missed at least that part of the relationship and found me searching for someone to calm my own raging energy level. We didn't want anyone to know about the relationship and so would leave the Cavett taping separately, then meet up at one or the other's apartment a few minutes later, or at a screening or with Oliver for dinner. The next morning, we'd taxi to the Cavett offices, and I'd get out a block away and we'd walk separately into the office. To the best of my knowledge, no one found out until years later, and this skulduggery inadvertently made the relationship juicier. Bridget went on to become an executive at the upstart HBO, married, had two daughters, and divorced. We're still friends, at least partially because she's inexhaustibly curious and she loves to cook.

Back in the musical days, I told her I thought Oliver and I had a real shot at Broadway and fantasized entering some junior version of the Loesser-Lerner-Hammerstein pantheon, and even entertained quitting the Cavett show. "Most amazing is that Oliver has pretty much done the whole thing himself," I told her. "I come up with brainchildren, he has better ones. I had no idea he could write music. And he's so clever with lyrics."

"This is amazing," she said. "But don't leave Cavett just yet."

I sang "our" songs constantly. After I'd announced our musical to several friends and was about to go seriously public with our boffo smash, Oliver became less inspired in his tunesmithery. I was sure he was becoming inhibited by the possibility of success, and encouraged him every time we did our hands-clasped promenades. Then one night he stopped by my apartment, an LP tucked under his arm. "Listen to this, my lad," he said, plopping the record onto a turntable.

For those of you even less perceptive than I, what happened next may be a surprise. Out from the speakers came brassy, orchestrated maxi-versions of our songs. The lyrics differed slightly from ours, but only slightly. I was stunned. "What is this?" I said. Had he had our songs recorded?

"No, Jonathan. It was on Broadway. It was called *Redhead*."

I think my dropped jaw was the funniest thing he'd ever seen. *Redhead*, with a score by Albert Hague and Dorothy Fields, starred Gwen Verdon and Richard Kiley, was directed by Fosse, and was a memorable innocuity that opened in 1959 and ran for a year. Oliver was beside himself with laughter and dined out on the story many times. I wasn't angry, just bewildered—and felt foolish. When I told Bridget, she laughed for what seemed like a month. Actually, she laughed for months, just not all the time.

"What I loved most," said Oliver, laughing now as he swirled the rigatoni into Malcolm and Kelley's pink sauce, "is that you actually sang the songs for people!" We sat down to the meat loaf—direct, flavorful, and bursting with juices—and the subtle, delicious pasta, and chortled again over the many curious things we'd done together. Like the time in the seventies when he got me to invest in an antique Rolls just as the oil crisis hit . . . but that's another story.

At about that same time, Oliver moved to Los Angeles, landed his series and dozens of parts in movies-of-the-week and features. He also became one of the three or four leading cast-iron-mechanical-bank collectors in the country and a successful folk-art dealer, and bought three houses. I didn't see much of him during that decade, but when my screenwriting career took off in the eighties, and I had to be in L.A., we spent many evenings together. We'd dine either at Musso & Frank's, which reminded him of New York and at which he had a table, or at The Palm, where his caricature adorned the wall. He had arrived.

Seven years after the great *Redhead* fiasco, I decided to marry. There was no second choice for best man. At the rehearsal dinner at Lutèce, he could have charmed the jewelry off my aunt Maymie's throat, persuaded my future father-in-law to put up seed money for his growing folk-art collection, and levitated the room. He did none of those things, except for the levitation of the room.

OLIVER CLARK'S MEAT LOAF

4 cloves garlic, chopped fine

4 tablespoons olive oil

2 medium onions, chopped fine

Salt and pepper

1 ½ large portobello mushroom caps, chopped fine

1 green pepper, chopped fine

2 pounds ground beef

1 pound ground pork or sausage

1 cup unflavored bread crumbs

½ teaspoon onion powder

1 teaspoon Dijon mustard

½ teaspoon Cajun seasoning

⅓ cup grated Parmesan cheese

4 tablespoons ketchup

1 tablespoon mayonnaise

2 tablespoons whipped cream cheese

3 eggs, beaten

½ pound bacon

1. Preheat oven to 350 degrees.
2. Sauté garlic and onions in 2 tablespoons of the oil until the garlic is lightly brown and the onions translucent. Remove to a bowl. Add a dash of salt and pepper.
3. Sauté mushrooms in the remaining oil until liquid is released, about 2 minutes, and remove them to the bowl. Add more salt and pepper.
4. Place the remaining ingredients, except the eggs and bacon, in another bowl. Paw at the mixture with two forks, combining thoroughly but not overmixing.

5. Add in the eggs and the mushroom-onion mixture and blend.
6. Bake in the oven for 30 minutes.
7. Meanwhile, sauté the bacon till half cooked, then adorn the meat loaf with it and bake for another 30 minutes.

Yield: 6–8 servings.

Malcolm and Kelley McDowell's Pink Rigatoni
(Adapted by Oliver Clark)

10 cloves garlic, roughly chopped
6 tablespoons olive oil
10–12 plum tomatoes, quartered (canned may be used off-season)
½ teaspoon salt
½ teaspoon pepper
½ cup red wine
1 pound rigatoni
¾ stick salted butter
½ cup grated Parmesan cheese
½ teaspoon sugar

1. Over medium heat, sauté garlic in oil till brown (but no darker).
2. Add the tomatoes, salt, and pepper and sauté for 30 minutes or until the liquid begins to evaporate.
3. Pour in the wine and cook an additional 20–30 minutes until thickened, then remove from heat and let stand for 10 minutes.
4. Boil the rigatoni until al dente.
5. Fold the butter, Parmesan, and sugar into the sauce until it turns the famous pink. Dump in the rigatoni, mix, and serve.

Yield: 4 servings.

Dinner for Kings

I WAS FIRED from the Cavett show in January 1972, after fourteen months, under circumstances about which I'm unclear to this day. One version is straightforward and political, the other tawdry and juicy. In the first, the producer of the show, John Gilroy, had been suddenly demoted by the arrival from *The Tonight Show* of Marshall Brickman. Brickman had been wooed away from Carson with the promise of taking over as producer, but his contract wasn't up for a few months, and during that time Gilroy had been appointed. Brickman, who went on to write *Sleeper*, *Annie Hall*, and *Manhattan* with Woody Allen as well as direct his own movies, was immensely entertaining, and one of the funniest monologue writers ever. Bridget and I immediately gravitated toward him when he arrived and unburdened ourselves of the many complaints we had regarding the stodginess of the Cavett show, which, we felt, kept us third in the ratings behind Johnny and Merv.

Cavett was a wit from both Nebraska and Yale; he had written for Jack Paar and Johnny Carson and starred on his own successful daytime talk show. ABC had been trying to figure out how to use him for some time. When elevated to the magic 11:30 P.M. slot, he quickly threw together a staff, a desk, some chairs, and the Bobby Rosengarten band. But, like Frost, he had no second banana (Frost had already broken the interior-design rules by not sitting behind a desk). Johnny had Ed McMahon and Merv had a butlery Englishman named Arthur Treacher. These number twos not only laughed at jokes and encouraged the audience to do so, but gave the host a pal to talk to and fence with. Frost's ebullient personality didn't need this shoring up, but Dick was and is a reactive comedian who plays best off strong personalities. Although he desperately wanted the show to be funny, it became the repository of serious topics and second-choice guests. Dick was comfortable with Gilroy's steadiness but was irritated that the shows weren't more exciting. The show became a critics' favorite—the kiss of death in television—and quickly earned considerable snob appeal, but the audience stayed away.

I wanted to bring some Frostian zest to the enterprise, pit warring factions against each other, and generally stir the pot; Bridget had similar notions. Gilroy resented Brickman's arrival; he'd been successfully producing the show for several months and protested to Dick that he should continue, and that Marshall should become head writer. Individually, Bridget and I told Dick that we thought Marshall becoming producer would enliven the show, and we backed him vehemently. Dick eventually lived up to the contract he'd made with Brickman, but erroneously didn't fire Gilroy, which meant he had a sniping second-guesser rolling his eyes in a "This didn't happen when I was producer" blamelessness whenever something went wrong.

We zipped up the show, all right—one installment featured a shouting match among onetime segregationist and ax-handle flailer Governor Lester Maddox of Georgia, black footballer and angry activist Jim Brown, and Truman Capote; in another, Gore Vidal and Norman Mailer verbally bitch-slapped each other for an hour; in another, Fred Astaire was the sole guest. Feeling my oats and beginning to appreciate the limitless possibilities of the medium, I somewhat legendarily suggested that in order to viscerally demonstrate the horrors of air pollution, we should put a rat in a plastic bag, tape the bag to a running automobile's exhaust, and watch with the rest of America how long it would take for the rat to die. After collapsing with laughter, Brickman said simply, "No."

The shows were more exciting—but more unpredictable as well. In our attempt to arrange theme shows and guests that fit or fought together, we frequently couldn't book them till the last minute, which unsettled Dick almost as much as being told to put on Rosencrantz's costume had me. We went to London for a week, hoping to book Laurence Olivier, Diana Rigg, and the Prince of Wales. Instead, we got Laurence Harvey, Fenella Fielding, and a random earl. Most of the guests were available in New York, so it appeared there was no reason to go to London. It was a disaster. Upon our return, Brickman decided producing wasn't for him and became the head writer. Gilroy was reinstated as producer and as first order of business fired his most vocal critic, who happened to be me. He couldn't fire Bridget, because she was Dick's favorite.

That's the first version. The second was told to me three years later, just as I was pulling out of my depression over the firing.

Gilroy had what was then called a secretary, whom I'll call "Jackie." Jackie was what is now called a babe, with extra-long legs emphasized by her skirt—not so much a wide belt, as wide dental floss. Dick taped two shows on Thursday so he could have a long weekend at his home in Montauk, but we had to come to work on Friday anyway, and every Friday afternoon, Jackie would disappear from her desk outside Gilroy's office *into* Gilroy's office, and the door would be locked. Twenty to two hundred minutes later, depending, I guess, on enthusiasm and acrobatics, Jackie would emerge red-faced and disheveled, smooth herself out, and assume her position behind her desk. A few minutes later, Gilroy would emerge, adjusting his necktie. The routine was so obvious it became comical, and whenever I'd ask Jackie why she was in Gilroy's office with the door locked, she'd say with quadruple entendre, "John had some . . . notes he wanted me to take."

Other days, Jackie would walk into my office, her naked right thigh pressing my left forearm as I tried to type, and would initiate an inane conversation.

JACKIE

Oh, hi. What are you doing?

ME

Typing up the notes on Erich Segal.

JACKIE

Oh, I loved *Love Story.*

ME

He's very pretentious. And now, he's very rich.

JACKIE

He has such a way of, you know . . . writing.

ME

We're putting him on with John Simon. That should cause some sparks.

JACKIE

Can I look?

ME

Sure.

JACKIE

(Leaning over me and the typewriter, her shirt appearing to be more unbuttoned than usual, knee now on the arm of my chair, underwear exposed)

I love John Simon.

When we got to London, my first visit was with Bridget to Piccadilly Circus. I hadn't been there for five years, and I wanted to roam every street.

My second visit was to Jackie's hotel room. She was having trouble with her orgasm, she said. She'd never had one with a man. And then she told me how boring it was to have slept with Peter Lawford, a recent guest on the show.

When we got back from London, Gilroy fired me. Jackie told me three years later that he had found out we had spent several nights together in London, and though he was seriously seeing another woman had become enraged. It didn't seem plausible, but he's since died, so Jackie is the only one who knows for sure.

Being fired for whatever reason was devastating, made considerably worse by Bridget firing me, too. I wasn't a particularly faithful boyfriend—never claimed to be, too many heebie-jeebies—but when she heard of my liaisons with Jackie, her contempt knew no bounds. Besides, she was becoming involved with a heavyweight newsman at NBC who took her to NASA liftoffs and promised for the next several years to leave his wife. But then, this was the seventies, when all STDs could be cured with penicillin, and drugs were actually thought to be good for you. (Kerouac became liberated on pot; Freud and Sherlock Holmes got smart on coke; Gaudi did Barcelona on mushrooms—how could they have been wrong?)

Once fired, I suddenly had no life and no identity. I'd expected some of the perks to keep up—screenings, play openings—but they abruptly halted with my dismissal from the show. You mean all those PR people were interested only in the show all along, not in me? Yup. So there I was, alone on the Upper West Side, with a bedroom, a living room . . . and a kitchen. So I picked up a pot.

I began cooking to ward off uncertainty and depression, and it worked. But one of the drawbacks of cooking is also one of its joys—as creative works go, it's done quickly . . . and it's over quickly. Palliated as I was when planning and executing dinner for others (and even for myself), there was always a junkie's letdown the following day, when the euphoria evaporated and there was nothing tangible to show for it except garbage bags. I was faced not only with joblessness but aimlessness, and cooking's brief injection of purpose and a parade of brief and thrilling but ultimately hollow relationships didn't quite make up for the empty clamminess of free fall. I attempted several television and film projects, none of which got anywhere.

In 1974 I began writing a play, never planning to show it to anyone who might produce it. I simply enjoyed writing it. It was a lengthy one-act about a baseball pitcher at the top of his form who, for no discernible reason, talks himself into failure in the middle of a game at Yankee Stadium. It reminded me of me. It was bold, in that it took place right on the mound, and the character actually pitched a baseball to his offstage catcher twenty-seven times while articulating his woes in a stream of consciousness, many of them politically infuriating by today's standards. I had recently seen a Richard Foreman play, *Sophia = (Wisdom) Part 3: The Cliffs*, and so liked the title I gave mine the same syllabification: *Yanks 3 Detroit 0 Top of the 7th*.

When I finished the play, I gave copies to Oliver and cousin Lee, solely for their amusement. Oliver gave it to Wynn Handman, who ran the American Place, at the time one of the top not-for-profit theatres in the city. Wynn phoned to say he wanted to produce it. I couldn't believe it—this had been written for my pleasure alone, a sort of psychic bloodletting. Lee, living in London, sent it to Stephen Sondheim, who phoned.

"Jonathan, I'd like to give this play to Hal Prince. I think he should direct it." This was impossible, part two! Hal was one of the leading directors on Broadway and *the* leading producer. He phoned the next day to say he wanted to direct it; we met with Wynn, and they agreed to do it at the American Place Theatre. Hal took me aside.

"Jonathan, Broadway's future is all about musicals. There's room for one straight play a year, no more. This is going to be it. This is the wave of the future—try out a play at a not-for-profit theatre, save all the out-of-town expense and gamble, and if the reviews warrant, move it to Broadway." This is conventional wisdom now, but no one had Hal's foresight thirty years ago.

Wynn told me, "We can put this on with someone else's one-act, but it's much better for you if it's on with another play of yours. Do you have one?" I didn't, but an item in the *Times* had caught my eye: A bill had been introduced in the New York State legislature in Albany forbidding the public display of contraceptives for fear of alarming children and easily offended grown-ups. It was hilarious, and all true! I wrote the first draft of *Rubbers* in a week. Both Wynn and Hal were enthusiastic, and I now had an entire evening to myself.

Jerry Orbach did a reading of *Yanks* and it was hot; he was perfect but unavailable, so Hal and I cast Tony LoBianco and the rest of the characters. Meanwhile, Hal's designer, Eugene Lee, planned a lavish set with an electronic scoreboard; Wynn balked—his budget for a set was $5,000, max, and this would cost $25,000, min. They argued. Wynn phoned.

"Jonathan, Hal doesn't understand your play. I don't like his way of working. And it will bankrupt us. I can't have him working in my theatre." He was adamant.

There were aspects of the production I didn't like, either. It seemed fraudulent, as I thought much of Hal's dramatic work was. He knew everything about the theatre but not about the world outside, and his productions often looked like tasteful reproductions of other productions, not life. "Wynn, this probably means no Broadway," I said.

"I don't care. I never did care whether this went to Broadway."

As usual, I was unmindful of the economic possibilities. I was itching to see what another director would do with it. "Well, you can't let Hal go until you've got someone else," I told Wynn.

Wynn phoned Alan Arkin, who said he would like to direct the plays, then phoned Hal and told him he was out. I phoned Hal. He was incredulous, but not angry. Amused.

"I can't believe it—for the first time in my life, I've been fired. And by Wynn Handman!" He started laughing. It was odd, all right—sort of like my boyhood friend Michael Eisner being fired by the ride operator at EuroDisney. "Well, good luck," he said.

Yanks and *Rubbers* did well by Clive Barnes, the chief critic at the *Times*, but were lionized by Jack Kroll at *Newsweek* and John Simon at *New York*. Initially scheduled to run six weeks, the show ran nine months. Among the people who saw it was Francis Ford Coppola, who said he wanted to put it on in Candlestick Park (then the San Francisco Giants' stadium), starring Jack Nicholson, and hang television monitors all over the stands so the crowd could see close-ups. Francis had recently finished *The Godfather: Part II* and was festooned with Oscars and generally considered creator of the universe, at least in southern California. After some badgering on my part, he suggested I join him in the Philippines, where he was about to start shooting *Apocalpyse Now*. "I don't get it," he said. "The Vietnam War is the most traumatic event in American history, and nobody except John Wayne has made a movie about it."

Tom Sternberg, an executive who worked for Francis, told me Francis wanted my opinion on a script. This was exciting.

"I'll read it right away and phone him."

"No, read it and fly out to San Francisco and meet with him." Couldn't it be done on the phone? Not how things work in the movie biz. And who'd want it any other way?

The script was written by Steve Martin, then primarily a stand-up comic, and Carl Gottlieb, who'd written the screenplay for *Jaws*. It was a comedy about the settling of California, and I didn't find it particularly funny, largely because I didn't know the California history the authors were satirizing and had never heard of Father Junípero Serra. I arrived in San Francisco just in time to accompany Francis, Tom, and some friends to a Steve Martin performance. Francis was energetic, filled with ideas outlandish and sensible, and seemed extremely interested in my opinion about things. I kept looking over my shoulder to see who he was talking to, but it was me.

Martin was truly fresh onstage and completely silly, with an arrow in his head and a cutting take on all things show biz, into which he saw the whole world descending. At the show's climax, he led the audience snaking through the San Francisco streets, and the show continued for another half hour.

"That's the funniest stand-up I've ever seen," I said to Francis. "But I have to say I wasn't crazy about the script."

"No, I don't like it at all," he said. So why exactly was I there if he'd already made up his mind?

The following day, Martin, Gottlieb, and I appeared in Francis's office on Kearny Street. Francis proceeded to talk about the screenplay as though he were eager to produce it. I kept my mouth shut. When Martin and Gottlieb left, I said, "I thought you didn't like it."

"I don't. We're not doing it." First lesson of Hollywood: You never do the dirty work. Your people do the dirty work.

Francis invited me to his mansion in Pacific Heights for dinner. He was attempting to start a Hollywood North with his film-school buddy George Lucas, with whom he'd had an enormous success on *American Graffiti*. His entrepreneurial vision, coupled with the two *Godfathers* and the cult hit *The Conversation*, plus the Oscar he'd already won for the screenplay of *Patton*, made him the hottest single figure in the industry. But film wasn't his only interest. He'd just announced the end of *City* magazine, a literary publication he'd founded, and though unhappy about closing it, his vision for the future was brilliant. What made his ideas unusual was not only their range but their practicality: He could actually pull them all off. We sat around an immense table with his petite wife, Ellie, their three children, Roman, Gio, and Sofia, and a few other friends, and talked about movies, television, magazines, food, wine, Italy, and how he hoped to realize his childhood dream: "Just one more hit, and I can start my own studio," he said. "And what do you like to do?"

A bit out of my league, I said sheepishly, "Well, I like to cook . . ."

"You do? You do?" Food was his favorite subject, except for all the others. "Cook tomorrow night! Take the whole day, use my staff, use my kitchen, whatever you want!"

A staff? Occasionally a friend helped me out in the galley kitchen of my one-bedroom in New York, but I had no idea what to do with a whole staff. But the next day, I found out.

I wanted to impress the hell out of Francis and Ellie and so remembered a few things from the S.S. *France*, like *tournedos Rossini*, and from my own repertoire, like the killer-diller *bavarois Clermont*, with all the glacéed chestnuts in the middle and the whole candied chestnuts dripping with chocolate spikes around the center.

His staff of four—one also took care of the children, another was his flirtatious projectionist, two others did whatever jobs needed doing around the house and office—and I spent the entire day making the stocks for the *tournedos* from scratch, then wrestling the chocolated *marrons glacés* to the earth. The kitchen was the first I'd ever worked in in which there was actually room and equipment to do everything. Sharp knives! A Chinese hat! Stockpots that didn't have to be stored under the bookcase!

I started off with Shrimp Toast à la Rothschild, creation of Raymond Oliver, chef at the Michelin-three-starred Grand Vefour in the only city where the guide's stars are remotely helpful, Paris. Loaves of bread are sliced fat, hollowed out, sautéed in clarified butter, then filled with a reduced, buttery fish stock made with crushed shrimp shells and fish frames, adorned with shrimp sautéed in more butter. I placed a truffle slice on top, then broiled these little toasted shrimp boxes till brown, and sped them out of the kitchen, feeling like a pro.

They're rich but small—three bites, perhaps—and they vanished immediately. The *tournedos* are incredibly rich, too—but also incredibly small, and Francis is a man of large appetites in every area of life. When he spotted the two little fillets on his plate, he began screaming in mock fury, "That's it? That's all there is? You spent the whole day cooking and this is all we get?" Ellie laughed and shushed him, but the *tournedos* were inhaled in seconds. Out came some sautéed green beans (boiled in water for thirty seconds, then sautéed till blackened in cast iron to remove all moisture, then slathered with butter, which they drank in like anxious sponges) and potatoes Anna, and they, too, were gone in an instant. I thought Francis was going to order up a couple of bowls of rigatoni and roll out some gnocchi to hold us all over until dessert, but the richness of the food began to take its toll, and by the time the *bavarois* made its *haute* appearance, the crowd was sufficiently butterfatted and mellow.

We sat and talked for another hour or two or three. Francis Coppola is certainly one of the ten greatest dinner guests in the world—or, in this case, hosts.

I lingered in the kitchen afterward, my eye caught by the flirtatious projectionist, and after the day's work we were on intimate terms. We eventually went upstairs to her room. It was a perfect day and a perfect night, except for one thing.

Around 3 A.M., I couldn't sleep (Etoile hadn't provided hypnagogics for every insomnious neurosis) and decided to go to the apartment Francis's company had arranged for me. I snuck quietly down the stairs . . . and the moment my right foot hit the floor at the bottom of the staircase, all hell broke loose. The entire mansion was suddenly alight, and a siren started shrieking. Then the lights began to flash. The whole place was one big security zone! I didn't want to ruin my relatively impressive introduction to the director of both *Godfathers*, panicked, and opened the first door I found. In true Feydeau fashion, it was a closet. The second led to another door, and that one led down some more stairs, which for all I knew could have opened onto a spewing Linda Blair. Finally I found a door that led out back, and I jumped a fence onto a back street just as two police cars pulled up to the front of the house. I walked away with as much nonchalance as I'd had all those years before, in Miami Beach, and made it to the apartment a free man.

The next day, the projectionist phoned and, assuming I had left her side before the alarm system was switched on, said, "The weirdest thing happened last night after you left. About three A.M. the alarm went off and the whole house went wild for about an hour. The police came and everything. Francis was pretty upset."

"Really? Hmmm, how bizarre."

"What time did you leave?"

"I forget. Around one. Two . . ."

"How are you?"

"Oh, fine, fine. How are you?" I didn't know Francis well enough then to realize he probably would have broken up over the story. But just to be on the safe side, I never told him.

I met with him that afternoon to discuss the movie he hoped would give him the clout to run his own studio, *Apocalypse Now.*

We sat in his San Francisco office while he tried to talk Al Pacino into playing Willard, the special-forces officer sent up the river into the heart of darkness to bring back Marlon Brando. "No, no," Pacino said good-humoredly into the speakerphone. "I know what's going to happen—I'll be down on the ground swimming around in the mud for three months, and you'll be up in a helicopter giving everybody orders and having a great time." Francis cast Harvey Keitel, a former marine.

Francis had already finished the screenplay with John Milius, so we worked out a generous arrangement in which I would write a book about the making of the movie. Francis wanted no financial participation in it, promised me total access to him except when sleeping or in the bathroom, and guaranteed no one from his camp or from United Artists, the financing studio, would look over my shoulder or insist upon reading my notes.

The following three months of '76 were almost as surreal as what eventually appeared on the screen. I practically lived in Francis's skin, accompanying him on every jaunt, boat trip, and plane ride, not to mention his own helicopter lessons, his bouts with the flu, and a loss of fifty-plus pounds. I witnessed directorial bravura and pettiness, brilliant cinematic insights and breathtaking sequences that he created with his good buddy Dean Tavoularis, the production designer. Movie sets are notoriously boring: Hours pass waiting for the right natural light or the construction of artificial light. Not this one. It was full-throttle pandemonium almost all the time, as extras misbehaved, choppers wouldn't take off (or went missing), explosives didn't detonate, props were stolen.

Francis is a professional Italian and had hired two Italians as his first assistant directors. "Firsts" (Lee's husband Kip was one) execute what the director wants—setting up the shots, arranging the background and foreground, marshaling the extras. But these Italians spoke neither English nor Tagalog (the

Filipino language) nor Vietnamese, and there were hundreds of Vietnamese and Filipino extras. After a month, Francis fired his two firsts, and, while waiting for a new one, appointed . . . me. Suddenly I was explaining to the extras (through a translator) how to dive into the dirt when the helicopters swooped in for attacks and staging scenes of village treachery—under Francis's instruction, of course, though he gave me wide latitude. It was heady stuff; nine months earlier I'd been grappling with sanity, scribbling a play onto yellow legal paper and making Roy Andries de Groot's *bifteck de Gruyère* and Simone Beck's *salade de broc*; now I was halfway around the world eating mangoes and being a general in the restaging of the Vietnam War! (About the only food I found edible in the Philippines were the golden, sun-bursting mangoes, sweetest fruit I've ever tasted. I had one every morning with a squeeze of lemon. The lunches on set were mostly local street food and much ground beef, reminiscent of boarding school.)

From the moment Harvey Keitel appeared on the screen in the dailies, it was clear he was the toughest soldier ever to appear in a war movie. He was actually frightening, both in person and onscreen, and seemed to me perfect casting. He wasn't an actor from New York playing at being a grunt; he was the real thing. After a few weeks' shooting and much of the movie in disarray, Francis told me he was firing Harvey "because he isn't sympathetic. We don't want to go up the river with him." I respectfully disagreed, and years later Harvey told me he was discharged because Francis wanted to put him under contract for his next venture—his own movie studio (megalomania doesn't get much more megalo)—and Harvey said no. Whatever the reason, Francis shaved his beard off over Easter weekend so he wouldn't be recognized at LAX (I was never sure exactly who would recognize him even with his beard) and snuck back into Los Angeles to recast.

"Who would you cast," he asked me, "Jack Nicholson or Marty Sheen?"

"Jack Nicholson, of course," I said.

Two days later he returned, having cast Sheen. I didn't think then and don't think now that Sheen was particularly believable as a military commander and murderer, and he had none of Keitel's mercurial ferocity; but since the movie became a theatricalized—if frequently astonishing—version of the war, he fit the style better. This was clearly an actor playing a soldier, and the movie was clearly an inspired director's vision of the war.

The production couldn't have been further behind schedule. Though it was initially slated for a three- or four-month shoot, at the end of three months, there were eight minutes of film in the can. During an early bout with the flu, Francis said weakly, "All the studios are betting against me. I don't even want to direct this anymore. I've asked about the availability of Steven Spielberg and Billy Friedkin—they're the only ones who could take this on. Well, George Lucas could, too, but he's in Africa shooting a sci-fi movie called *Star Wars*." I don't know if Francis had a change of heart or neither Friedkin nor Spielberg was available.

Spring is monsoon season in the South Pacific, and several days of pounding rain and unbelievable windstorms ransacked the Philippines. Many died in Manila, many more in the hinterlands, where we were shooting. Four of us were holed up in a completely safe house with Cyndi Wood, a former *Playboy* Playmate of the Year who had a tiny role in the movie along with two other Playmates. When the rains stopped, Francis surveyed the damage to the set. It was completely devastated. Boats, planes, huts, villages, all wiped out. After a few days of conferences, he announced a two-week hiatus for everyone. We would all be called back once the sets were rebuilt.

I was glad to get out of there and wondered whether I really wanted to finish this picture, as it looked as though it would take another year. Six weeks passed without word from the staff. Finally, a phone call from Tom Sternberg, an exec with Francis's company.

"Are you ready to go back?"

"Yes . . ." I said reluctantly.

"Good. The only thing is, U.A. is very concerned about what you're writing. They want to have a look at your notes."

"You know what that means—they want to change anything they see as unflattering. They want a puff piece."

"Maybe not. But those are the conditions. You ready?"

"Nope. I'm not doing it." He tried to talk me into going back, but returning would have been spineless.

I didn't go back and am glad I didn't. As Francis later said, "Little by little, we all went crazy." Stories that poured out of there indicated a crew gone berserk, lots of drugs, general looniness. Francis's wife, Ellie, who had been making a documentary about the movie, ended up writing the book about the making of the movie. When *Apocalypse Now* opened in 1979, it drew wildly conflicting reviews but was generally considered a major work by a major director and wound up an enormous success. After defying odds and gods, Francis felt, with some justification, that he could do anything. Although he was the first (aside from John Wayne) to start a movie about the war, he wasn't the first to release one. Michael Cimino, who began shooting after Francis, stole much of the *Apocalypse* thunder. His *Deer Hunter* was a financial and critical success, going on to win the Oscar for best picture (not that Oscars necessarily bestow critical merit; they usually indicate more heat than light).

I didn't talk to Francis for fifteen years. Though we'd been as close as two people not married to each other could be for three months, he never phoned or wrote after I'd said I wouldn't be returning. Though he's only two years older than I, his entrepreneurial soul reminded me of Dad's, and so he became something of an unwitting father figure. Oddly enough, when we got together in the early nineties, he followed through on his earlier plan, having convinced CBS that it should air a reworking of *Yanks 3 Detroit 0 Top of the 7th* at Dodger Stadium, live. Jack Nicholson was too old, but Kevin Kline and Alec Baldwin weren't. We spent several months rewriting the script on and off, only to have Francis abandon the project at the last minute in favor of an expensive production of *Pinocchio,* a pet project of his, in France, which never happened, either.

A few months after leaving the Philippines, I started a play centered around four men and a Playmate, working in the Philippines on a movie called *Parabola of Death*, who are stranded in a house during a typhoon with little to do but torment one another. At the end of the second act, the production designer, frustrated by the Playmate's refusal to sleep with him, attacks her and beats her savagely. In the third act, she turns the tables: Not only is she paid off handsomely by the all-powerful director, but she gets to beat up the designer.

The play was called *Geniuses*, and I hoped it was funny and dark and a little scary. The structure was based on Shaw's *The Devil's Disciple*, complete with a deus ex machina in the form of the director (my version of Shaw's Gentlemanly Johnny Burgoyne). It was turned down at every theatre in New York—except Playwrights Horizons, then run by André Bishop, who was in the process of becoming the most important producer off-Broadway after Joe Papp. *Geniuses* was preceded at his theatre by Chris Durang's *Sister Mary Ignatius Explains It All for You* and A. R. Gurney's *The Dining Room*, and was followed almost immediately by the amazing musicals *Herringbone* and *Sunday in the Park with George*. André knew exactly what to do with my play and suggested Gerald Gutierrez as director, which was exactly right.

Geniuses received strong support from *The New York Times*, first from Mel Gussow, then Walter Kerr, and it ran for nearly a year. In the second act the men gather 'round to feast on dog—a Filipino specialty that I tried once and found highly agreeable and rather sweet (and actually environmental, since there were thousands of stray dogs running around the Filipino backwaters where *Apocalypse* was shooting).

Dad came to the opening night and walked away with several copies of the *Times* review under his arm and was, I think, pretty proud. Francis heard about the play and was reportedly apoplectic. I assume he felt betrayed by its satirical perspective—he thought he had the copyright on what happened offscreen in the Philippines as well as on. (Actually, he had neither—no director does. The studio owns the copyright to the property. God owns the copyright to what happens offscreen.) Francis was also angered, so I heard, because he assumed the production designer Dean Tavoularis, his great friend in real life, was made the assailant in the play. We've never talked about it.

Simplified Shrimp Toast à la Rothschild

(Adapted from La Cuisine, *by Raymond Oliver, Tudor, 1969)*

4 slices firm white bread, crustless, 1 ½ inches thick
4 tablespoons peanut oil
½ cup butter
1 pound small shrimp (rock shrimp preferred)

2 tablespoons minced shallots

1 medium onion, minced

1 carrot, minced

1 tablespoon tomato paste

$\frac{1}{2}$ cup dry white wine

$\frac{3}{4}$ cup fish stock or clam juice

1 bouquet garni

Salt and pepper

2 tablespoons crème fraîche

2 tablespoons Cognac

$\frac{1}{4}$ cup grated Gruyère cheese

4 thin slices truffle

---

1. Scoop out center of each slice of bread so it looks like a lidless little box. Sauté each box on all sides until crisp and golden in 3 tablespoons of the oil and 3 tablespoons of the butter, then drain on paper towel or rack.

2. Shell the shrimp, then pound the shells to a paste in a mortar or whiz them in a blender.

3. Cook shallots, onion, and carrot until golden in 1 tablespoon each of oil and butter. Mix in the shrimp-shell paste, cook for 3 minutes, then add tomato paste, wine, fish stock or clam juice, and bouquet garni. Cover and simmer over low heat for 20 minutes, then strain into another saucepan and reduce to $\frac{3}{4}$ cup. Add salt and pepper.

4. Sauté the shrimp in 3 tablespoons of the butter until just barely pink, then transfer them to the sauce and heat for another minute. Remove the shrimp with a slotted spoon and divide them evenly into the bread boxes.

5. Stir crème fraîche into sauce, then the Cognac, and bring to a final boil. If sauce is runny, reduce further. Remove from heat, add remaining butter in bits, and ladle sauce over shrimp. Top with grated cheese and a truffle slice and brown quickly under a broiler.

YIELD: 4 servings.

Starter Marriage

~~~~~~~

Shortly after leaving the Philippines in 1976, I had said to my friend Jack Temchin, "I'm tired of dating all these show-business people. I want an heiress!" Remarkably, Jack produced one. He had been to college with her. I made countless phone calls to Chatzie Kirk and received a few back, but it took months for us to get together. I finally learned how to use the post office to my advantage: Two funny letters actually convinced her she should drop everything and meet me.

The decade was fast, the sexual revolution (Part 8,403) in full swing, AIDS only an undercurrent. Usually the idea (mine, anyway) was to open a bottle of wine and as quickly as possible start convincing the woman I was with to spend the night. This worked exactly 24% of the time, which meant it didn't 76% of the time. When Charlotte walked into my apartment on West End Avenue and said, "Water," when I asked her what she'd like to drink, I knew this was not your typical seventies girl. She was striking, with an angular jaw and splendid cheekbones and a carriage that exuded confidence, even arrogance, and professional success. She possessed a selectively photographic memory, was much smarter than I was, and was, in the best sense of the word, a dilettante. She knew about art and architecture (minor at Vassar, when it was the women's Yale), classical music, literature, history, politics local and international, sports (played several), had been president of her high school senior class, and made the impression on everyone she met that she was a woman destined for glory. She had formed a producing company with a partner, and wanted to become the next Sol Hurok, impresario of classical music and dance events. She loved to talk, and to listen, and to argue, as did I. I'd never met anyone like her.

As far as I was concerned, girls had long graduated from biological curiosities to potential lifelong companions and inspirations. I was thirty-four when I met Charlotte but had been part of only two long-term relationships. I think I was so tentative because I had grown up surrounded by divorced and single women. Unfortunately, like a good liberal, I could see both sides of my parents' divorce. I could see that Mother felt betrayed and wounded, and I could see that Dad felt tricked and gypped. My solution was simplified Chekhovian: work! If a woman worked as hard as a man and was treated equally, she would be less susceptible to the swooning depressions that had swallowed up Mother, and she would be able to stand on her own two feet financially, therefore having no need to bankrupt and infuriate her husband. I never thought to substitute the word *desire* for *need*.

I had been a feminist for as long as I could remember—but not one with an agenda Robin Morgan or Kitty McKinnon would appreciate. I believed not only should women be allowed to work, they should be forced to work just as men are (not by law, but by custom), thereby protecting themselves from dependency. Though Chekhov meant it ironically, I didn't: Work made people value themselves. I didn't want more women winding up like Mother. Later, when some critics (in Los Angeles, of course) criticized *Geniuses* as sexist for showing a vapid blond woman beaten up onstage, my response was that yes, she is, but by the end of the play she has fought back and emerged victorious— she hasn't stayed in bed like Sarah Crouse or collapsed onto psychiatric couches like Mother. Many feminists of that time would rather women be defeated by men and become martyrs to be pitied. Not my brand of feminism. And Charlotte was a living example of it. Her own vivacity, coupled with her family's comfort level, meant (in my simplistic interpretation) that I'd never need worry about her passivity or depression or financial dependency. She would always stand on her own two feet and perhaps exorcise my own temptations toward narcissism and depression.

Her family was as impressive as she was: handsome, as aristocratic as a southern family can be, immensely entertaining, athletic, filled with the confidence of the blessed (if not the chosen), Ivy Leaguers all; and most important, it was functional. They loved one another.

Cf.

Charlotte and I went to the theatre and the movies, and on trips to Europe, the Maryland shore, and California. Once things got going after a month or two, we ate dinner together almost every night. We each had wagonloads of friends and they all had to be introduced. We briefly tried cooking together, but the competition was fierce and we became testy. We examined this to see if it was symptomatic of deeper troubles. I worked out of my apartment—by then a three-bedroom in the Village—and had more time to cook, not to mention read up on how to cook. She saw what cooking meant to me and gave it up agreeably (I think) in exchange for making the apartment look beautiful when we had some of our wagonloads over to eat and watch the World Series or an election or the Oscars. And always, there was provocative conversation. Both of us were sensualists, but our lives were liveliest above the neck.

Shortly before proposing, I went to her apartment on a perfect spring day with two truffles poached in a combination of champagne and sherry, then smothered with a mousse of foie gras and placed inside puff pastry with a thin slice of ham. I baked them in her oven, and her response to this extraordinary dish, called *truffes en feuilletage Cendrillon* (Cinderella Truffles), from the kitchens of the Parisian restaurant Lasserre, was so appreciative and sexual that the afternoon was gone completely, and I knew this match would work.

A few weeks before or after we were married, Charlotte's producing company failed. I don't know how; I reasoned it was overambitious to expect windfall profits from producing John Curry, the Olympic Gold Medal–winning, classically trained ice dancer, and the Royal Danish Ballet. Her partner grumbled about something Charlotte had done, but I never found out what it was. I assumed the whole thing was a minor setback, and that she would entrepreneur another venture right away. She never did.

When I was talking to my cousin Lee about her failed first marriage and some disappointments in her second, she had told me, "Everything is there in front of you right at the beginning. You just don't choose to see some of it. You choose to keep the bad things in the background, out of focus, while all the good things about the person are in ECU (extreme close-up). But it's all there. Then, as the years go by, the background comes forward into focus"—she moved her hands, one sliding far in front of the other, indicating a near image receding—"and the ECU goes into the background."

Charlotte and I both thought we had our focuses sharp, and we were married on June 10, 1978, at Grace Church in New York City, the Reverend Paul Zahl presiding. The place was full, the day a cool and sunny seventy-four degrees. Oliver didn't drop the ring, and the bride and groom rode uptown in a hansom cab, she looking like a Victorian angel, he wearing her father's top hat.

HOW TO GET A WOMAN TO MARRY YOU

TRUFFES EN FEUILLETAGE CENDRILLON (Cinderella Truffles)
(From Secrets of the Great French Restaurants by Louisette Bertholle, Macmillan, 1974)

Four 1 ½-ounce truffles, fresh (brushed and peeled) or canned
1 cup dry champagne
¼ cup sherry
3 ounces fresh or canned mousse de foie gras
4 ounces puff pastry
4 thin slices boiled, sliced ham
1 egg yolk, beaten and diluted with 2 drops of water

1. Preheat oven to 350 degrees.
2. Poach truffles gently in champagne and sherry 15 minutes. Cool. Mash foie gras with a fork and coat each truffle evenly with it.
3. Roll pastry into a 16-inch square and divide into four parts. Place a slice of ham on each sheet and a coated truffle in the center of the slice.

4. Moisten pastry corners and pinch them together to seal, twisting at the top to form a bundle. Brush each bundle with egg yolk and bake on a baking sheet for 15 minutes or until golden brown.

5. Serve immediately on a dish lined with a white napkin.

YIELD: 4 servings.

Birthday Nut

~~~~~~~

DID YOU PHOTOGRAPH your first child more than the succeeding one(s)? If he was a boy, did you believe him the only one ever born destined to play the violin, quarterback the Giants, read at six months, speak Czech at two? I did.

Frank was born in 1980 during performances of our well-intentioned but ridiculously inept revue of the songs of the great Broadway and movie composer Jule Styne. Jule composed the scores for *Gentlemen Prefer Blondes*, *Peter Pan*, *Gypsy*, *Funny Girl*, and a bunch of others. He also won an Oscar for the treacly title song of *Three Coins in the Fountain*, one of his weaker movie efforts.

Our show, which Jule called with a somewhat wooden ear *Styne After Styne*, was produced at the Manhattan Theatre Club, hot on the heels of its success with *Ain't Misbehavin'*. It had been decided that our show needed a book—even though we all should have realized that one of the reasons for *Ain't Misbehavin'*'s success was its lack of a single line of dialogue. Just all those wonderful Fats Waller songs exuberantly sung by a sensational cast.

The highlight of the rehearsal period for me came with what seemed like my eighty-seventh rewrite of the very inane concept dreamed up by the director, Fritz Holt, and agreed to by me because I couldn't think of anything better. I also couldn't think of anything worse: A group of show guys and gals are about to put on a musical, but gosh darn it, lacking an eleven-o'-clock number, the guys 'n' gals sing Jule's catalog, before—eureka, at the eleventh hour—finding one. This simple-minded story line was augmented by unmemorable staging and a competent but unexciting cast.

Jule didn't like Rewrite #87, and said he was thinking of withdrawing the show. "Oh, this version is shit," the artistic director, Lynne Meadow, said to Jule in front of me, endearing her to me forever, "but the show will work anyway." Jule was convinced because he wanted to be convinced, but the show *didn't* work anyway (musicals with bad books never do). The rehearsals had been unpleasant, the previews frustrating, the reviews dismissive.

Normally, I would have been wrecked, but our son's birth superseded everything, and against my will I became a jubilant and dutiful—if somewhat selfish—father. After a lengthy discussion of names, Charlotte said, "Let's name him Frank, after your uncle." When I called Uncle Frank to tell him, he broke down. Many tears followed on both ends of the phone.

I had heard about babies before Frank was born but hadn't had much business with them and considered them as dangerous to hold as porcupines (still do, sort of). At his birth, I concluded that he was unique—and not by the standards of *Rosemary's Baby*. Had there ever been such fascinatingly tiny feet, intricately wrinkled fingers, ebullient smiles, or riveting breathing even while asleep? I photographed and videoed incessantly and still have a forty-minute tape of my giving him a bath that would rival Warhol's *Empire* for torpor-inducement. I submitted adorable head shots to modeling agents and, when he wasn't chosen, turned my back on show biz forever and deliberately sabotaged most of the scripts I was then writing. (Unfortunately, the studios decided it wasn't so deliberate.) I put his name up for Harrow and Eton and insisted that he be clothed by Rowe's of Bond Street, a ridiculously expensive store specializing in Spoiled Children's Clothes so fancy that they were suitable only for coronations—and which were outgrown in a matchstrike.

I also determined that he would have an epicure's palate and so made sure all his food was fresh and puréed by hand, occasionally sprinkling it with seasonings that might have pleased Fredy Girardet but didn't particularly please Frank. Charlotte, the eldest of four children, was well aware that there were other babies besides Frank but humored me nonetheless, even allowing me to make his first three birthday cakes with chestnuts.

I'd always thought chestnuts were indigenous to France, because that's where I discovered them, on a break from LAMDA. The trees grow all over the

world, but a blight wiped out most of our American ones in the early twentieth century, forcing us to import fresh chestnuts from Europe.

Here, we generally associate them with Christmas and roasting, thanks in
no small part to Mel Tormé's song about Jack Frost nipping at your nose. But
in French hands they become a marvel of subtlety. The *mont blancs* (puréed
with cream), *coupe aux marrons* (in syrup, over ice cream), and the fat and crys-
tallized *marrons glacés* (candied) from Lyons all exploit the natural sugar of
chestnuts, and by luck or the lack of it, dessert served as my introduction to
them. I loved their smooth, starchy taste (they have less oil than other nuts)
and crumbly texture and the way sugars and syrups clung to them, softening
them in sweet embrace. Years later, I made many friends by bringing forth a
bavarois Clermont, a spectacular Bavarian cream studded with candied chestnuts and surrounded by candied chestnuts dipped in chocolate—which was
also served to Coppola.

Since then, I've discovered the virtue of unsweetened chestnuts, as in the
delicious soup devised by Patricia Yeo at the departed AZ restaurant and a
supremely complex chestnut-flour farfalle that Alain Ducasse surrounds with
slivers of pork breast, tiny chicken quenelles, cèpes, foie-gras grease, white-
truffle shavings, and more chestnuts. It wouldn't take you or me more than
three days to make, but it is one of the great dishes in New York. You should
sell the family liver and go to the restaurant and order it.

If there's a chestnut on a restaurant menu, I order it.

Chestnuts are so special and so difficult to deal with—it's practically impossible to shell them without crushing the meat—that they have their own
knife (with a curved, sharp edge) and their own roasting pan (with small per-
forations so the shells won't explode). Neither is of much use for anything
else. Slitting the shells and roasting the chestnuts is the traditional method of
separating one from the other, but the shells may also be slit and the nuts
dropped into 350-degree oil for twenty minutes and then cooled.

Back when Frank was about to be a year old, I determined that the best
was almost good enough for him and came up with an old recipe from the legendary French chef Paul Bocuse for a *gâteau aux marrons* that isn't difficult but
is unusual and sets off the nut's mild and chewy pleasures with a fail-safe film
of chocolate. And though it can be made with the more common chestnuts in

syrup, which you then purée, or a can of the purée itself, I opted for the billion-dollar candied version. I whipped it up for him and several of his closest one-year-old associates, and he wolfed it right down. So did his buddies. Their parents were amazed that this would be served as a birthday cake for onegenarians, but I thought, superciliously, What else would you expect for a Czech-speaking, violin-playing pro quarterback? Besides, Payard Patisserie hadn't opened yet. At his second birthday, the scene repeated itself, happy children gulping down this special dessert and parents who stayed just to taste it.

On his third birthday, however, a little snag developed. Flanked by apparently wiser friends, Frank dove into his birthday cake with glee once more, having advertised it at nursery school for days. He then asked rhetorically, "Isn't this great?" and his best friend, Jasper or Julian or Kenneth or something, took one bite, made a face as if he'd just swallowed a full glass of soy sauce, and emitted a noise something like "Eeeyoueccccchhh!" He dropped his fork and said, "This is *awful!*" Frank, who is today quite a freethinker and dazzles and infuriates the Upper West Side with his contrarian views on international politics, was not immune to peer pressure at age three. He suddenly realized that he was eating something weird, possibly poisonous, something that might lose him friends, and that certainly had no place in the junk-food duchy to which he'd become accustomed (his father having sometime before given up on the puréeing of fresh produce, unable to fight what was served at nursery school and in other people's homes). He looked at the *gâteau* in shock, as if double-crossed, and dropped his fork. All of his friends dropped their forks. We lived near Washington Square, but you could hear the crashing of cutlery in Washington Heights. Amid demands for ice cream and "real" cake, the wheels quickly came off the party.

I quietly put the recipe away in a drawer and never had the nerve to try it out on him again—or on his less-photographed but equally adored younger brother, Eddie.

Until '02.

Mindful that fall and winter—and particularly Christmas—are optimal seasons for the warmth and earthiness of chestnuts savory or sweet, and that nineteen years had passed since that "friend" brought my son's culinary world (and belief in his father's taste) crashing all around, I decided to spring the cake on Frank's considerably more experimental palate once more. The occasion wasn't Frank's birthday but his soon-to-be stepbrother Dodge's. Dodge Landesman has exceptionally precocious taste buds. And so, with some trepidation, I looked up the old concoction, scoured the city for *marrons glacés* (a seriously disappearing breed but available at Payard and Fauchon), whipped up batter for two cakes, and melted chocolate. My memory had rusted. The timing was off (longer baking was required), and I laid the chocolate on too thick, but the cakes were a success. "Great, Dad!" Frank exclaimed. Both he and twelve-year-old Dodge, whose mother, Red, I was main-squeezing—and the sixteen grown-up guests—polished off their cake and nibbled the dishes clean.

However, if I was expecting a Proustian remembrance, it didn't happen. Frank didn't recall that third birthday (or the preceding two), which once again made clear to me that individual moments shared by parent and child are so evanescent and subjective that what is indelible and traumatic to one might fail to crease the brain of the other. But that wouldn't be the worst thing.

GÂTEAU AUX MARRONS

1 cup candied chestnuts (*marrons glacés*), or drained chestnuts in syrup, or chestnut cream or spread

4 tablespoons unsalted butter, plus extra for greasing the pan

6 tablespoons heavy cream

4 eggs, separated

4 ounces bittersweet chocolate

1 teaspoon apricot jam

5 or 6 macaroons (preferably made with pine nuts), for garnish

5 or 6 *marrons glacés*, for garnish

1. Preheat the oven to 350 degrees. Butter an 8-inch round cake pan and line with a round of buttered parchment paper.

2. Purée the chestnuts in a food processor. Add the butter and cream and process until smooth. With the machine running, add the egg yolks, one at a time. Transfer the mixture to a large bowl. Beat the egg whites until stiff and fold into the mixture just until blended. Pour into the pan and smooth the top. Bake until the cake is firm to the touch, 30–40 minutes. Cool completely on a wire rack, then place on a serving dish.

3. Melt the chocolate in a double boiler and stir in the jam and enough water to thin mixture to a spreadable consistency. Ice cake with a thin layer and decorate with macaroons and *marrons glacés*.

YIELD: 6 to 8 servings.

SQUASH-AND-CHESTNUT SOUP WITH CHIPOTLE CREAM
(Adapted from AZ)

For the chipotle cream
1 cup ruby port
½ cup dry red wine
1 teaspoon chipotle peppers in adobo sauce or crushed dried chipotles
2 tablespoons tomato paste
1 cup crème fraîche or sour cream

For the soup
2 ½ pounds kabocha, acorn, or butternut squash
2 quarts chicken stock
10 ounces whole chestnuts (before peeled), roasted and peeled
2 tablespoons pure maple syrup
Kosher salt and freshly ground black pepper to taste

1. Combine the port, wine, chipotles, and tomato paste in a medium saucepan, bring to a boil, and then simmer until the mixture is a thick paste, about 15 minutes. Let cool, then whisk in the crème fraîche and refrigerate until serving.

2. Preheat the oven to 350 degrees. Cut the squash in half lengthwise and remove the seeds. Place cut-side down on a foil-lined baking sheet and bake
   until soft, about 1 hour. When the squash is cool, scoop out the flesh and
   place 6 cups in a large saucepan. Add the stock and the chestnuts and simmer until the chestnuts are soft, about 30 minutes. Stir in the syrup and
   purée with a hand blender or in batches in a blender. Return to the
   saucepan and season to taste.

3. Reheat the soup and ladle it into bowls. Drizzle with chipotle cream.

YIELD: 8 servings.

NOTE: The soup and cream can be made ahead and refrigerated for up to 3
days.

Right Turn on Red

I MET FRANK RICH while he was a film critic at the *New York Post* in the late seventies, and we hit it off immediately. We shared a great interest in movies, food, and the theatre; in fact, I was surprised when he told me he had wanted for years to be the drama critic at the *Times*. He found plays more exciting than movies (I didn't then but do now), and, having grown up in D.C. in New York's cultural shadow, knew only too well that there were hundreds of film critics across the country—but only one important theatre critic. He is a great raconteur and conversationalist, and I considered him a good friend. I couldn't have predicted then that he would wind up the most popular general columnist at the paper twenty-five years later.

Still, I was surprised when he told me during dinner one night that the *Times* had made him an offer to be a second-string critic with no promise of taking over Walter Kerr's position when Kerr retired a few years down the road. As it turned out, Kerr had a heart attack, and after a little jockeying, Frank was appointed chief drama critic within months of moving to the *Times*.

Frank and I went to the theatre several times, though not nearly as frequently as he went with his friend Rafael Yglesias; the two ditched their wives every Thursday night, saw something Frank was to review, and then had dinner and got pleasantly drunk, sometimes with me tagging along at least for the food and booze. Elaine's was the favored watering hole for a year or two, then Orso was.

Frank disqualified himself from reviewing *Geniuses* because he'd read an early draft of it, but Gussow's review was so uncharacteristically effusive, it read as though Frank had given Mel some of his Kool-Aid.

André Bishop opened *Geniuses* at Playwrights Horizons less than a year after the little-noted but still embarrassing *Styne After Styne*, and since Hollywood likes plays that take notice of it, pro or con, the studios came calling.

Rafe Yglesias and his wife, Margaret, lived two blocks from Charlotte and son Frank and me, and we became instant friends. As Frank Rich and I fenced over his reviewing *Geniuses*, Rafe and I became closer. Rafe had dropped out of school at fifteen, written his first novel at sixteen, and had three novels published by the time he was twenty-one. He is smart and snappy and funny, and a good friend to this day, unless we get into a political discussion, at which point he becomes a serious combatant.

Although he had the markings of a New York liberal when I met him, he told me many times, "I'm not a liberal, I'm a Marxist." But he was the only cheerful one I'd ever met. I was becoming suspicious of the Left's hypocrisy: Everyone from every campaign seemed primarily interested in making lots of money and sending their children to the best private schools while vehemently criticizing greedy capitalists and privileged children. Most of my friends were great advocates for civil rights but no one actually knew anyone black. And for all the talk of peace-and-love, the malicious treatment of returning Vietnam veterans was appalling. The Left's self-righteousness seemed as anal and dictatorial as the Right's (hello, Elia Kazan), and every bit as obsessed with controlling other people's lives.

In 1974, William Shockley, who had won the Nobel Prize for physics some years earlier, was invited to speak at Yale about his theory that intelligence was determined by racial genetics. This flew in the face of everything I had been taught and believed, and I thought this excuse for segregation had been disproved years earlier. But since the question lurks at the unmentionable core of every racial debate (Are whites genetically smarter than blacks? Are Asians smarter than whites? Are Calcuttans born with a better business gene?), I was interested in hearing it disproved again, as it no doubt should be at least once per generation in order to set it to rest. But student Lefties at Yale not only protested Shockley's appearance, they heckled him so thoroughly that he was unable to speak. This paradoxically gave his theory new currency: What were the students so afraid of? Why wouldn't they allow him to voice these opinions and have them countered? I began to see more hypocrisy on the Left, which insists on free speech but, as Nat Hentoff so clearly limns in *Free Speech for Me but Not for Thee*, frequently won't tolerate the practice of it. It is precisely this unwitting hypocrisy—and the delusion that their actions were taken "for the greater good" (i.e., to prevent innocent victims from being exposed to Shockley's unbearable ideas)—that mushroomed into the culturally crippling political correctness of the last thirty years.

If my mother and sister didn't discuss politics growing up, Rafe's family had all the time, it seemed, so he was considerably more invested in it than I had ever been, even though I'd gone out and campaigned for mine. My religion was a sloppy Episcopalianism; his was an unflinching Marxism. As long as he and I stayed off the subject, we couldn't have been more congenial and frequently hilarious together. When I took an office two stories below his on East Eleventh Street, we had lunch several times a week. He was continuing to write novels and, together with his half-brother, Lewis Cole, made screenplay deals, though none were produced.

When Hollywood showed serious interest in me after *Geniuses* opened, I asked for help. I'd been an avid moviegoer, hookeying through many a tutoring-school afternoon, and had written a couple of passionate but formless screenplays. I didn't really know how they worked. At breakfast one morning, Rafe sat me down over a bagel and smoked salmon (oh, all right, lox), and said, "The first and most important thing you need to know is that all screenplays can be broken down into three acts." The scales fell from my eyes. Next? "There are many more characters in a movie than there are in a play." Of course, and not just because Actors Equity charges too much per actor. Unless you're a salmon, you see many more people in the course of a day than you see onstage in a play not by Sydney Kingsley. "Characters don't talk nearly as much as they do in plays." That much I knew. "Scenes are much shorter." Yup. "There must be conflict. There must be jeopardy. There must be somebody to root for, and there must be change." Though it sounds simple, it was exactly the structural underpinning I needed to know about.

"Also, screenplays are fraudulent. Producers and executives always want the leading characters to be sympathetic, and let's face it, people basically aren't sympathetic." He laughed in triumph.

I went to Hollywood and commuted for most of the eighties. After months of flailing around with a script, I somehow managed to get a Columbia project called *Micki & Maude* right. Dudley Moore was in my mind during the writing of it—and, by God, they cast him and made the movie. A writer is never as hot as when he's written a script that's being made—not *has been* made (unless it's hugely successful), but *is being made*. If the movie has been made, it's a real object with real success or lack of it, as measured by the box office. But in Hollywood, fantasy is the stuff of life, and everyone's reputation becomes better or worse than the wearer of that reputation could ever possibly be. Before *Micki & Maude* was released, I had two other assignments, and they were also green-lighted. During the next five years, I wrote five movies that were produced—three written by me alone, one a rewrite, and one that was rewritten by someone who turned it into pap. All but one were signed before *Micki & Maude* was even released.

I'd signed on with a business manager when my first screenplays hit, and he was worth every percentage point he took. Not only did his real estate advice prove wise and his investments pay handsomely, he looked after all the details of the money, which, now, since I can no longer afford him, consumes 10–20% of my day. He is just as lively today as he was twenty years ago, and flourishing. And so I wrote about him for one of my columns:

THE FABULOUS BAKER BOY

CLOSE YOUR EYES and listen to him, and you're back under the Third Avenue El in a white T-shirt on a roasting summer's day with the guys, mostly Jewish or Italian, smoking Luckys and screaming about ball and Marciano and money, whistling at the skirts. WW2 just ended, your hair's all curly, you're about to marry your best girl, and the world is yer erster. And now, fifty-five years later, in his kitchen, after a thirteen-hour day in the office—"Four hundred fights I got into today! Four hundred!"—Bert Padell relaxes by baking, a stress reduction probably unimaginable back in the days under the El.

Midnight baker, poet, former Yankee batboy, friend of DiMaggio and Mantle, Joe Cocker and Montgomery Clift, business manager and lawyer to eminent enterprises as varied as Britney Spears, Jackie Mason, John Berendt, Mikhail Baryshnikov, P. Diddy, the rapper Rakim, and the restaurants of Robert De Niro (but not De Niro himself), Bert is as New York a New Yorker as New York has ever Yorked. Sometimes as soft-spoken as a courtier, he is usually a walking exclamation point, either surprised or outraged. And I love talking to him.

While stirring a pound of chunked chocolate into a pound of butter melting over the heat of his electric stove one night in 2003, Bert tells me about Madonna's lawsuit against him in 1999: "The BBC kept trying to get me to say something bad about her, but I wouldn't." He nudges the chocolate gently with a spoon. "Go slow now—don't burn it." He wheels around and pours sugar into a stainless-steel bowl filled with eggs. " 'But I got nothing against the woman,' I told them. 'Most people would say something bad about her,' this interviewer kept prodding me, and I said to him, 'Well, I'm not most people.' "

As they said in the thirties, I'll tell the world.

For years his pastries went—free—to several of the restaurants he handled (most notably, One if By Land, Two if By Sea), but now he bakes mostly for his family. He used to start at eleven at night and finish up at two but now limits that to Fridays. Tonight he is making chocolate-chip cookies and the densest, creamiest, most-likely-to-make-your-cardiologist-rich chocolate cake ever to be unavailable to the public (until now).

An easy-listenin' version of "You Were Meant for Me" plays softly on the radio, followed by "Everything's Up to Date in Kansas City" and a bunch of other show tunes. Would Jellybean Benitez, Kid Creole, and Alicia Keys drop themselves from Bert's client list if they were aware of his musical tastes? Doubtful. And what about rap? "I don't like it, but I accept it," he says, paddling the eggs in his Dito Dean mixer. Bert's is not the kitchen of a pro but of a successful couple whose kids have moved out—which he is one of and who have. "When I first started baking, all my people were guinea pigs. I'd bring an apple pie into the office, and when it fell on the floor and broke the floor, they'd say how much they liked it. So I didn't know who liked what.

"My tofu cheesecake was good, but then one night by accident—by accident!—I put it in the freezer, and that was it! I found the secret of making it jell. See? You understand what I'm saying? You have to learn and learn." Bitten by the pastry bug, Bert went to the Culinary Institute of America in Hyde Park, which normally turns out cookie-cutter chefs prepared to oversee two hundred covers at a big hotel, and took a weeklong accelerated course— what else would you expect from someone who gets into four hundred fights a day?

"A lotta people like the taste of coffee with chocolate," he says, anticipating my own recent addiction—and pouring boiling water into espresso powder— nothing better than the darkest 91% chocolate mixed with a black espresso. He pours the coffee, then the chocolate and butter, into the eggs, lets the mixer work until the batter is the texture of heavy cream, and looks at me impishly. "Are you ready?" he asks. I nod, and he pours the mixture into a buttered and floured springform pan and carefully walks it to his oven. It's soupy, and there's a danger of spilling.

After baking the cake, he refrigerates it for thirty minutes, then gives it to me and kicks me out with an admonition: "Don't eat it till it's cool. Hot cake is very bad for you." I never heard that one before, so on my way home, I swipe a finger through it and suck—it's a cream dream!—and sleep the sleep of the just with no digestive eruptions.

The next two days running, Bert phones to remind me to whip the tofu for his famous cheesecake until it's very creamy and to take the chocolate cake out of the fridge twelve to twenty-four hours before serving.

A few days later, having made the cheesecake—warmly and incredulously received by friends for its lightness and lack of tofuishness—I visit his offices, a full floor opposite the Carnegie Towers.

There's not an inch of space on the walls—they're covered with hundreds of gold and platinum records he's been involved with, autographed posters and pictures not only of his clients but of presidents FDR, JFK, RMN, GRF, and WJC. ("I don't take sides in politics," he says.) There is a private bathroom with a letter about personal freedom from Charlie Chaplin, a conference room filled with hundreds of signed photographs from Cy Young and

Christy Mathewson and just about every Yankee ever as well as sixty-five baseball bats, belonging to everyone from Stan Musial to Garth Brooks (who once went to spring training with the Mets). The most extraordinary artifact is a framed collection of 1937 Yankee photographs, *with each player's original signed contract!*

I had asked Bobby, Bert's wife of forty-four years, mother of their three children, grandmother of six, and an interior decorator, where she thought his collecting mania stemmed from. "He didn't have when he was a kid," she said, "so now he can, and he gets everything." My genes kick in: another self-made man.

He is seated about three feet from two secretaries. Liz has been with him for thirty-three years, Douglas only two. Everyone talks on various phones at the same time, and between Bert's instructions to me about the proper way to serve pinwheel cookies, he illustrates what a business manager does besides crunch numbers.

He sprinkles his sentences with a vocabulary enriched not only by a childhood in the Bronx but by his 1949–50 Yankee batboy stint, which job he acquired when his predecessor was killed in a hunting accident. (Bert secured his place in the record books in the sky by being the first batboy ever ejected from a game for stealing signs from the opposing team's catcher and coaches.) One word in particular—which I'll euphemize as "handkerchief" but whose referent wouldn't get past the elevator operator of a family publication—is used about as often as most people use *the*.

"Seymour," he shouts into the phone, "the guy can't appear in a concert, he's in the handkerchiefin' hospital! He's got no leg! . . . But, but, he's got no handkerchiefin' leg! It was a terrible accident! The bone is lying there in the street!"

An accountant who hasn't been putting in enough office hours is reprimanded in front of me. When he leaves, Bert says: "He's been doing that a long time. The nicer you are, they put a bullet up your keister."

Another call comes in on the speakerphone. "That house she moved into, the hot-water heater doesn't work. Do you get a warranty with a used house?" the caller asks.

"You don't call a house 'a used house,'" Bert says. "It's a resale. And no, there's no warranty on a house. But call up the guy who sold it and tell him there is."

Liz places a call for him, and he turns courtly. "Marty, I'm sorry for breaking your chops the other day. . . . No, but I'm saying I'm sorry. And I sent him the mortgage." An employee rushes in to say the underwriter of a client's insurance policy has been pocketing the premiums but not paying the benefits. Bert picks up the phone and gets the underwriter's broker on the horn. "You tell that underwriter guy I want him in this office Monday or I'm going to the handkerchiefin' district attorney and file a complaint." (Lots of protests from the phone.) "You tell him I'm going to ask the handkerchiefin' DISTRICT ATTORNEY to examine his books. Do you understand? . . . YOU DON'T UNDERSTAND! HE'S GOING TO JAIL!!" He hangs up and says to me, "You gotta get your demand in first—that keeps them on the defensive, which is what you want." Liz gets him another number, and his voice drops in decibels as he becomes concerned. "Hi. I need a good lawyer to represent someone's son against his mother. He's in a psychological ward, poor kid."

And it's then I remember why his clients pay him the 5 percent—it's not just for keeping their accounts straight and their taxes paid and the hot-water heaters repaired; it's because he connects with them. He has a heart as big as the Bronx—just read some of that poetry—and he's an unflagging optimist.

Eighty-six problems confronted and solved, more or less, in an hour. "Sometimes I think I should go to handkerchiefin' China and be a monk and help everybody—I never seen such a business where everybody just wants one handkerchiefin' thing."

He has a lunch date, and I walk him to the street. "Bert, I have two questions. First, what happened with Madonna?"

"She sued me for two-point-five million dollars because New York State said she'd been living here for a hundred and eighty-three days and I had her in California." He won't tell me the figures, but they settled. He smiles confidentially. "But it wasn't very smart of her people to do. What's the other question?"

"Did the Giants steal the signs from the Dodgers in the '51 playoffs? Did Thomson know Branca was going to throw a fastball?"

"Of course," Bert says—no question. "They did it from the outfield, with binoculars. Now don't forget to take that cheesecake outta the fridge an hour before. And bring me my handkerchiefin' pan back."

BERT PADELL'S CHOCOLATE CHOCOLATE CAKE

1 pound unsalted butter, plus extra for greasing the pan
Flour for dusting the pan
12 ounces bittersweet chocolate
4 ounces unsweetened chocolate
1 bar (3.5 ounces) milk chocolate with cappuccino filling
8 large eggs
1 cup plus 2 tablespoons sugar
2 tablespoons espresso powder dissolved in 1 cup boiling water
Whipped cream for garnish

1. Preheat the oven to 350 degrees. Butter and flour a 10-inch springform pan and line the bottom with parchment paper. Set the pan on a square of heavy-duty aluminum foil and bring the foil up around the sides of the pan to prevent leaks. Set aside.
2. Combine the butter and chocolates in a medium saucepan and melt over medium heat, whisking until smooth. Transfer to a heatproof measuring cup.
3. In the bowl of an electric mixer with the paddle attachment, beat the eggs and sugar for 5 minutes at medium-high speed. With the mixer running, pour in the espresso and beat until blended, then the butter-chocolate mixture, again beating until blended.
4. Pour the batter into the prepared pan and bake for 55 minutes. (The cake will crack around the rim.) Remove from the oven and cool on a wire rack for about 20 minutes. Cover with plastic wrap or aluminum foil and refrigerate for at least 30 minutes (or up to 1 month).
5. Twelve to 24 hours before serving, take the cake out of the refrigerator. Re-

move the sides of the pan, slide a metal spatula under the parchment paper, and slide the cake onto a serving plate. Serve with whipped cream.

Yield: 12–14 servings.

BERT PADELL'S TOFU CHEESECAKE

1 tablespoon butter, softened, plus 2 tablespoons, melted
11–12 graham crackers, crushed, or 1 ¾ cups graham-cracker crumbs
2 cups plus 2 tablespoons sugar
¼ teaspoon cinnamon
2 pounds soft (silken) tofu
1 ½ cups plain yogurt
1 teaspoon vanilla extract
3 tablespoons flour
Pinch salt
4 egg whites (½ cup)

1. Say to yourself, "No, just because it's tofu doesn't mean it can't possibly be good. Trust this guy—he tells Alice Cooper what to do with his money."
2. Roughly 36 hours before serving, preheat oven to 400 degrees. Smear the tablespoon of softened butter over bottom and sides of a 10-inch springform pan. Set prepared pan on a large square of heavy-duty aluminum foil and bring up foil around sides of pan to prevent leaks. Set aside.
3. In medium bowl, mix the 2 tablespoons melted butter with graham crackers, 2 tablespoons of the sugar, and cinnamon.
4. Cover the bottom of the springform pan with half the crumb mixture.
5. In a large bowl of an electric mixer, whisk the tofu until creamy, about 5 minutes at medium-high speed. Gradually beat in the 2 cups sugar, then the yogurt and vanilla. Sift in flour and salt.
6. In another mixer bowl, at medium-high speed, beat egg whites until soft peaks form when beaters are raised and fold into tofu mixture using a rub-

ber spatula. Pour batter into prepared springform and top with remaining crumbs.

7. Place in a large roasting pan and add enough boiling water to reach two thirds of the way up the sides of the pan. Bake 30 minutes. Reduce temperature to 300 degrees and bake an additional 90 minutes.

8. Remove from oven, bring to room temperature, then freeze overnight, or for at least 8 hours.

9. Defrost cake in refrigerator for 24 hours. To serve, remove cake from refrigerator 1 hour before serving. Remove sides of pan, slide a large metal spatula under parchment, and slide cake onto large, flat serving plate. Cut into slices and serve.

YIELD: 12–14 servings.

Will the Soufflé Rise?

~~~~~~~~~~~~

WHILE I WAS proud of my plays, I was damn disappointed in my movies. Although *Micki & Maude* was respectable critically and financially, I'd really only enjoyed working on one film—*My Stepmother Is an Alien*—because its director, Richard Benjamin, was so much fun. He laughed at everything I said, and I laughed at everything he said. And the movie is loopy and out there. But Dan Aykroyd was an overweight leading man and his love scenes with Kim Basinger were creepy. The movie got moderate reviews, and opened the same weekend as the blockbuster *Twins*, starring Danny DeVito and the governor of California. It quickly fell off the radar screen. *Micki & Maude*, directed by Hollywood's most unappreciated director, Blake Edwards, wasn't any fun because Blake didn't much like me after I told him I thought one of his lines wasn't funny. It was a simple line, and a big mistake on my part: I believed him when he said he wanted to know how I felt about his rewrite, which is director-speak for "Tell me how good my rewrite is." In my version, rather than fictionalize names of minor characters, I threw in the names of people associated with Playwrights Horizons—Gurney, Durang, Wasserstein, Innaurato, Lapine, Bishop—and at the beginning of the script, while riding in the back of a limo, Dudley's character asks the chauffeur his name. "Finn, sir," the driver replies, using the composer Bill Finn's name. In response, Blake wrote that Dudley should say, "Well, Finnsir . . ." I thought it wasn't funny but looked as though it was trying to be.

"I don't think that line's funny, Blake," I said into the phone. Silence.

"Gee, I thought it was pretty funny," he said, muted. I could tell he wasn't used to being challenged. Directors aren't in Hollywood; hence the second re-make of *King Kong* and the bloated length of *The New World*. But I plunged ahead. I mean, he *said* he wanted to know my opinion.

"I think it's forced. It's asking for a laugh."

"Oh," he said, and despite my being invited to all the casting sessions and many of the sets before that conversation, I wasn't invited to a single one after-ward. But the movie was the best-realized of anything I wrote, both because Blake was brilliant at staging physical farce (though less so at verbal), and be-cause Dudley Moore, the only actor since Cary Grant able to play farce with sexuality and intelligence, was its leading man.

For the record, the other pictures were *Switching Channels*, *Leonard Part 6*, and *The Distinguished Gentleman*.

Despite what appeared to be success, I was miserable. I'd wanted to be some kind of serious cultural force in New York, and instead was being dis-missed (if mentioned at all) as a writer of trivial, throwaway comedies. I ranted about these highly enviable problems to Charlotte, but she had trouble understanding my gripes.

In 1983, our second son, Edward, was born. Frank had been a feisty baby given to waking in the middle of the night with terrors; he burned almost hy-peractively. By comparison, Eddie was quiet and loving and doted on his par-ents. I felt both boys deserved better than New York, and probably better than me, both of which were in chaos in the eighties.

But for the first time in my life, serious money arrived on the doorstep. Oh, not Bill Gates money or, God forbid, Dadmoney, but bags of it larger than you get for writing off-Broadway plays. I bought a house on Jane Street in Manhat-tan. It was Charlotte's dream to raise our family in as warm and bustling a home as the fairy-tale farm on which she'd grown up, in Elkin, North Carolina. The Jane Street brownstone was built for a single family in the mid-nineteenth century but had since been converted into seven studio apartments. It now looked like a tenement. It needed a near-gut renovation, which didn't interest me. But Charlotte wanted to attack the job.

About five years, a million dollars, and 64,000 arguments later, we moved in. It was a nasty experience from beginning to end. I felt Charlotte wasn't moving fast enough, and she had complaints about me of her own. For one

thing, every time I'd come home with another 10 G's, I'd see something that
could be improved and would request a change—a better lighting fixture that
took three weeks to order, a wider staircase when one had already been built,
a ten-burner Garland industrial range with two ovens and a salamander instead of the G.E. we'd decided on. The Garland was so big and heavy it had to
be disassembled outside, carried in in pieces, then reassembled inside, and
there was some question whether the floor could support it. All these events
caused architect and contractor alike to tear their hair out at the roots. Finally,
as the thing approached completion, I looked at the back wall of the house,
not unlike the artist Gully Jimpson in *The Horse's Mouth* looking at people's feet
and seeing a potential canvas, and said there was nothing exciting about it. I
brought in Joe D'Urso, a visionary designer, and asked for help. Joe produced
three sweeping French doors that made the entire floor magical.

But I was an apartment kid who'd never lived in a house, and it was overwhelming: What do you do if the boiler goes wrong? How do you fix a roof?
What's this about shoveling snow? Besides, it wasn't even finished when we
moved in—not a stick of furniture in the wondrous D'Urso living room. The
boys' schools and my office once around the corner were on the other side of
town now and suddenly much farther away, and the new neighborhood was
scary. Hard to believe now, since Woody Allen has christened Jane Street "the
second most beautiful in New York" (I forget the first), and as of this writing
it's become one of the central boulevards in the horrifically trendy, unhappily
regentrified meatpacking district. It swarms with people and traffic day and
night—now.

But in the late eighties, we were in the more menacing Koch-Dinkins era,
and the meatpacking district was considered the transvestite-hooker capital
of North America. Now I can understand the appeal of a female hooker, and
of a male hooker; but I cannot for the life of me understand the appeal of a
male hooker who looks like a female hooker but won't once you get to know
her. But somebody can. Quite a few people can, in fact, because we found used
condoms and syringes in front of our door just about every day. In addition,
the police department had successfully chased the "Joints . . . loose joints!"
sales force out of Washington Square Park, and it had moved west, near us. So,
easily influenced by the *New York Post*, recently purchased by Rupert Mur-

doch, I'd return from my office every night with images of our young sons with axes in their heads. No doubt my overheated imagination presented this image as a defense against a more realistic catastrophe.

Then one winter night, I got held up at knifepoint by a pair of what seemed like eighteen-foot-tall African-Americans. They'd followed my solo self home from the subway, one as lookout, one as knife-wielding perp, and demanded money. The exchange was almost funny.

"Give it up," the wielder menaced, his foot-long jackknife glinting in the streetlight. This was shortly after Arsenio Hall popularized the expression, so I briefly thought, "You mean, applaud?" I didn't know what he meant. I really didn't. The wielder's eyes darted between me and his lookout.

"Give what up?" I said. I probably could have disarmed him with a feather, because his shoulders sagged and he came close to laughing. He was suddenly not as frightening as he was disgusted at this street-unsavvy honkie. But still scary.

"Your money," he said with contempt.

Which I gave him. Eleven Andrew Jacksons.

He was about to run off when he stopped and looked through the glass panels of our front door. I imagined that he considered for an instant forcing me to open the door and murdering my children. This was funny no longer. Then, almost whimsically, he ran.

I opened the door, not frightened but crestfallen. "What happened?" Charlotte said.

"I just got mugged. At knifepoint." I was defeated, but she wasn't.

"Call the police! Call the police right now!"

She was right. Even though there wasn't a prayer of catching them, the police came in five minutes, and together we prowled the neighborhood; no luck. By simply calling them, I felt my depression lift. I was suddenly less powerless. Active, not passive. Left to my own, I would have sulked into a stew.

A month or so later, my pocket was ripped open in Times Square and picked. The thief made off with fifteen Jacksons this time, and the change that flew about was quickly picked up by the onlookers—and pocketed.

A few months after that, I came home after a midday Sunday movie with Eddie, then age five, to find our electronics stacked in the living room—a

VCR (valuable in those days), a record player, tuner, amps—and the curtains of a living-room window blowing in the breeze. Apparently the thief heard us enter and jumped out the window. This time I called the police without any urging, and again they came in less than five minutes. The search was again futile.

I had begun to dislike the city for reasons other than its curiously personal hostility toward me and my family. Although New York is arguably the most cosmopolitan city in the world, it can also be the most provincial. It's imperious and condescending toward those who don't live there—particularly if they live somewhere between the coasts. It brags of its tolerance toward various lifestyles—unless someone disagrees with that tolerance and actually doesn't approve of abortion or gay marriage or favors church attendance. It touts its urbanity while disdaining those who don't share its enthusiasm. Politically, it's as close-minded as a small town in Alabama, only from a different point of view; and if you're in show business, you will asphyxiate from the lack of fresh political ideas and go deaf from the sound of lockstep.

By the end of the seventies, I was disheartened by the local and federal policies that seemed to idealize codification and restriction and the rusting of gears. The Democrats ruled all branches of federal and local New York City government in 1976 and hadn't had a fresh idea since FDR died—except for the Peace Corps and landing on the Moon. They seemed stale and claustrophobic, chanting the knee-jerk mantra that we must be more like Europe. And in New York, we were. Municipal unions controlled the city almost as much as the theatrical unions and *The New York Times* controlled Broadway. The desire to squash the appetites of those who would express themselves fully, whether in the arts or in business or in foreign policy, had led to what Jimmy Carter correctly called "a national malaise"—at least some of which he caused. It was suffocating.

In 1980, I did the unthinkable. I pulled the lever for Ronald Reagan, whose buoyancy and humor and challenge to the old way of doing things lifted my spirits. I, who had campaigned without end for Eugene McCarthy and Stanley Sheinbaum, who'd flown back to New York on Election Day, 1972, sure that my vote would help George McGovern upset Richard Nixon, who'd pulled the lever twice for Lindsay and once for—arrgghh!—Abe Beame, had come to this. I was the only one I knew who voted this way—and I knew lots of people. When I told friends, arguments inevitably followed—heated and angry arguments, as if I had insulted the Pope in a cathedralful of Catholics. This was no lighthearted matter to them. This was religion. They felt betrayed and furious.

I saw myself as entwined with the city, both clogging ourselves in cobwebs and grime, the city frozen into inaction by political correctness, the divisive racial demagoguery of Al Sharpton, and the inability to break free from union strangleholds that have led to its becoming, as of this writing, the worst state in the union in which to do business. The worst! Fiftieth! In that regard, at least, I was becoming my father's son.

I thought my friends had little curiosity regarding the rest of the country. Occasionally someone would fly to Miami for a weekend or, of course, to L.A.—but interest in finding out something about the national character, not merely the local, left them cold and contemptuous of anyone who felt otherwise. I wanted out.

My play *Fighting International Fat* began as a comic jab at the coming phenomenon of afternoon TV talk shows, then exemplified by Phil Donahue, Sally Jessy Raphaël, and hundreds of narcissistic guests. In the play, all the characters except the host belong to International Fat Fighters, a group run by a character named Roz and loosely based on Weight Watchers International. Each character has a horror story about being overweight, and each successfully has lost weight through Roz's strategy: Not unlike that of Alcoholics Anonymous, each character is assigned a Food Governess, whose responsibility it is to prevent her from eating—whether that meant smashing all the food in her house, running her up hill and down dale, or becoming sexually involved with her. As I delved deeper (or some might say, shallower), I began to see the play as a metaphor for individualism. When Roz's nemesis, a beautiful woman named D'Raleigh Bell, who has lost weight and became ravishing through hundreds of surgeries, teases the group members away from International Fat Fighters with promises of their favorite foods, Roz sees how weak people are and appreciates the person who can stand alone without the aid of others. No doubt this was somewhat inspired by my father's independence, somewhat by the thoughtless and clunky avarice of corporations, and somewhat by the unions that so throttled New York and show business. I gladly joined the Dramatists Guild, which represents playwrights, lyricists, and composers and is not a union. As owners of their own copyrights, playwrights are entrepreneurs; and because the Dramatists Guild is not a union, each can act individually for him- or herself—and for the good of others if he or she so chooses (I doubt many other DG members view themselves as small businessmen and businesswomen; most would rather the Dramatists Guild were a union). Artists, by and large, function as individuals, and I began to see small businesspeople as artists, too—those who, as Stephen Sondheim writes in "Finishing the Hat" from *Sunday in the Park with George*,

> Look, I made a hat
> Where there never was a hat

create an enterprise. I doubt Sondheim or his collaborator, James Lapine, would view their show or this song as a capitalist manifesto, but artists, visionary businesspeople, mathematicians, and scientists often create something where there was nothing, and to me, anything that wasn't corporate, governmental, unionized, or federated became worth championing.

The play wasn't well received by critics, mostly because it was sort of a goofy mess, with half-formed ideas bouncing off walls and exaggerated characters camping around. I hoped GBS would approve, but I don't think he would have. Certainly audiences didn't. There were walkouts every night, even though I thought, "If they'll only wait for the big food fight, they'll love it!" Unfortunately, the ones who waited for the big food fight didn't love it, either.

THE BEST HOLLYWOOD COMEDIES are anarchic, whether made in the thirties like most Marx Brothers movies or in the forties like *Sullivan's Travels* or in the fifties like *Sunset Blvd.* or in the sixties like *Dr. Strangelove* or in the seventies like *Animal House* and *The Heartbreak Kid* or in the eighties like *Ghostbusters* or in the nineties like *Dumb & Dumber* and *Flirting with Disaster*. First among comic equals is probably Charles Lederer and Howard Hawks's *His Girl Friday*, the rapid-fire, gender-switching, verbal gymnastic made in 1940 and based on *The Front Page* by Ben Hecht and Charles MacArthur. Remakes aren't usually an improvement on the original, but *His Girl Friday* proves the rule, and in my opinion is considerably better than any of the *Front Page* versions. Lederer and Hawks changed the original from a male-buddy picture featuring a battling editor and his star reporter to a romantic comedy featuring a battling editor played by Cary Grant who's been married to and separated from his star reporter, Rosalind Russell, who, in turn, is about to marry a stiff played by Ralph Bellamy. Wearing my hubristic screenwriting hat, I was wooed by Columbia into trying to rewrite it into an update for Michael Caine, Kathleen Turner, and Christopher Reeve.

Unfortunately, I succeeded, and it was made into something seriously unfunny called *Switching Channels*, though without Michael Caine, which was crucial.

Comedies need surprise, edge, wit whether physical or verbal, and helium. Instead of the wit and high wires of *His Girl Friday*, my script was heavy-handed and obvious, more or less like the actors, who were club-footed and showed no understanding of the nimble acting style Hawks elicited. Largely due to the influence of the Actors Studio, today's actors often feel they have to show the *process* of arriving at their emotions—the great effort they've exerted—rather than the emotion itself. This is why light-footed comedies are so rare nowadays.

Also rare in movie comedies of any era is the length of the *His Girl Friday* script—as much as 240 typed pages, almost all of it slam-bang dialogue. Most scripts in the eighties were about 120 pages in length and today come in at slightly over 90 pages. Hawks managed to have his actors spit dialogue at a machine-gun pace without drawing attention to it. They appeared to speak and act just as naturalistically as in any action-comedy of the time, giving this picture a sort of loony, heightened theatricalism and an amazing unity of style. In our version, the actors were only too happy to show how hard they were working.

The director, Ted Kotcheff, and I watched this disaster unfold during the shoot and tried to figure out how to combat it every day. We couldn't.

Part of its failure artistically (it was a complete failure at the box office) was due to the absence of Michael Caine. It's difficult to find a leading man in his forties or fifties who isn't an action hero and impossible to find Cary Grant, certainly my favorite movie star of all time—and not just because he looked like Uncle Bus. Dudley Moore and Michael Caine came close as comic actors, and I'd written it with Dudley in mind. He wasn't available. Michael was, and when he agreed to play the lead, jubilation broke out among Kotcheff, the producer, Marty Ransohoff, and me.

We had a reading of my script at the Ritz-Carlton in New York, and it was thrilling—hard to imagine when you see the finished result. Kotcheff had wanted another writer to take a pass at the script, and it turned out Kathleen liked the other writer's version. So we had a script-off. The three actors read both scripts back to back. When it was over, Michael said, "Well, there's no question which one is better—yours."

"That's the one we're doing!" said Marty. Ted agreed. My head swelled, and I was a Cainiac for life.

"I always alternate pictures—do one because I like it, then one for the money," Michael said.

"And this is for the money?" I kidded him.

"No, this one I like. *Jaws 4* is for the money." I was tickled. I really hadn't wanted to write this script since the original film was already perfect, and I knew the critics would be gunning for it because of its presumption. (I continue to believe that the only movies that should be remade are ones with promising premises that were botched; you can never hope to better the good ones. Look at *Sabrina*.) But my ego was flattered because of agents and producers calling and blowing in my ear and, of course, offering money. And now the future Sir Michael said how much he liked it.

I had written the first draft a year earlier and sent it in to Ransohoff. I was in midtown New York the next day when I picked up a message to phone him and darted into the Princeton Club, where I was permitted because my father-in-law was a graduate, to make the call.

"Hi, Marty."

"Where are you?"

"In New York—I'm calling from the Princeton Club."

"You went to Princeton?" It turned out Marty, who was not Jewish but was annoyed when anyone thought he was, highly prized the Ivy League.

"No, my father-in-law did. I went to Denison." He chose not to hear that, and from that moment on referred to me as a Princeton boy. I think he got the picture green-lighted so he could brag about his author's collegiate genealogy.

"I love the script," said Marty, who is almost as enormous in legend as he is in physical size. "I've sent it to Michael Caine."

"He'll be great!" I said.

"And he's British, so there won't be all that actor bullshit," Marty said.

"And he'll say all the words!"

Marty laughed. "Yes, I don't want them changing one line of your script." He sounded pugnacious. "It's too good."

"Thank you, Marty," I said, knowing he'd forget he'd said those words as quickly as he'd forgotten I hadn't gone to Princeton.

Michael would shoot our film as soon as he finished *Jaws 4* (*Jaws: The Revenge*), which would be in plenty of time.

Only it wasn't. The payoff in *Jaws: The Revenge* included the shark jumping out of the water to bite the wing off an airplane . . . and they couldn't get the shark to work.

We began shooting in Montreal, then moved to Toronto, made as usual to look like someplace else—sort of Atlanta, since the newsroom from *His Girl Friday* was now a cable-TV station not unlike CNN, a fresh idea in 1987.

The wizards at Universal couldn't get the shark to work. We shot every scene that Michael wasn't in for two weeks, praying the damn shark would jump up and bite off that fucking wing.

Somewhere during the first couple of weeks of shooting, Kathleen announced she was well into a pregnancy.

Marty, one of the toughest of the tough, became apoplectic. "That bitch! That cow!" he said to me over the phone from L.A. "She knew she was pregnant before we started—she just made sure there was footage of her so she couldn't be replaced!" I thought he was going to come through the telephone from Holmby Hills and choke me in place of her. For the rest of the shoot, Kathleen had to be costumed so she wouldn't look like a mother-to-be. When she was sideways, her jacket was always open so it would hide the extra inches.

I wasn't a Kathleen Turner or Christopher Reeve fan. I've known several actors who've spent a year or two on TV soap operas and become so used to manufacturing emotions quickly (literally, overnight) and repeating them so frequently (two to five times a week) that they have nothing fresh to bring up. Kathleen suffered from this. She always did a lot of heavy breathing in her serious roles, which I found unbelievable and which eventually were treated as camp. In the dark comedy *The War of the Roses*, she found a wonderful blend of humor and menace that was perfect, but this wasn't a dark comedy, and in her other comic roles such as *Romancing the Stone*, she was frantic and loud but not funny. Although not sexually attractive to me as, say, Kim Basinger was in *My Stepmother Is an Alien* or Amy Irving and Anne Reinking were in *Micki & Maude*, I thought she would do a workmanlike job, and she did.

Although it's heresy to say so now, Chris wasn't any better. He was a lousy actor in his non-Superman roles and very full of himself offscreen, which was perfect for the role in *Switching Channels*. However, sometimes the hardest thing for a bad actor to play is himself onscreen or onstage because he isn't aware that's who he is—particularly if the role is unflattering. So he plays an exaggerated version of himself, which is what Chris did.

I hoped the anticipation of working with Caine would keep Kathleen and Chris on their best performing behavior. He would be their mentor in the film, which we all believed would bring out better performances than they'd ever given. Michael could be superb when properly challenged, and they knew it. I hoped he'd get there soon. I stroked Buddha's belly that the actors would try to rise to his level—and I knew his observations would make the script better.

And I still think they would have. But I never got to find out. A few days before we had to shoot his scenes, Marty jetted in and said he had to replace Michael with Burt Reynolds. I pleaded with him not to—not because Burt couldn't be good in certain roles, but because he was in no way a nimble, verbal comedian and certainly not a Brit, for whom the lines and rhythm had been written. Marty said he had no choice—we had to shoot his scenes.

Two days later, *Jaws: The Revenge* wrapped. I again begged Marty to get Michael.

"But I've already hired Burt."

"Well, unhire him—he's not as good as Michael for this role."

"Jonathan," Marty said, for the first and last time in his life sincere, "I couldn't do that to Burt. Think of the man's feelings. I mean, he's a human being." Marty is a very funny man, and I thought he was joking, but he wasn't.

I gasped for air. Marty was a man famous for incinerating the carcasses of studio heads, CEOs, and the Spielbergs of the world and had just chewed out Kathleen for becoming pregnant without his permission, and who had fired me temporarily for a rewriter Kotcheff wanted without reference to the possibility that I was a human being or his pledge to change nothing in the script, then rehired me on Caine's say-so after the script-off. For Marty, steak tartare was too well done. And here he was, turning mawkish. The fact was, he'd already guaranteed Burt's price, and to have two leading men on the payroll would have sent the budget into the red.

"But if the movie's no good because of the casting, it'll be a lot further in the red," I said.

"No. Have a heart."

Kotcheff and I were despondent.

Burt showed up and went to work like a pro—just a different kind of pro from Michael. He'd been the top box-office star in the world for nearly five years but had recently been brought low by a couple of failures and a strange jaw disease the press had described as AIDS, which it wasn't. He had lost confidence. And after years of one-liners opposite Johnny Carson, with whom he was charming and funny, he was unable to speak a sentence longer than three or four words. Sweet as Burt was, what would have been warm-up stretches for Michael became Olympic lifting for him. Ted and I knew from that moment that the picture was doomed.

Oh, and Burt and Kathleen hated each other. He resented her top billing; at a cocktail party, he informed her he'd been nominated for an Oscar, expecting her to be well aware of it.

"Oh, for what?" she said tactlessly.

"A little thing called . . . *Deliverance*," he said between clenched teeth and stomped out. The war was on. See for yourself.

About halfway through shooting, Marty phoned.

"I want you on that set. I've seen the dailies. You can't let them change your lines."

"But, Marty, I can't make anyone stick to a script. I'm the writer. They won't listen to me. That's the director's job."

"I'll tell them to listen to you. I've phoned Ted. Protect your script!" He hung up.

I sweated through most of the night. I didn't mind if the actors changed my lines all they wanted if it made them funnier.

The next day I duly went to the set. Kotcheff wasn't particularly glad to see me but was courteous. Unlike the theatre, in films, writers do not overrule or even consult with directors unless summoned by the director. So Marty had put Ted's balls in a vise, which Ted was handling as gracefully as he could.

In a scene Chris has with Burt, Chris says superciliously of Kathleen's character, "She'll make a great wife. It'll be like having an extra appendage— another arm or a leg." And Burt responds sarcastically, "Make sure to tell her that," knowing she'll explode. It wasn't going well, and Ted called me over.

"What's the matter with this scene?"

"Chris shouldn't say it as though he thinks it's funny. He should say it as though he's thrilled with this observation. To him it makes perfect sense," I said. "And it's sort of Acting 101, but if Burt laughs after his line, the audience won't. He's hoping Chris will tell her that." By now I was thinking maybe the lines weren't funny after all. Was any of it funny? Had we all been on nitrous oxide at the Ritz-Carlton script-off?

Ted ambled over to Chris, who shot me a threatening Superman look. Writers aren't supposed to interfere. They did another take. It was still unbelievable and still unfunny. This time I walked over to Ted, unasked. "He's still saying it as though he thinks it's funny." Now Ted looked at me unhappily. He suddenly weighed twice as much and slowly went over to Chris again and whispered. Chris stiffened.

"I'll get it from him," Ted said to me. "Why don't you step into the next room during the next take?"

I left, and after the take, Chris found me in the hall. "My character would never say that, you know," he said curtly. I tried to accommodate.

"Well, he's very full of himself. He doesn't really realize what he's saying is so self-centered. He thinks it's a compliment, as if he's just said, 'She's a great lawyer. We'll make a great team.' But what do you think he'd say?"

"Never mind. It's done," he said, and walked off. In the final version, of course, Chris tips his hand to let the audience know he knows it's a comedy, and Burt keeps the laugh.

The following morning, I got a call from the line producer, Don Carmody. "You're banned from the set. Chris doesn't want you around. And that goes for the scenes he's not in, too."

I was stunned and zoomed out to Pluto again. It was pretty funny, considering the universe of the movie world. "But Marty said—"

"Marty knows and agrees with Chris," Carmody said.

I phoned Marty. "Chris kicked me off the set. What do I do now?"

"You fucked up, Jonathan. You can't talk to an actor that way."

"But you told me not to let them change any of my lines."

"Yeah, but you gotta give in every now and then."

I spent the rest of the shoot in a singularly unattractive hotel room with thin walls in Toronto. Toward the end, a couple fond of very audible lovemaking moved into the room next door. Occasionally Ted would ask for additional dialogue, which I dashed off quickly because by then I was way more fascinated by the couple on the other side of the wall.

Michael Caine's high standards (at least on every alternate movie) might have lifted all boats, mine included—I screened the movie recently, and it's a dud from page one. Without realizing it, I had copied the structure of *His Girl Friday*—almost scene for scene—but left out the fluff. Michael Caine might have turned it into a soufflé of a dud, but the minute it was out of the oven, it still would have collapsed.

1,095 Bread Puddings

Professionally, I felt glummer than ever. *Fighting International Fat*'s hilariously disastrous reviews were not so hilarious to me at the time. Despite the money, the dismissive reviews and minimal box office for *Stepmother* and *Switching Channels* had been painful and dispiriting. And unimportant as it may now seem, a sketch of mine scheduled to appear in a revue at the Manhattan Theatre Club (home of "this version is shit") was suddenly dropped from the show, which proved to be the last straw.

Charlotte and I argued all the time, mostly about the house. We almost never argued about the children: She wanted them on an Ivy League track, and I saw no reason they shouldn't be. I had missed the Ivy League, and I didn't regret it (surely it would have meant another expulsion for something or other), but I thought Frank and Eddie might profit from it—though I also knew it made little difference where you went to college in terms of education, but a big difference in terms of contacts afterward. I thought Ivy League contacts didn't matter, since both boys showed artistic gifts—Frank appearing in school plays, Eddie revealing a sensitivity and wit beyond his years.

Charlotte hadn't recovered professionally from the collapse of her company a decade earlier and never ventured out on her own again, at least not while we were married. She became a real estate broker, but missed appointments and found that nothing moved. I thought she was wasting her enormous potential and worried she might be sliding into the passivity with which I was so familiar.

One night I announced to her that we had to leave New York. I thought we all needed recharging. I didn't want my children growing up knowing only New York, as I had. The uniqueness of America did not spring from this city—this city was Europe. I love Europe, but it's not America.

I was furious at the world for not recognizing my genius and rattled on about the boys' safety. I now hated the city where I'd spent so many exciting years in and out of trouble, love, gastronomy, and success. Charlotte wasn't enthusiastic—she'd grown up outside New York and already knew more about the country than I did. But at one point, as she reminded me several times later, I shouted, "I'll kill myself if I have to live in New York!" and she gave in when she saw my desperation. And maybe a move would freshen the marriage.

The idea began to feel good. I'd lived in several places—London, Paris, college in a small Ohio town, months in Los Angeles, San Francisco, Atlanta, New Orleans—and still felt I didn't know America. I wanted to move someplace exciting—like Las Vegas!—or to a town we'd never been, like Butte or Durango. I knew I didn't want to move to the company town of Los Angeles, fearing that familiarity might breed contempt—theirs. I was more exotic to the studios as a playwright from New York and therefore more attractive—at least until the movies mostly bombed. Darryl Zanuck, the legendary chief of production at Fox, said to me when I interviewed him for the Frost show, "Hollywood is a town of proven failures," which I was about to discover.

Charlotte was more down-to-earth. No Las Vegas, no Montana, no burg in Colorado. "Winston-Salem," she said. She knew her way around Winston-Salem because she had been born there and grew up thirty minutes away in the tiny town of Elkin. With what remained of the movie money, a few years before, I'd bought a house and twenty acres just off the Blue Ridge Parkway near Sparta. Sparta is not only featured as Charlotte Simmons's hometown in Tom Wolfe's novel; it's a few miles from the Roaring Gap Club, where my nonfiction Charlotte and her family spent summers. Her parents owned a house on club grounds, and we'd visit every summer. I loved the area but wanted us to be on our own.

Charlotte had moved to New York from North Carolina twenty-five years earlier to go to Vassar and had decided to stay. One of her dreams had been to host a literary salon through which all types of New York characters would wander. Though close to her parents, she didn't really want to live near them, so moving back was a considerable sacrifice on her part, for which she made me pay over the next few years.

I've loved the American South since age eight minutes. I was born in Fort Smith, Arkansas, though Dad dragged us out after six months for the rivers of San Antonio and hills of Virginia, where he attempted businesses. Once the divorce was definite, Mother moved us to New York, where southerners are often caricatured as either racist or redneck or ignorant. I've always thought it the most mysterious, romantic, and tragic section of the country. Dad and his family were from the Southwest, and though Yankees don't differentiate between the South and the Southwest, natives do. The South is older, it's greener, and it has a more literary history. There is no aristocracy in Oklahoma.

And then there were all those bread puddings! The simplest, comfiest, most versatile sweetgoo ever concocted into which you could throw just about anything as long as somewhere in there were bread, eggs, milk, and sugar. And in the South they did throw in everything—every restaurant had its own—bread puddings with bourbon, rum, or just about any booze except Fernet-Branca; with whipped cream, butterscotch, molasses, vanilla, and nutmeg sauces; with bananas, pineapple, bananas *and* pineapple, walnuts, raisins (of course), apricots, lemon peel, coconut, cayenne, even cocoa (reminding me of Mother's noble effort); bread from yesterday's dinner, leftover biscuits, buttered Wonder bread, for Pete's sake, Irish-soda or any other bread or muffin (except maybe rye), and you could cook it on the stovetop, in an oven, in a Crock-Pot, or probably in a solar cooker. Loved it since a child, probably through a very strong bread-pudding gene pool. And because it was available everywhere all over town, I never had to make it!

As much as I was drawn to the South, I've never understood it. I certainly didn't understand segregation or Jim Crow or how anyone could come up with laws that wouldn't allow people to drink from the same water fountain or kiss one another. I'm not saying I just didn't agree with it—I didn't *understand* it. What did those lawmakers think would happen if two races drank the same water? I'm not particularly *laissez-faire*, and I'm happy not to be—if I can make up my mind, I sit *in judgment*; but this cruel foolishness I just couldn't fathom: I couldn't understand why they did it or what they got from it. But the region fascinates me and always has.

I find the South's literature, the fondness for conversation and stories compelling, and its history completely absorbing, flaws and all. I continue to love Faulkner, think Willie Morris's memoir *North Toward Home* is masterful, and find Tennessee Williams endures as our most beautiful playwright. He lacks the tin ear of O'Neill and the earnest social conscience of Arthur Miller and shares the spirituality of Thornton Wilder. I like Charlie Rose and Bob Schieffer and used to like reading Tom Wicker and thought senators Sam Ervin, Howard Baker, and eventually Fred Thompson saved the country. David Brinkley was the best broadcaster ever. It's a broad generalization, of course, but I find a sweetness and fragility in the southern character that struggles against its outward masculinity and often redeems its meanness. It's not just the cordiality of the English, though there is that, but—they'll kill me for this—an effeminacy and appreciation for intellectual thoughtfulness that no other part of the country embodies in quite the same way.

In New York, I grew up feeling combat the moment I opened the front door—real and imagined. People in the street seemed fighting mad just getting out of bed. Every day was a struggle against other people, whether you knew them or not. Most of the South wasn't like this.

So it didn't take much for me to agree with Charlotte. If we had to move, the familiar South was preferable to the Wild Blue Yonder.

ONE OF THE GREAT BREAD POODS

1 cup raisins

4 ounces Maker's Mark bourbon

1 loaf of day-old white bread in 1-inch cubes (6–7 cups)

2 cups milk

2 cups heavy cream

3 eggs, beaten

2 cups sugar

2 tablespoons Mexican vanilla (Madagascar will do)

¼ teaspoon allspice
½ teaspoon cinnamon
½ teaspoon cayenne
1 cup chopped pecans or walnuts
3 tablespoons unsalted butter

1. Soak raisins overnight in bourbon.
2. The following day, preheat oven to 350 degrees.
3. Soak the bread in milk and cream until absorbed. In a separate bowl, beat eggs, sugar, vanilla, and spices together. Add nuts, raisins, and soaked bread, stirring gently.
4. Grease a 9 × 13-inch baking pan with the butter and pour in the batter. Bake 35–45 minutes, until edges brown and pudding looks set (it's also fine if it's a little runny).
5. Serve hot with Bourbon Sauce (see below).

YIELD: 6–8 servings.

Bourbon Sauce
½ cup unsalted melted butter
1 cup sugar
1 egg
1 cup Maker's Mark bourbon

1. Whisk together butter, sugar, and egg in a saucepan over low heat until it thickens. Whisk in bourbon.
2. Let cool, then whisk again and serve immediately. It should be creamy, and don't let the eggs scramble!

YIELD: About 2 cups.

Daddy Dearest

~~~~~~~~~

I eat my peas with honey
I've done it all my life
It makes the peas taste funny
But it keeps them on the knife.

—Anonymous

ABOUT THE ONLY PERSON I know who doesn't like peas is my son Eddie, and in Winston we once had a Joan Crawford showdown over them. When we were entrenched in Winston in the early nineties (anybody who's been there more than five minutes drops the "Salem"), we were frequently confused with the local royal families—either the R. J. Reynoldses, who introduced the first nationally successful pre-rolled cigarettes, Camels, or their cousins the R. S. Reynoldses, who made the foil destined to become Reynolds Wrap, which was initially used to wrap the pre-rolled ciggies. This was of no advantage to us whatever and regularly resulted either in keen disappointment when others found out we weren't royalty or in being overcharged twenty-five bucks for service calls by appliance repairmen who didn't believe us.

But the boys lived an idyllic childhood that Norman Rockwell would have envied—unlocked front door, bicycles in the yard, skinned knees for all the right reasons, friends and kids down the block, water and nature all around. When I wasn't in L.A., we had dinner together every night, a Rockwellian conceit I continue to recommend to even the most virulent Schnabelian.

At first, Frank and Eddie were distraught—yanked out of school, separated from beds and friends they knew in New York, forced into classes and onto sports teams where the only faces belonged to strangers. After only a month, our Jack Russell terrier, Louis, was hit by a car and killed. I thought I had ruined the lives of three people and murdered the family dog. But after the second month, when the boys realized how liberated they were from the confines of New York, how all the greenery and camaraderie was available to them without a parental escort, how they could trust strangers, and, most important, that TV was the same down there as it was up here, they grew into it. As far as I was concerned, I could open the front door and not feel confrontation in the air. People were polite, both by heritage and because they thought it was a better way to live. In Winston, at least the days *started* happy.

I would usually throw together breakfast for the boys, who'd watch with disbelief as I'd eat a faddish health-food concoction of broccoli and oat bran (eggs were against the law in the eighties). Charlotte would pack their lunches. At night, we discussed what they'd eat. No fish, of course, potatoes and creamy things, yes, burgers, chicken, an attempt at a green vegetable (could corn be considered green? They'd both eat that). I'd write during the day, then take a break around five to go to the Fresh Market in search of something that wouldn't result in protest.

Neither boy had particularly adventurous taste buds and had yet to appreciate anything foreign like, say, Chinese, Indian, or Italian outside of spaghetti marinara or carbonara. But with the mac-and-cheese served at Duke's and the brilliant butterscotch pie from Roy's in Elkin, thirty-five miles away, why should they? Southern cooking is mostly soothing: cheese grits, chicken-fried steak, fried pies, creamed corn, Mr. Pibb, and all those cakes and puddings.

I was certain that peas fresh from the pod—English peas, or garden peas, as they're sometimes called to distinguish them from dried peas like the black-eyed, the chick, and the cow—would seamlessly initiate my sons into solid green vegetables, which they ate willingly in infancy, when Gerber puréed them into custard. Besides, peas are naturally sweet, can be mushy and comforting, and, in the generally green-loathing preteen years, are harmless. (I know the country would be better-governed if people weren't allowed to vote until they passed a stiff green-vegetable-appreciation test.)

But Eddie despised them, as I found out one spring evening. Soothingly buttered and spooned next to some G-rated mashed potatoes and a forgotten brown meat, the first pick of the spring couldn't possibly offend.

But it did. Eddie refused to eat them, even with threats of limited television that night, extra piano practice, and banishment from playing in one of those five-hour Saturday baseball games in which the catcher misses every pitch, and the pitcher misses every throw from the catcher who has walked leisurely to the backstop, and the second baseman has retrieved the missed throw, only to throw it over the pitcher's head, so that each pitch takes about ten minutes, first to last.

It became a shootout worthy of the O.K. Corral between a supposedly mature adult and a seriously determined seven-year-old. I decided this might be the inevitable confrontation Philip Roth insists must take place between father and son if the son is to become a man (though in Roth's version, the son is considerably older). I dug in. Eddie dug in. His mother implored him to at least *try* the peas, and I attempted cowboy recklessness, swearing we'd both sit there all night till he finished the peas. Freeze frames of Faye Dunaway and the congealing beefsteak flashed through my head, followed for no logical reason by the "No wire hangers!" tantrum. As I became Faye Dunaway, he became The Rock.

Finally, after three or four minutes, he took a forkful, gagged, rolled his eyes, and made several gurgling noises that under different circumstances would have admitted him to an emergency room. Either this was a superb operatic performance or he really hated peas. He bravely started to take a second forkful. I caved pathetically. "I guess you really don't like them," I said. He looked at me with the equivalent of "Hel-LO" (right before it took over from "Duh") and put down his fork.

To the best of my knowledge, no pea has passed his lips since.

I've never known whether it was the grandstanding emotional gauntlet I foolishly threw down in North Carolina (and thankfully never repeated) that made it impossible for him to like peas, or a genuine dislike of the things. But at 23, he's got another 113 years—if he drinks his green tea and eats his dark chocolate—to shape up.

In *Jane Grigson's Vegetable Book*, the late British author introduces what is certainly the simplest and friendliest method of eating this supreme springtime vegetable: You boil the peas, in their pods, in salted water for ten minutes, drain them, and serve them in a big bowl, family-style, accompanied by a couple of bowls of melted butter. Each pea-eater takes a pod by the stem end, dips it into the butter, and sucks out the peas while pulling off the soft outer layer of pod with his teeth. Totally delicious, totally effortless, certainly Rockwellian.

JANE GRIGSON'S PEAS IN THE POD

(Adapted from Jane Grigson's Vegetable Book, *Penguin Books, 1998)*

2 pounds fresh young peas in their pods
8 ounces (2 sticks) butter

1. Boil peas in their pods in salted water for 10 minutes. Drain and divide into individual bowls.
2. Melt butter over low heat and place in two or more serving bowls.
3. To eat, take a pod by the stem, dip it into the butter, and suck the peas out while scraping the thin, sweet layer of the pod.

YIELD: 6 servings.

Elevating the pea to gastronomic divinity doesn't need my help, but it might need Alfred Portale's. Portale, proprietor and chef of Gotham Bar and Grill in New York, makes a stunning creation that will make you look at the formerly trivial pea in amazement and say, "This . . . came from . . . *that*?" Complicated but celestial. Might even impress Eddie.

ALFRED PORTALE'S SPRING PEA SOUP WITH MOREL CUSTARD AND WHITE TRUFFLE OIL

Morel Custard
1 ounce dried morels
1 teaspoon white truffle oil or extra-virgin olive oil

¾ cup heavy cream
2 egg yolks
¼ teaspoon kosher salt
⅛ teaspoon freshly ground white pepper
Sprig of chervil

1. Preheat oven to 300 degrees. Lightly butter four 2-ounce ramekins.
2. Wash morels carefully with cold water, making sure you get all the sand and grit out.
3. In a medium-size saucepan, bring morels, truffle oil, and heavy cream to a boil over medium heat. Reduce the heat to very low and simmer slowly until the mixture thickens, about 12 minutes.
4. Place the mixture into a blender and purée until smooth. Add the egg yolks and strain through a wire sieve or a strainer. Add salt and pepper to taste.
5. Place the ramekins in a large baking dish. Pour the mixture into the prepared ramekins and put the baking dish in the oven. Carefully pour enough hot water into the dish to come about ½ inch up the sides of the ramekins. Cover the pan with aluminum foil. Bake until the custards are set, 1¼–1½ hours. (The centers will still seem a little loose.) Remove from the water bath. If not serving immediately, cool completely, cover with plastic wrap, and refrigerate for a day, possibly two, but no longer.

While custard is cooking, prepare the soup:

Pea Soup
1 tablespoon olive oil
1 onion, chopped
½ rib celery, chopped
1 quart chicken stock
4 cups shelled fresh peas
Coarse salt and freshly ground pepper to taste
2 tablespoons sugar, or to taste (optional)

1. In a stockpot, heat the oil over a medium heat. Add the onion and celery and cook, stirring, for 3–4 minutes, or until softened. Add the stock, raise the heat to high, and bring to a boil.
2. Add the peas and return to a boil, reduce the heat, and simmer for about 12 minutes, or until the peas are tender. Remove from the heat and season with salt and pepper.
3. While the soup simmers, set a strainer over a bowl large enough to hold the stock. Set another bowl in a larger one holding ice cubes and ice water to chill the soup. Also, have a blender and ladle on hand. When the soup is ready, strain it into the bowl. Transfer the vegetables to the blender and purée, adding only enough of the strained stock to make a fine, thick purée.
4. Scrape the contents of the blender into the bowl set in the ice bath. Add the remaining stock, a little at a time, until the soup reaches the desired creamy consistency. Season with sugar, if desired, cover, and refrigerate.

To Assemble:
1. Turn custard upside down in the center of a round soup bowl. It should come out easily. If not, use a paring knife along the ramekin to loosen custard.
2. Carefully spoon the soup around the custard. The soup should come up to three quarters of the height of the custard.
3. Drizzle white truffle oil or virgin olive oil. Add chervil sprig for additional color if desired. The soup may be served at room temperature or warm.

YIELD: 4 servings.

I WAS PRETTY SURE I was a wretched parent, running off to L.A. all the time, but it turns out I suffered from the typical daddy fear: dependency. Men are generally terrified of anyone relying on them for emotional support. I was no exception. And if there's one word synonymous with *baby*, it's *dependency*. I assailed diaper-changing valiantly, attended all sporting events when in town, even became assistant basketball coach for Frank's team in Winston, went to school fairs, and drove the boys to sleepovers. I also paid for a lot and enjoyed being able to. I actually *loved* paying for things as long as I could.

Still, I never minded when the movie business pulled me away. We lived in Winston for three years, during which I spent about two thirds of the time in North Carolina and one third executing or pursuing screenplays in Los Angeles. My professional tide was turning after those five movies were made right in a row, and my ego, which was once too large to fit in the room, could now squeeze easily through a keyhole. During an earlier disastrous period, when I was writing a television pilot for Diana Rigg in London, a British lawyer said to me, "You're odd, Reynolds—you're arrogant but not confident." I hadn't learned my lesson. I continued to get assignments but not to have any of them made. And making movies—not just writing them—is the barometer of the industry. It seemed the more time I spent in L.A., the less successful I got.

I had lavish experiences in the hotels of Los Angeles and managed two weeks in a suite at the Dorchester in London while working with the director on *Leonard Part 6*. I ate at the hotel daily or else at The Connaught and the usual Indian joints in Soho and lamented that the working period was so short. It meant leaving those surroundings. In fact, I felt certain the movie bubble would burst sooner rather than later and spent just about as much time dreading the end of it as I did enjoying its luxuries. I spent a week in an enormous, marble-floored bungalow at the Beverly Hills Hotel convinced I was there under fraudulent circumstances and would be found out, until I realized everyone in Hollywood was there under fraudulent circumstances. I spent a deranged month at the Bel-Air watching Peter Bogdanovich systematically turn a green-lighted screenplay that I'd been hired to punch up back into a development deal. Criminal. He was in his Springsteen-worshipping period and arranged for us to fly clear from L.A. to Syracuse, New York, to see The Boss's final concerts of the year, stopping in Manhattan aboard the MGM plane to pick up Charlotte (we hadn't yet moved to Winston at this point). This had absolutely nothing to do with the movie we were working on, but was the movie business at its most delightfully zany, and only adds a penny or two to the price of a ticket. Jim Carrey adds the extra dollar every year, just as A-Rod does at Yankee Stadium.

By far the worst of these experiences was the ten-week shoot of *Switching Channels* in Montreal and Toronto, during which period I was alternately being told by Marty Ransohoff to keep the actors from changing a single line of my sainted script and being banned from the set. I was welcome at the director Ted Kotcheff's table but not at Miss Kathleen Turner's, bless her basso profundo, or at Chris Reeve's. Kotcheff, who is Canadian, introduced me to the most memorable of Toronto dishes, the great smoked-meat sandwich, which resembled a Reuben without the cheese and sauerkraut. Mostly, I spent solitary days in an undistinguished hotel changing all the Michael Caine lines to Burt Reynolds lines.

Charlotte and the boys came up for a weekend and ran around the set. Frank and Eddie were dazzled that their dad was working on a picture with Superman, though Superman wasn't dazzled in return.

Trips back to New York and Winston from these surrealistic sites were as different as waking and dreaming. The boys were in a bucolic school in Winston, they had playdates in the afternoons and on weekends, as well as practices and games, piano lessons. Weekends we'd try to spend at the house on the Blue Ridge Parkway (christened "Bullhead" by Charlotte, in reference not only to a nearby mountain of the same name, but to our willful personalities). I grew to love that house and the simplicity it represented much more than the Jane Street house, which we'd rented to a family and was a continual headache. It represented complication, New York, and the need for money to keep it up. We looked into selling it, but during the week we talked to brokers, a man was shot and killed making a telephone call at Jane and Greenwich streets, and *New York* magazine's cover story the following week not only sensationalized the murder but outed the lurking violence and rampant transvestite-hooker community of the area. Prices fell and stayed that way for ten years. The house took an inordinate amount of time to landlord, and it never made a dime.

Charlotte chose not to work in Winston, put on weight, and dove headfirst into a depression that lingered on and off for the next decade. I drank aquavit late at night and at least once mentioned—shouted, actually—I would trade the Jane Street house for a divorce. No takers.

It was easy to make friendly acquaintance with people in Winston, but, like London, it was a difficult place for deep friendships to develop. Charlotte's brother, Donny, and his wife, Ruthie, and their three children were regular companions, and a joy to be around. It's surprising on whom children model themselves. Charlotte and I were seldom publicly affectionate, but Ruthie would sit on Donny's lap after dinner, and he'd call her "Sweets." Years later, Frank replicated not his own parents' cordial aloofness with his most serious girlfriend but his uncle's playful-natured warmth. She sits on his lap, and he calls her "Sweets."

Despite the many attempts at hosting dinners, I still felt like a stranger in Winston, and Charlotte just plain didn't want to be there. We rented a searchlight and threw an Oscar party attended by thirty or forty people and featuring Frank and Eddie with Instamatics pretending to be reporters and snapping photos outside as the guests arrived. It would have been a smashing success had I managed to get Fredy Girardet's *blanquette de saumon et crevettes* on the table before the Best Actor was announced around midnight, but such was my timing that I didn't.

At Bullhead, we hosted assorted Kirks, Remicks, and Reynoldses, who came from New York and Boston and Winston, on Thanksgiving and Christmas. Those were the best times: our house overstuffed with people, the people overstuffed with crisply roasted turkey or goose, pies or plum pudding, and spider cakes and mountains of pork products for breakfast. We were at our familiest then.

When summer heat chased us up to our house on the parkway, we left the rented house in Winston and welcomed friends who passed through for the camaraderie, the German Johnson heirloom tomatoes, and a flank steak smothered with chilies and cooked on the grill. We were away from real life (though I realized too late that this was also real life and could have been ours) and untroubled by financial and real estate arguments.

Shake It Up, Baby

~~~~~~~

O F THE FOUR most perennially puzzling culinary mysteries—how do you cook perfect rice, who separates the juice of the pomegranate from its seeds, what the hell is in marshmallows, and where did my malted milk go—the only question I can answer with any authority is the last. Like Nesselrode pie and Danish pudding, Nicole Brown's real killer, Salinger's talent, and the friendship between Woody and Jean, malted milk has disappeared.

Well, almost. (But then, the same can still be said for Nicole Brown's real killer, still out there somewhere.)

Nothing conjures the small-town America of Andy Hardy, Thornton Wilder, and Norman Rockwell like a malted milkshake served in a carbuncular soda glass and blissfully slurped through a straw—unless perhaps it's the four-fingered baseball mitt or the blueberry pie cooling on a Kansas windowsill. I don't know if there's actually malt in all the Rockwell shakes or in the famous drugstore scenes from *Our Town* and *Shadow of a Doubt* or when Andy and Polly roll their eyes at each other, but I'd like to think there is, because those blessed drinks sure seemed to bring families close.

Though there is no single greatest American playwright or greatest play, there is none greater than Thornton Wilder or *Our Town*. The play transcends the brilliant realism of *Long Day's Journey into Night* and *Death of a Salesman* and will satisfy the test of time even more enduringly than the inspired language of *A Streetcar Named Desire* and *The Glass Menagerie*. Because of its sudden leap into spirituality, detailed atmosphere, and theatricalism and its deceptively bone-simple style, *Our Town* resonates universally. It also captures the uniqueness of the American character that isn't urban—as does *The Music Man*—by lovingly memorializing, with its own spare realism, the nation's vanishing small towns.

The country's ills are harder to salve these days. We've pretty much rejected Wilder's religion, Louis B. Mayer's comforting (if ultimately bogus) platitudes, and Rockwell's masterfully simple reassurances, mostly to our detriment. While I'm not suggesting we airlift refrigerated trucks of strawberry malteds to Baghdad or Tehran or Omaha (where bin Laden is actually hiding), the case can nevertheless be made that such an international policy would certainly make the principals feel better. A roomful of Mahmoudijan, Abdullahs, Faisals, Condoleezzas, and assorted mullahs all sipping date or figgy malteds with flexible straws could only speed up the peace process. You simply can't do war with a malted milkshake in your mouth. Cognac and bourbon, yes (Churchill and Truman), but a malted banana smoothie, never. The earthy, nutty contribution malt makes to a shake cuts the shrill sweetness of ice cream and syrup. (Some throats—mine, for one—get sugar burn from too much sweetness, whether from ice cream or candy bars. Mine burns after two or three slugs of a shake, and malt soothes it. And speaking of ice cream, if you eat too much too fast and your head aches or your throat swells terrifyingly, grab something really cold—ice or the glass the ice cream's in—and press it to an artery at ankle, wrist, or neck, and it will disappear.)

Malt adds not only complexity and maturity to an otherwise infantile concoction but also surprise and a smile to pies and puddings and cakes and muffins—no one ever expects it because they think it's dead.

Malt is usually made from barley that has been soaked and allowed to sprout, converting much of the grain's starch into sugar. Further roasting the barley caramelizes its sugars and gives malt its unique taste. Malted milk was initially created in 1887 by the Horlick brothers of Racine, Wisconsin, as an easy digestible for invalids and infants. They combined malted barley with wheat and added dried milk and a few thousand other ingredients like sugar, whey, various oils, and that old standby thiamin mononitrate. But malted-milk powder is not for the faint of heart—literally. Though a tablespoon of pure malt has 21 calories and 4½ grams of carbohydrate, Horlicks has 60 and

12, and who wants to stop at one tablespoon? The pure malt is just as good—though stronger and less rich-tasting—and is eminently worth trying.

The closest I came to a corner soda fountain *was* a corner soda fountain, though it was on the corner of Madison and Eighty-fifth, not Grovers Corners. Sipping a vanilla malted and watching two short-order cooks whir up ten or twenty burgers, eggs, and hash browns seemed the height of excitement and glamour. But there wasn't much of a soda-shoppe culture in New York; I got most of mine through the Andy Hardy series of movies, which I watched eagerly, hoping they would instruct me how to be a teenager since Brando and Dean weren't helping much. But there weren't any jalopies in my neck of the woods or dazzling beauties like Lana Turner, and though there was a sister who could be annoying and a maiden aunt in Quincy, there was definitely no Judge Hardy to turn to for advice. The series took place about fifteen years before my time, and in a small town so remote it might as well have been in Greenland, but I yearned for the experience. Instead, I got life lessons from Steve McQueen, Burt Lancaster, Montgomery Clift, and Ernest Borgnine, and in place of Judge Hardy, I had the role model of Frank Sinatra.

I hadn't had a malted in twenty years, when, sometime during the summer of 1990, I was motoring around the mountains of North Carolina in search of a camp meeting. I was doing research for a screenplay in which Dolly Parton—with whom I had fallen in complete but unrequited love—would play an evangelist who sings with divine inspiration, performs healing miracles for real, and becomes a national phenomenon. Then, at the height of her success, she is brought low by some human failing.

Paramount wanted her character, Sister Sunshine, to be a fraud, but both Dolly and I thought it would be more original and challenging if she was a true believer, which made the execs nervous, since in Hollywood the only valid and commercial religion until *The Passion of the Christ* was a zealous atheism. The scandalous Jimmys Bakker and Swaggart were all over the front pages then, casting more doubt than ever on organized religion.

Bakker was an apple-cheeked preacher who appeared on a daily television show called *PTL* (which alternately stood for *Praise the Lord* and *People That Love*) with his wife, Tammy Faye, a heavenly choir, and several seriously religious guests. I don't remember him healing anyone, but I do remember him selling time-shares in a vacation community in South Carolina. He was enormously popular and great fun to watch, even when he went on one of his to-the-right-of-Beria rants about homosexuals, masturbation, and women with loose morals. Supposedly, the show pulled in $500,000 a day in contributions and earned the envy of other prominent televangelists like Jerry Falwell and John Ankerberg. Our friend the actor Ian McKellen came to visit us at Bullhead and wanted more than anything to drive to the *PTL* studios a few miles away but didn't have time. I think Sir Ian, who is famously gay, wanted to look the devil in the face and laugh at him. Bakker was eventually accused of molestation by Jessica Hahn, a local girl who claimed to be a devout Christian. Bakker's empire was investigated, and it turned out Jim had oversold the properties, spent wildly on personal luxuries (supposedly $60,000 for gold bathroom fixtures and an air-conditioned doghouse), and may have been a practicing homosexual himself. Too neat for fiction. Off he went weeping to prison. Jessica Hahn went to Hollywood, bought breast implants, and posed for *Playboy*. You can't make this stuff up.

Though Bakker wasn't much of a scholarly Christian, Jimmy Swaggart was a highly regarded biblical specialist. His regular television show pulled in eight million viewers and somewhere between $100 million and $150 million a year in his heyday—which was, coincidentally, parallel to Bakker's. Swaggart began as a gospel singer and was given to tear-jerking, emotional sermons. After publicly denouncing Bakker as "a cancer on the body of Christ" and defrocking a fellow minister for an extramarital affair, he was photographed by that minister picking up hookers, after which he took them to motels and masturbated in front of them. That's all he did, but it was enough. He went on the air, cried, prayed that his wife and family and God and the public would forgive him, which they all seemed to . . . and then he went and did it again. He went on television again, cried again, and asked for forgiveness a second time, and it was again granted. But he lost his enormous flock and as of this writing was back in the Assemblies of God church's good bosom, though more as a scholar and admitted sinner than as the rabble-rousing fund-raiser of old.

The story of the man rising from the dead always fascinated me, as it has billions. I knew it wasn't possible, but now and then I'd say to myself, "Of course it isn't possible . . . but what if it happened? I mean I know it couldn't . . . but what if it did? The disciples who claim to have seen Him may have been true believers and were at least superb at PR, but it couldn't happen. Only, what if it did? How come all those brilliant minds throughout the centuries thought it happened? It couldn't be true . . . but what if it was? It would certainly end all argument about religion. And if it wasn't, the story at the very least espoused a great philosophy."

Most (all?) movies about evangelists set out to prove them crooks—most famously, *Elmer Gantry*—and Dolly and I wanted to make one that didn't.

I've been wildly disposed toward southern women since childhood. My very first serious backseat session took place on a double date in New York at age fourteen with a girl from Tennessee. Her willing clotheslessness, the languor of her voice and gesture, the ease with which she succumbed to every frenetic maneuver I made (I was a Yankee, after all), made me feel older, stronger, more triumphant than my years would suggest. I wrote her several passionate and explicit letters after she went home, all unanswered. Deliriously in love, I finally phoned her. She said, "You got me in a whole lotta trouble. My daddy opens all my mail, and I can't ever talk to you again." My heart was broken. Undone by the post office again!

Dolly recorded a song called "He's Alive," told from the viewpoint of a visitor to the tomb where Christ was laid. The rhythm pulsates with mystery until she discovers the tomb is empty and realizes He's risen from the dead—which means He's alive. Here the song hits a smashing crescendo that Dolly rides beautifully, and with my own questions of faith whirling around, this thrilling song—what if it were *true*?—made me wonder if writing this film was more than coincidental.

When I first met with her in Los Angeles in 1989 (me already primed to fall, her mind so swift, perception so honest, self-invention so extraordinary, heart so pure, and inside a little girl so terrified occasionally peeked out . . . *and* she was a southerner), we talked over her character's Achilles' heel—alcohol, drugs, money, power, doubt, loss of faith—what would it be? She looked me gently but unapologetically in the eye and with a beguiling innocence said, "Jonathan, my weakness is . . . men," thereby setting in stone what would undo Sister Sunshine, as well as, I hoped, me.

Dolly wrote wonderful music and lyrics for the film but ultimately wound up disliking the script almost as much as Paramount did. I never found out why. As with most Hollywood rejections, you never do. I think she thought the role too complicated, and indeed she was at her best live onstage or on television, where she could be direct, extempore, and sincere. At any rate, without her participation, Paramount was only too delighted to shelve a project that had made them so anxious in the first place. Needless to say, my heart was completely broke, as it is by all southern women.

But months before that, there I was, somewhere near Dobson, North Carolina, searching for that camp meeting (a small revival with a minister going at it), and I found a little dinette selling chicken-fried steak—a slab o' beef battered and deep-fried—and also featuring malteds. I ordered one as a curiosity, recalling that soda fountain on Madison and Eighty-fifth. It was so cold and so thick and probably so bad for you that I ordered another, and almost every day for about two weeks returned for what was rapidly becoming a very fattening addiction.

And ever since then, two associations pop into my head every time I put straw to lip—my own childhood and Dolly Parton. It's not that the malteds in Dobson were so extraordinary—after all, you just shake a little powder into milkshake fixin's—but that they existed at all. Ovaltine contains malt, but unchocolated malt is difficult to find. The Vermont Country Store sells Horlicks, and I've occasionally seen jars of Carnation's version, and the pure stuff can be found in health-food stores. In Philadelphia, you might get lucky and come across a Dusty Miller—coffee ice cream sprinkled with malt. At places whose food curve changes glacially—like, say, country clubs—it can still be found, but malt isn't carried in most supermarkets.

Easier to find are malted-milk balls—a single detractor of which I have yet to find in North America or the British Isles after an extensive, though admittedly anecdotal, survey. Among the best purveyors—aside from the cinemas that mark up Whoppers so astronomically I once thought of scalping them outside—is Dylan's Candy Bar on the Upper East Side, named after and run by Ralph Lauren's daughter (and a person in her own right). There, among other delights, you can find balls covered with dense, dark chocolate. About 96% of the time I prefer dark or semisweet chocolate, but in the case of malted-milk balls, dark overwhelms and yields a slightly bitter taste. Milk chocolate isn't so competitive. At Oren's Daily Roast you can feast on ones shellacked with espresso. The Brits enter the competition with Maltesers, which even some patriotic Yanks prefer.

But don't eat them all from the bag if you can help it, because they can be taken home and chopped and crushed and strangled into delicious cakes, pies, ice creams, puddings, and muffins. If you can't find malted-milk balls easily, go to the movies and see anything with Gene Hackman or Keira Knightley or Diane Lane in it. Buy several boxes (or if sold in bulk, several pounds).

But whether you invest the time and effort to make a pie or cake or even a shake, use malt to flavor something, because it's a snap to use: Open the jar, insert the spoon, remove a heaper, and dust it on anything, ranging from oatmeal to the peanut butter of a sandwich. If you like sweet alcoholic drinks—a piña colada, say, or a good rum punch as the sun sinks over the yardarm late in July—malting them gives you the experience of being a child and an adult at the same time, possibly one in love with Dolly Parton. And bourbonless, it's a great remedy for a hangover.

A Great Malted

3 scoops (about 8 ounces) vanilla ice cream, slightly softened (aficionados claim the ice cream should be vanilla regardless of the flavor of the syrup)

½ cup 1-percent, 2-percent, or whole milk

¼ cup chocolate, strawberry, or any other flavored syrup

2 tablespoons malted-milk powder, or to taste

½ teaspoon vanilla extract

Pinch nutmeg or whipped cream (optional)

In a blender, pulse all the ingredients on low speed just until smooth, about 20 seconds. (Don't overblend—the shake will become too soupy.) Pour the shake into a soda glass and top with nutmeg or whipped cream, if desired.

YIELD: 1 serving.

NOTE: For a vanilla malted, increase the milk to ¾ cup and omit the syrup.

CHOCOLATE MALTED ICEBOX PUDDING

4 slices pumpernickel bread, torn into small pieces
4 ounces milk-chocolate squares
1 ounce semisweet chocolate squares
3 cups heavy or whipping cream
3 tablespoons malted-milk powder
1 tablespoon confectioners' sugar
½ teaspoon vanilla extract

1. In a food processor, pulse the bread into crumbs (you should have about 1 cup). Transfer to a bowl. Using the large holes of a grater, grate the two kinds of chocolate. Add to the bread crumbs and set aside.
2. In a large mixer bowl, beat 2½ cups of the cream, the malted-milk powder, confectioners' sugar, and vanilla until stiff. With a large rubber spatula, fold half the bread crumbs and chocolate into the whipped cream just until blended. Repeat with the remaining bread crumbs and chocolate.
3. Spoon the pudding into a 1½-quart soufflé dish or serving bowl; smooth the top. Cover and refrigerate overnight.
4. Just before serving, beat the remaining ½ cup cream until stiff and decoratively spread over the top of the pudding.

YIELD: 8 servings.

Lee and Me

BUT WHEN IT CAME to true love, there was only one.

I fell in love with her the way most people who met her did—at first sight, passionately, like a sheepdog. I was maybe three years old, and she was probably nine, and we were on a beach somewhere, and had anything come of it, we both would have been in a great deal of trouble in every state except Louisiana, because we were first cousins.

Those of us who adored her were transfixed not only by her perfect Episcopalian beauty, and the alluring carnality underneath, and that laugh—head thrown back, mouth open, teeth flashing the sky—but also because being with her made us feel so good. It's been said of Frank Sinatra that if you were ever around him, in whatever mood he was, you were by definition at the hippest spot on earth. With Lee, you were at the happiest.

She reminded me of a Fitzgerald heroine, and we were all wearing the gold hat and bouncing as high as we could to move her. She had many friends and loved nothing more than girdling her dining table with them and feeding them, though you'd never guess it from her waist, which, until the end, simply wouldn't expand. People fell for her, just fell for her; she was surrounded by the aura of the Charmed, chosen by God or one of His best friends for the graceful and glamorous glide through life afforded to a handful. No heartache, no setback, no sadness. Or so it seemed through my inverted binoculars from the other side of the family. Was it self-pity, resentment, or envy that made me idealize *those* Remicks so and excoriate *our* Remicks?

Those Remicks were golden—handsome Uncle Bus, his lively beauty of a first wife, Pat, their children of such promise and zest. Why did they seem untouched by the depression and uncertainty that cloaked us like a comfortable and familiar duvet? For one thing, Dad had rejected us, and though he never saw them, he hadn't rejected them.

Of course they were beautiful. The older child, Bruce, was all boy, full of mischief, and wanted to be a rancher and work with animals. Lee was training to be a ballerina, but when she converted to acting, she became successful in what seemed like minutes, but inevitable minutes—seasons of stock, out of town with Broadway shows, then appearing on Broadway at seventeen in a few-night wonder, *Be Your Age*. I wasn't jealous. I was in awe.

And then she was chosen in '57 by Elia Kazan, the greatest director of his generation and certainly the best manipulator of actors in the history of the medium, to be in *A Face in the Crowd*. He saw in her not only the spoiled, erotic teenage baton-twirler she played in that movie opposite Andy Griffith but also the repressed, erotic spinster in her best picture, the seldom-seen jewel *Wild River*, with Montgomery Clift.

Lots happened after *A Face in the Crowd* was released. She married a dashing television director with a bright future, Bill Colleran; she got pinched by Prince Philip and wooed by the president of the United States; she made one movie after another; she had two children. She and Bill invited me out to movies like *Sweet Smell of Success* and plays like *Long Day's Journey into Night*, the original—and if you think the recent run was something, you shoulda seen Fredric March and Jason Robards. You shoulda seen Lee. It wasn't just that every head turned; it was that every head turned and she still focused on you. On me, actually.

Even her failures were honorable: There hasn't been as respectable a financial disaster on Broadway since *Anyone Can Whistle* lasted only a week. She met Sondheim, and there were rumors of a romance with him. If true, it wouldn't have been her first or last involvement with a gay man. She made *Days of Wine and Roses* and was nominated for an Oscar.

No life is a glide, of course, and my cousin Lee's trajectory jerked. While driving home alone one night in Los Angeles, Bill smashed up his car—and his body. Lee, who was filming *Wild River* in Mississippi, flew to his hospital bed. "His head is the size of a watermelon," she told her father, "and he doesn't remember anything." She spent the better part of the next year nursing him. Bill had a short fuse and though he'd been very successful in television directing what used to be called "spectaculars" as well as the weekly *Your Hit Parade*, he was never popular with executives. The accident, coupled with his reputation, prevented him from regaining his position. He was no longer "promising"; he was Mr. Remick.

In those days, homosexuality was considered a neurotic disease that could be conquered, and Bill "had been" gay before he married Lee. He wanted a heterosexual family life and, for a while, succeeded. Lee knew about his past but also believed the contemporary psychiatric evaluation that someone gay could change if only he thought the right thoughts and disciplined himself. In the sixties, Bill re-exited the closet and shortly after I returned from London in '67, the two split up, after nine or ten years of marriage.

In memory, it seemed more difficult to tell who was gay and who was straight in those days; the assumption was that people were straight. Maybe .5% weren't; but they adopted straight mannerisms because being gay was so terribly, terribly horrible. Despite his occasional wild idea for a comeback—"How about this for a show? Lee and Harry Belafonte in a musical of *Rain!*"—I never thought Bill was anything but a good family man; I don't know if Lee's mother and father did or not.

Lee loved that I had spent fifteen months in London and wanted to hear every detail, night after night—about every stage performance, a description of every street corner, and not the number of times it rained but the size of the drops. So when she made the film *Hard Contract* in Spain in 1969, she was primed to fall for an Englishman—and did. His name was Kip Gowans, and he was the very straight assistant director on the film, a handsome and tough working-class bloke with sideburns and a flat stomach. I warned her about English food, but she said, "I don't care! I'll cook."

She moved to London with the kids, who proceeded to have what might be called extreme adolescence: constant nightmares, experimentation with sex and substances, confusion. Neither liked her second husband because he was a tough disciplinarian and wanted his wife all to himself. The household filled with repressed fury. Lee tried to side with everyone.

Her movie career waned as she hit the wall most actresses run into: the age of forty. She made small movies in England and played Churchill's mother in the miniseries *Jennie*. But she miraculously rebounded on American television, where she soon became the queen of the made-for-TV movie for more than a decade. It seemed that the American public responded to her essential decency, and whenever she went astray onscreen, it was not without conflict; her personal morality always came through.

Though Kip was in demand as an A.D. (assistant director) in England, when they all moved to Los Angeles to take advantage of her newfound television career, American unions wouldn't allow him to work. Always a man proud of his trade, he became a heavy drinker. Lee defended him all over town, made him her producer. But he, too, became Mr. Remick. Upper-middle-class Los Angeles can be a trap for teenagers: too much money, too many cars, guilty parents, competitive escapades, unlimited sex. The kids suffered from too much freedom.

I visited her and felt instantly close again, as I always did. This is how close: I took her to lunch one afternoon when I was thinking of marrying Charlotte, whom she knew and liked.

"Do you think I should get married?" I asked her. Her blue eyes danced—she thought I was kidding. People don't ask their cousins for permission to marry. But I thought she'd know—was there something I was missing? She reminded me that a few years earlier, she'd told me about her failed marriage to Bill: "Everything is there in front of you at the beginning; you just don't choose to see some of it."

Lee realized now I wasn't kidding, and that her response would make a difference.

"Yes," she said.

"Do you think I will?"

"I think you better!" she said, laughing. And I did.

She bought a splendid house in Osterville, on Cape Cod, and after Charlotte and I had Eddie and Frank, we spent Christmases there with her. She was an enthusiastic cook, and her house was filled with cookbooks. "I read them before I go to bed," she said, "the way other people read mysteries." When her daughter, Kate, turned eighteen, Lee handwrote a cookbook for her with special instructions, which included: "1. Always read entire recipe from start to finish. . . . Nothing makes you crazier than getting halfway through and finding out there's something missing. 2. When in any doubt, it's better to cook on a lower flame than a higher one—because burning things is boring. . . . 7. The most important single thing to remember is to clean up as you go along."

Then, in the spring of 1989, as I was trying to sell a pitch to Paramount, I visited her in her Brentwood home. She was filming a TV movie and said in passing, "I've had this temperature about one degree above normal for a few days."

I didn't know what this meant. "How many days?"

"About a month."

When the film wrapped, she was told the cancer had metastasized from her kidneys to her lungs and brain.

She was more astonished than upset. Her New England upbringing taught her to face this as she had all the other challenges in life: forthrightly and without bitterness. Isn't this curious, this happening to me, she thought. There was no question that she would recover—just a little chemo and some surgery, just another little hurdle to clear—and, by God, she did, and with good cheer. She was in remission, and she was signed to do Sondheim's *A Little Night Music* at the Ahmanson in L.A.

Then, during a follow-up scan, she was told that she had seventeen new tumors in her brain. Her longtime friend Karla Champion was at the hospital and remembers Lee being annoyed but asking her doctor, "Well, what do we do now?"

"Denial" is psychobabble jargon and currently in disrepute, but sometimes it's one of the more useful weapons in our arsenal, as Ibsen illustrated in *The Wild Duck* and O'Neill in *The Iceman Cometh*. And Lee's refusal to clearly see or believe her fate wasn't foolish—it was thrilling.

Also thrilling was the reaction of her friends. As her body and face became swollen from the steroids and she gradually lost the ability to walk, we gathered nightly to feed her—body and soul. And ours. She actually had rolling, raucous parties centered on her and food, at once comforting and uniting, and on laughs and enjoyment of her last days on earth. Roddy and Bobby gossiped, and Glover massaged her feet, and Nanny and David reminisced, and the Guests and Axelrods told funny stories, and Beverly helped make her favorite shepherd's pie, and everybody brought food.

After she died, I wondered if her constant attempt to accommodate, to absorb the problems with children and husbands and friends as her own, made her more susceptible to the disease, or if her weakened resistance allowed it in. She blamed herself for poor judgment with Bill, for Kip's unemployment and alcoholism, for being away on a set while her kids went haywire.

Did she do it to herself? What if she had said, "Fuck off! Rescue your own damn selves!" Would she have avoided the cancer? Unknowable, of course. But if she had, she would have been a different person.

I was tantalized by Chinese food then and made her one of her other favorites—a seriously Szechuan hacked chicken. Her children, Kate and Matt, and Kip and Karla nursed her. Of course, when anyone took a breath and stepped back, there was incredible sadness—but lugubriousness isn't allowed in New England, even if it is in Hollywood, and it wasn't in that Brentwood house. We watched her die, and in its curious way, it was uplifting. She wasn't "brave" or "valiant," but of course, she was. She watched her demise with the curiosity and wonder of a child. Occasionally there was a shriek of terror from the bedroom, and concern for her children's future, but little anger.

She would have thrilled to see her daughter, Kate, a landscaper and contented married mother of two girls, Remick and Georgia; and her son, Matt, a bicycle fiend and an important digital-sound recordist in the movie business.

I haven't wanted to see any of her movies since, preferring to keep her alive in my memory, which she is to this day as much as she was before she gently stopped breathing on July 2, 1991, at age fifty-five. But I keep being reminded how good she is in *Wine and Roses* and as Churchill's mother in *Jennie* and in her funniest role, in the miniseries *Nutcracker*, so one of these days I will, and you shouldn't wait for me.

LEE REMICK'S BARBECUED CHINESE DUCK

Four 1-pound duck breasts
1 cup sherry
2 tablespoons brown sugar or honey
3 tablespoons soy sauce

1 teaspoon powdered ginger
1 teaspoon powdered mustard
Toasted sesame seeds for garnish

1. Trim excess fat and skin from the duck breasts. Combine the sherry, sugar, soy sauce, ginger, and mustard and pour over the duck. Marinate several hours or overnight, turning occasionally.
2. Drain the duck and reserve the marinade. Grill 20–25 minutes over medium heat, turning and moving duck to avoid flare-ups while basting frequently.
3. Allow the duck to rest for 5 minutes before slicing. Sprinkle with sesame seeds before serving.

YIELD: 6 servings.

SZECHUAN HACKED CHICKEN FOR LEE

1 tablespoon Szechuan peppercorns
1½ cups peanut oil
2¼ pounds chicken breasts
9 tablespoons peanut butter
3 tablespoons sesame oil
3 tablespoons soy sauce
3 tablespoons white vinegar
3 teaspoons MSG
4 teaspoons cayenne (or less, to taste)
4½ teaspoons minced ginger
5 teaspoons chopped scallions
5 teaspoons minced garlic
2–4 teaspoons crushed red-pepper flakes
2 tablespoons chopped fresh cilantro

1. Fry the Szechuan peppercorns in the oil for 15 minutes. Discard the peppercorns, and reserve 4½ tablespoons of oil for this recipe. (Save remainder for another purpose. It will keep for months in the fridge.)

2. Skin and bone the chicken, then plunge it into boiling water and simmer till just barely cooked through, about 5 minutes. Cut into ¼-inch-thick strips 3 inches long.

3. Blend the peanut butter and sesame oil until smooth. Stir in all the remaining ingredients except the red-pepper flakes and cilantro.

4. Add 2 teaspoons of the red-pepper flakes and then taste, adding up to 2 more, according to your tolerance. Then add as much of the reserved oil as necessary to make a sauce that isn't overly greasy.

5. Arrange the chicken on a platter, spoon the sauce over it, and sprinkle the cilantro on top. Serve at room temperature.

YIELD: 6 servings.

Fear of Frying

~~~~~~~~~~~~

I NEVER SANG for my father, to quote my friend the playwright Robert Anderson, but I did finally manage to cook for him. Twice. The first effort was so unsuccessful that I was banished from his kitchens forever. It happened during a family gathering at his house in Kona, Hawaii, at Christmastime, 1991, nearly six months after Lee died. By then, family meant not only his three children, our spouses, and six grandchildren, but his gorgeous new girlfriend, Virginia McCartney, who actually loved the old weasel, and three or four aides who knew him infinitely better than the rest of us did.

Dad's mental decline had been noticeable back at his eightieth birthday party in 1986. He stared blankly for a few extra seconds, or his eyes welled up with tears for no apparent reason, or he simply didn't recognize people he'd known all his life. He threw himself the party because, he said, with that merry glint in his eye, "I wanted to see all my old girlfriends." And they and lots of others came to his Las Vegas mansion that night and ate huge amounts of lobster and drank booze from a table adorned with a bust of him carved in lard and an ice sculpture made of the company logo. Outside, where dinner seating was formal, the swimming pool was covered over so a stage could be erected for the stand-up performance of George Burns and the songs of the two remaining Mills Brothers, one of his all-time favorite groups. Of course, they sang his favorite song, "Paper Doll," which years ago the original four had made a hit, and the lyrics of which were startlingly revealing:

I'm gonna buy a paper doll that I can call my own
A doll that other fellows cannot steal
And then the flirty, flirty guys with their flirty, flirty eyes
Will have to flirt with dollies that are real.

When I come home at night she will be waiting
She'll be the truest doll in all this world
I'd rather have a paper doll to call my own
Than have a fickle-minded real live girl.

I think he'd always wanted a two-dimensional relationship with a gorgeous, never-aging woman who'd provide snappy dialogue at dinner, do everything he asked, let him alone when he wanted but also be there when he wanted. That he would publicly announce this sentiment in a song—with the financial contract spelled out ("I'm gonna buy a paper doll that I can call my own")—was unusually candid for a businessman who kept such a low and cautious profile that he shredded all his company papers every few years. His chief associate, Fred Smith, who was in charge of the party, had also arranged for the more generic "My Way" to be played and sung incessantly—same as at any party or bar mitzvah where the honoree once had an unusual idea.

I met my half-brother, Don Junior, for the first time at that birthday. I was in my forties, Don in his fifties. He was the issue of Dad and his second wife and spent too many years of his life working for him. He had Dad's stocky build and exuberant speech intonations, and it was a fascinating meeting. We strolled around Dad's grounds feeling each other out, trying to see what, if anything, we had in common, both genetically and psychologically. We got on right away. Don was funny and ironic about our father's influence on him and we laughed and sighed a lot. Under his gruff and bouncy exterior, I sensed a serious, lifelong hurt with which I was familiar, a feeling that whatever he did, he could never measure up to Dad or his expectations. Perhaps I was projecting, but as I see it, it wasn't until Dad died that Don Junior picked up a pencil, some chalk, and a brush, and began to draw. In his sixties, after a lifetime flailing around trying to please our unpleasable father, he became an artist!

Dad's three chief business associates (they weren't partners—Dad was the only stockholder and answered to no one) convinced him that he should now enjoy the fruits of his labor, relax, and gradually withdraw from the day-to-day operations of Donrey Media Group. This was contingent, of course, on Fred Smith keeping him informed on a regular basis. To cap this retirement plan, Fred suggested Dad surround himself with his loving family, and urged us all to fly to Hawaii as often as we could and spend time with him.

A stupider man than Fred might have tried to keep the children away from their father in case he uncharacteristically fell in love with them and changed his will to include them and lock out any associates. But Fred knew Dad well—he'd had only one job in his life, and that was working for "Mr. Reynolds" since the mid-sixties. He knew Mr. Reynolds wasn't about to get softhearted, and that Mr. Reynolds had long since made a gas- and water-tight will that favored Fred and two other associates and didn't favor the Reynolds children. Fred also shrewdly calculated that should the children protest the will, at least they (that is, we) couldn't accuse Fred of trying to keep father from children. In fact, he was practically forcing us together after years of lack of interest. And, incidentally, Dad would have companionship and plenty of distraction to keep his mind off Donrey Media.

So twice a year for four years, Charlotte and I would first-class Eddie and Frank to Kona, for the sort of vacations game-show contestants scream about. For the first two visits, Hawaii was an entertaining novelty; and the boys loved every second of splashing around pools and taking scary sightseeing trips in helicopters, and swimming with their medicated, sweet old grand-dad. For me, the charms of humid and dull Hawaii quickly turned into biannual obligations. Dad was beyond having a meaningful conversation, and the trips there soon became an endless routine of unexpressive meals together. He didn't have Alzheimer's, Fred explained, but he did have dementia.

That first attempt to cook for him was an overambitious disaster, during which I loonily decided that the Swiss chef Fredy Girardet's recipe for a blanquette of salmon and shrimp (the same one that took so long on Oscar night in Winston) needed the improvement of masses of onions sweated in butter, on the theory that everything that goes in or on the human body can be improved by the addition of sautéed onions.

Not only did this upset the delicate symmetry of the Swiss master's creation; it also made such a mess of the presentation that my father, already wandering agonizingly around his own mental Sea of Tranquility, took a look at his plate and cried out: "What am I eating? What am I eating here?" He was panicky and mad. While the other relatives seemed sincere in their praise, though bullied by Dad's fury, I realized I had forever gummed up my chances of so much as boiling water for him in any state where he owned a newspaper.

Dad was at that dangerous state of mindlessness during which you never knew whether he understood what you were saying or not. Gregarious as hell and an aggressive-aggressive before his dementia struck, he'd now often be violently silent, increasingly reminding me of my mother, a noted passive-aggressive. At lunch for the two of us one day, just as I'd mustered the courage to delve into the lifetime of dreams and disappointments that I'd always been afraid to tell him about, I threw in an off-the-cuff reference to a failed business venture forty years earlier in Alaska. He called in a couple of Black Hawks. "I didn't fail in Alaska!" he roared back at me. "Sold that paper for twice what I bought it for!" Steam flew out of every orifice, and for a moment his anger almost levitated him, like a wildly spouting balloon.

So the effort to cook for him was more loaded than, say, the night the Michelin man comes to your restaurant. I visited him once or twice in Hot Springs, Arkansas, where he had a house I don't think he recognized and a Thoroughbred racehorse with whom he felt increasingly *simpático*. Four or five of us would lunch with him at the track whenever his horse ran, and Dad would order fried catfish every single time. It didn't take too many races for me to realize that if I was ever going to show him I could do something on a stove besides make a mess, it would have to be with fried catfish, hold the sautéed onions.

I invited him to Bullhead for a few days one summer, and much to my surprise, he accepted. He'd long ago replaced the Ten Commandments with about thirty of his own, and the first was, "Fish and houseguests smell after three days," so I knew his stay wouldn't be long, just Armageddonian. The frantic housecleaning that ensued was rivaled in scope only by his arrival on the Donrey 727 at the airport in Winston-Salem. With an entourage that would impress the current resident of 1600 Pennsylvania Avenue, I motored him up the mountain in a fifteen-year-old Lincoln, which he liked because the front passenger area was roughly the size of Kenya, providing him enough room to swing his arthritic legs out to the pavement without all the bending and scrambling required in the next-largest conveyance, the Bradley Fighting All-Terrain Vehicle.

By now I knew something about catfish. He liked the muddier taste of the wild catfish he had grown up with, not the blander farm-raised that's generally available now, and he liked a good crackle. At this point, annoyances like cholesterol didn't concern him. Once I heard he was coming, I broiled several, deep-fried some, and sent away for mail-order breaders, coatings, and batters. Finally, I decided on a simple cornmeal-and-spice breading and held my breath.

As soon as he arrived that afternoon, Dad took a nap and woke up in a blind rage. He was brought upstairs to our living room, and, eighty-three years old and deep into his senility, suddenly shouted in panic, "Where's my money? Where's my money!" I certainly didn't know. He sure hadn't given it to me. His aides, Lee and Dennis, and his companion, Virginia, couldn't calm him down.

"In a bank in Little Rock?" I tried to cool the boil. "Or Las Vegas. Or Kona?" I was bewildered by this man whom Forbes had recently dubbed a billionaire at a time when a billion dollars was a lot of money.

But he was unmollified. "How do you know? Have you seen it? Have you?"

"Well, no, but what about your associates, surely Fred, and Ross and Pat—"

"Those guys have been robbing me blind my whole life!" he shouted. He was hyperventilating. It took several minutes to talk him down from that window ledge. We assured him his money was safe and that Fred and company weren't robbing him. And then, just as suddenly as he'd flared up, he calmed right down and the panic left his face. I offered him Scotch. He politely accepted. But the specter of winding up poor like his father never left him.

I quickly threw together the fried catfish, first soaking the fillets in buttermilk, then dredging them in cornmeal and spices, and pan-fried them up. Couldn't have been simpler.

Charlotte presented an overflowing platter to my father, his aides, and Virginia. He took several bites and mashed them in what remained of his teeth, and something clicked. He looked up at me suspiciously—where had I had this flown in from? But then his milky, alcohol-drenched eyes softened, and for an instant there was connection—even appreciation.

"You . . . did . . . this . . . for me?" those eyes seemed to say.

Which was about the best that could be expected, and all I'd been after all along. And the man who could no longer shave himself or find his billion dollars at last took satisfaction in something that cost $2.49.

Dad died three years later, on a cruise near Spain. Both my parents spared me the anguish of caring for them in their declining years—Dad, by virtue of his wealth, with plenty of people around him, all taking care of him; Mother, by dying of a heart attack, suddenly and young, at sixty-two, with no apparent health problems except glaucoma.

Though Dad left us three Reynolds kids enough money to pay the rent— literally, the rent—we were removed from his posthumous enterprises by Fred Smith, not to be confused with the founder of Federal Express. After a few months feigning interest in our joining the board of the Donald W. Reynolds Foundation and allowing us to make a single generous gift from it (I gave mine to Denison), Fred became president of the foundation, installed his own family (and Dad's doctor . . . hmmm . . . call *CSI*? Just kidding) on the board, and baldly shut us out. The foundation's assets were $800 million at Dad's death and have grown substantially since then, despite the annual 5% distribution required by law. Dad's name is now plastered on several medical and journalism schools, and Fred engineered the building of several edifices in states where Dad's businesses flourished—chiefly Nevada, Arkansas, and Oklahoma—glorifying Dad's good name. Among them, the Donald W. Reynolds Razorback football stadium for the University of Arkansas in Fayetteville and a geriatric center in Little Rock stand out. And Fred saw to it that at least one building was named after himself, also at the University of Arkansas. Dad achieved a mean reputation as a boss, in keeping with his union-busting activities, and in hopes of repairing his reputation, the foundation gave the Smithsonian a $30 million grant to buy Gilbert Stuart's Lansdowne portrait of George Washington, and in 2005 gave the Smithsonian an additional $45 million to restore the Old Patent Office Building and rename it the Donald W. Reynolds Center for American Art and Portraiture. Though Don junior and I chuckled over Dad's sudden and posthumous interest in art—mostly what I remember are portraits of the houses he owned that he hung over fireplaces, and a few Remington sculptures of the Wild West—it's clear the advantage private funding has over government subsidy. Didn't quite repair the lesions in *my* house, but with the good works the foundation has done, I don't think I'd get much sympathy as a movie hero.

But with Dad's death, gone overnight and forever was that extra little privilege that inflated my chest whenever I set foot in McCarran airport. To be near him for the little time I was was to be associated not just with power and money, but with ambition, amazing energy, a great sense of humor, astonishing cruelty, and the unflagging religion of individualism. I thought some of those things might rub off, but the ones required for gargantuan success didn't. And I'd begun to re-evaluate that individualism. The world can tolerate a few thousand people who think only of themselves, and might even be stimulated by them—but not a few billion. The line between total self-expression and social detriment is fine and etched with responsibility. America risks becoming too individualistic in the world, and without a balance between the absolute Darwinian and total altruism, will do great damage.

Dad's body was brought back to Las Vegas in his 727, and he was cremated. Almost before the ashes were soft, the three associates sold his company and became very, very, very rich men.

I tried to sort out what he'd meant to me. By disappearing, fathers convey that their children aren't important—not to them, not to the world—whether they mean to or not. I surely missed love and affection from Dad, but I don't think I'd have had it if he were around all the time; he didn't have it to give. My half-brother, Don, had Dad in his life till he was almost sixty, and it was calamitous for him. I missed Dad's not being around so that I could see him realistically—well, as realistically as any child sees any parent—and could experience more of him rather than turning his life into a fairy tale of exaggerated evil and Hollywood megawattage. I didn't see him take his shirt off at night and know his muscles weren't perfect or hear him be boring at the dinner table or watch him fail occasionally at business or, God knows, observe him being tender with Mother, which he must have been, once or twice. I never saw him naked.

Given that just about every child feels his parents should have loved him more, what I missed most became, by default, practical. All hows: How did he get so much exuberance? How did he come by so much self-confidence? How come he was so smart? And how the hell do you get the world to work for you the way he did?

Buttermilk-and-Cornmeal Pan-Fried Catfish

1 cup buttermilk or water
2 cups yellow cornmeal
½ teaspoon salt
½ teaspoon pepper
3 tablespoons Cajun seasoning (or to taste)
½ cup peanut oil for frying
Four 8-ounce catfish fillets

1. Place buttermilk in a shallow bowl. In another shallow bowl combine cornmeal, salt, pepper, and Cajun seasoning.
2. Heat about ⅛ inch of the oil in large skillet over medium heat until a pinch of cornmeal mixture sizzles quickly.
3. Dip catfish fillets into buttermilk to coat on both sides. Drain excess and dredge fillets in cornmeal mixture, coating both sides. Shake off excess.
4. Fry fillets in oil, 3–4 minutes on each side, adding oil as necessary, until nicely browned and crisp.

YIELD: 4 servings.

Red-Cabbage-and-Roquefort Slaw

(Adapted from Nantucket Open-House Cookbook *by Sarah Leah Chase, Workman, 1987)*

2 medium heads red cabbage
2 cups finely chopped fresh parsley (about 4 bunches)

1½ cups crumbled Roquefort cheese (about 8 ounces)

3½ cups mayonnaise

½ cup grainy mustard

---

1. Remove a few outer leaves of the cabbages, rinse, dry, and use to line a large serving bowl. Quarter and core cabbages; cut wedges crosswise into thin shreds. Place in a large bowl with 1½ cups of the parsley and 1 cup of the cheese.

2. Combine mayonnaise and mustard in a medium bowl and whisk until blended. Pour into cabbage mixture and toss to coat. Sprinkle with remaining cheese and parsley. Cover and refrigerate at least 2 hours before serving.

YIELD: 16 servings.

Eating with the ★ ★ ★

AFTER THREE YEARS in Winston, Charlotte insisted that we move to L.A. if I was to continue going there so frequently. I'd always enjoyed visiting L.A. but shied away from setting up house there because it made the movie world inescapable. You were there, in it, like spiders climbing up the smooth side of a greasy trash can, unable to get traction and unable to get out. In New York and Winston-Salem, there was retreat—and perspective.

We were both right. Living there was better for the kids and, for a while, for us; and it was excruciatingly enlightening. In 1991, we rented a house in Santa Monica, where we were assured that the temperature was always ten degrees lower because it was west of the 405. (A true Angeleno refers to the notorious freeways by number rather than by name—so we first had to jettison the San Diego Freeway and the Ventura Freeway from our vocabularies in favor of the 405 and the 101. But then numbers have always carried more weight than poetry in Burbank. Up north, they drop the *the*.) Real estate is more expensive in Santa Monica than in Winston, but we all managed comfortably, and I continued to work at home.

Frank and Eddie were, again, horrified. Having just put down roots in the South, and loving those roots, they were once more yanked out of the ground and thrown into a much bigger cauldron of strangers, odd customs, different and disturbing social hierarchies. Personality didn't matter as much in L.A. as it did in North Carolina; money, fame, position, and which car you drove mattered most. In Winston, "My dad writes screenplays" ensured an otherworldly reputation. Out west, it carried the same prestige as "My dad drives a taxi" (actually less, since taxis in Los Angeles are pretty otherworldly). It was as though we'd moved to the Moon: On Earth I weighed 170; Out There, 55.

Fortunately, we still had Bullhead, to which I anticipated we would all return for holidays, summers, earthquakes, riots, and terrorist attacks—most of which we encountered in our first two years in Santa Monica. The headaches at Jane Street continued. A new boiler was needed. New windows. The roof leaked, ruining the tenant's grand piano! Meanwhile, we tried to sink roots into the Pacific.

Fat chance.

During my painful incarnation as a resident screenwriter, I once found myself seated in first class right behind Michael Jackson at the height of his inventive powers, well after "Billie Jean" and *Thriller*, and right next to his chef, who told me that she nearly always flew with him. Flying first class is one of the great joys—most say the only joy—of writing for the screen.

On this particular trip, however, the chef regaled me for three thousand miles across the country with descriptions of her recipes for the Gloved One—leaves and acorns, giraffe-shaped radishes and space sauces, granola fasts and all-grape regimens—none of which would I have then considered putting in my mouth either singly or in combination. At the time, I thought, I'm trapped with an L.A. vegan[3] and her Newly Galactic food.

The truth now, of course, is that Los Angeles is one of the great eating cities of the world, and it's been ages since anyone could make fun of it for its cuisine. Yes, there are health-food stores and more than the average number of pasty-faced vegans, but there are also too many excellent chefs and educated palates braising and feasting every night in the southern 90000 ZIP code to dismiss its cooking. Besides, the tofu and baby spelt legs we on the East Coast once thought lunatic are now sitting on Manhattan tables just possibly saving our lives. And because southern California is the tail that so often wags the American cultural dog, be warned: The fricassee of lobster face you roll your eyes at tonight may just wind up on your plate tomorrow.

In Hollywood, restaurants are a gauge of how well you're doing. Not just which restaurants you're taken to by agents, producers, stars, and studio heads, but the time of day they choose to take you there. If you're invited to dinner by a potential employer, you couldn't be hotter. At lunch, true, your heat is measured by which restaurant the boss has chosen—in the nineties, Spago, Chaya Brasserie, and Ivy at the Shore were indicators of heat; studio commissaries and Musso & Frank's meant you were in trouble. Breakfast, unless it was at the Hotel Bel-Air, meant not even the best golf swing in the county could resuscitate your career.

When you're hot, you don't notice the food—the meeting is too highly charged for anything sybaritic to take place; when you're not, your diary notes became voluminous, or at least mine did. I could chart my success by the length of the food entries in my notebook. In the eighties my notes were short and clipped, and in the nineties, several forests were chopped down to record my increasing gluttony.

The sad but happy fact is, I never learned how to tell a film story, particularly at a pitch meeting. Too many digressions, irrelevancies, inconclusions. Not enough mystery. Sad, because from the outside looking in, I thought I wanted to be in the movie business; happy, because, once in it for a while, I realized that aside from cashing some outsize checks, I didn't want to be in the movie business.

After *Micki & Maude* was released in 1984, it was clear to me that the only artistic power in the business lay in supermoviestardom or directing; I was advised by agents, producers, and friends that because of the success of that movie and my background in the theatre writing and working with actors, all I had to do was come up with my own brilliant screenplay—not one originated or owned by a studio—one the money people would be so desperate to make that they'd be happy for me to direct. And in the twenty years I worked at it (on and off), I never could. At the same time that David Mamet successfully moved from playwriting to screenwriting to directing, I was trying to figure out cause and effect, rising and falling action, and what the hell character arc meant. And all along, where to get a good piece of Patagonian toothfish (a.k.a. Chilean sea bass).

Despite having all those movies made, I took a couple of screenwriting courses, which reduced beloved films of the past like *Casablanca* to mathematics. None of the writers and directors I admired had taken screenwriting or film courses—not Welles or Mankiewicz or Kubrick or Terry Southern or Arthur Penn or Kazan or Benton & Newman or Lubitsch or Wilder or Izzy Diamond or Charles Lederer or Wyler or Elaine May or John Ford or Paddy Chayefsky (but only *The Americanization of Emily*), either Sturges or Woody Allen or Hawks or the Coen brothers or Blake Edwards. Coppola went to USC but it hadn't become the constricted academy it is today. I don't know if David O. Russell or the Farrelly brothers or Amy Heckerling went to film school, but if so, nothing damaging seems to have rubbed off.

The teaching gurus at the time were Syd Field, Robert McKee, and John Truby. Ironically, not only did aspiring writers and directors attend these script courses, but studio executives did, too. This explains why so many movies resemble one another. The fatuous analyses promulgated by these dis-appointed writers who were now teachers resulted in a dog-chasing-its-own-tail mentality: Though these courses were initially conceived for writers, studio executives decided they needed a more systematic method of judging scripts other than "I don't know; I liked it"—though that was good enough for Zanuck, Goldwyn, Cohen, and Thalberg—so they began taking the courses, too . . . which meant the execs were deciding to green-light or reject screen-plays based on their interpretation of how well the screenwriters' interpreta-tion of the Field/McKee/Truby interpretation of what makes a good movie measured up. If the movie was ever made, this aping the shell of successful movies of the past resulted in nicely shaped, hollow films without an original thought in their heads. The unprecedented and the clever were reserved for the special FX of *The Matrix* and *Crouching Tiger, Hidden Dragon*.

I tried to conform to these rules but couldn't. They exemplified what I dis-liked not only about the movies, but all the pop culture I couldn't stomach—and my own inability to manufacture some of it. Like so many who wind up in Hollywood, I was in constant struggle between an intense, if fantastical, desire for easy money and fame—which making movies always seems to be from the outside looking in—and the need for some sort of spiritual nourish-ment professionally. What I could stomach—and like a truant, spent most of my time pursuing—was finding the best source for Brandywine tomatoes or the way to complicate the sharp flavor of a Virginia ham by striating it with spinach and garlic or which downtown bar made the best lamb sandwich, complete with its own *jus* for dipping (Philippe's on Alameda Street). That was sensuality and passion! That was living in the moment! That was fun! It just never occurred to me to make a living at it.

Just like you and me, Hollywood's stars and power brokers have to eat. They just get to do it first. L.A. restaurants are the purest of meritocracies: It doesn't matter who your parents are or where you went to school; if you're famous, you get seated first.

And prominently, just the way your car is parked.

In November 2000, after I'd left Los Angeles, *The New York Times* sent me a list of the city's dining hot spots and asked for an article. Herewith, a sampling of the whos, whats, and wheres on November 12, 2000:

Warren Beatty (whose fingertips Woody Allen reportedly said were what he'd most like to be reincarnated as) regularly orders the sushi without rice at Hamasaku. (Only in Los Angeles would someone dream up riceless sushi and not call it sashimi—sort of like fatless duck confit.)

Annette Bening prefers the intriguing Japanese bouillabaisse. Gina Gershon's bee-stung lips lovingly caress the lamb chops with tomato-mint salsa from Chaya Brasserie, where George Clooney and Matt LeBlanc go for the Chaya steak. Leo No-Last-Name-Needed-for-Another-Ten-Minutes tosses off pretensions with ham and eggs at the Griddle Cafe. It should also be noted that in this weathercock city, Wolfgang Puck's remarkable Spago remained hot longer than just about any other bistro, perhaps, among other things, because of its "Jewish pizza"—a thin slab of smoked salmon dolloped with caviar. None of these restaurants is as hot as it was.

On the set, a rigid class system rules. While the stars sip their strawsful of sugarless broth fumes and vapor of fetal watercress leaf helicoptered to their trailers daily, everyone else gets fat. Grips and gaffers don't usually have personal nutritionists. Because working on a movie set is about as exciting as seeing the movie of *Flower Drum Song* thirty times or *The Hours* once, you blindly reach out for whatever the craft service wagon has on display to quell the boredom—usually an endless supply of doughnuts, meat loaves, fries, burgers and dogs, things in gravies, and quite cosmic pastries drowning in sugars and jams. On a ten-week shoot (or a regular weekly TV series), you don't have to look above the belt line to tell royalty from commoner.

I never got any recipes from Michael Jackson's chef. Michael himself was polite and talkative and quite normal—until the plane landed, the glove went on, and the surgical mask was slipped over one of his noses. He didn't eat a thing the entire journey—perhaps that's the best secret of all.

SPECIAL "LOBSTER"

(Adapted from Mr. Chow of Beverly Hills)

½ pound fresh jumbo shrimp, peeled and deveined
½ egg white
1 teaspoon cornstarch
2 teaspoons salt
1 teaspoon plus ¼ cup vegetable oil
3 tablespoons rice-wine vinegar
1 ½ teaspoons sugar
1 teaspoon potato starch or cornstarch
½ jalapeño chile, seeded and minced
1 teaspoon slivered fresh ginger
1 celery rib, julienned
½ green bell pepper, julienned
½ red bell pepper, julienned

1. In a medium bowl, combine the shrimp, egg white, cornstarch, 1 teaspoon of the salt, and 1 teaspoon of the oil. Mix well. Refrigerate anywhere from 1 to 12 hours.
2. In a small cup, mix the vinegar, remaining teaspoon salt, the sugar, and the potato starch until salt and sugar dissolve. Set aside.
3. Heat the ¼ cup oil in a wok over high heat until hot and add the shrimp mixture, stir-frying 1–1 ½ minutes, until shrimp are pink and curled but not cooked through.
4. Pour shrimp and oil into a sieve over a bowl. Return 1 tablespoon oil to the pan. Add the jalapeño, ginger, vinegar mixture, celery, bell peppers, and

shrimp and stir-fry 1 minute or until shrimp are shiny and evenly coated. (Do not overcook shrimp and vegetables.) Serve immediately.

YIELD: 2 servings.

CHAYA RIB-EYE STEAK
WITH PEPPERCORN BUTTER AND BASIL SAUCE
(Adapted from Chaya Brasserie)

For the peppercorn butter
½ pound unsalted butter, softened
¼ cup black peppercorns, coarsely crushed
¼ cup green peppercorns (not in brine)
¼ cup pink peppercorns
¼ cup finely chopped onions
¼ cup finely chopped shallots
2 tablespoons minced garlic
2 tablespoons chopped fresh chives
2 tablespoons bread crumbs
2 anchovies, rinsed and mashed
Juice from ½ lemon
1½ teaspoons chopped parsley
1 teaspoon rock salt or sea salt

For the garnish
2 tablespoons olive oil
15 baby white potatoes
1 head garlic, separated into cloves and peeled
Salt to taste

For the basil sauce
4 tablespoons unsalted butter
½ cup veal stock

1 large basil leaf, finely chopped
Salt to taste
Five 1-pound rib-eye steaks

---

1. To make the peppercorn butter, 3 hours or more before serving, place butter in a bowl and beat with a mixer at high speed until fluffy, about 5 minutes. Fold in the remaining ingredients. Line a loaf pan with plastic wrap, spread mixture in the prepared pan, cover with plastic wrap, and freeze until firm, at least 2 hours.
2. To make the garnish, preheat the oven to 350 degrees. Coat the bottom of a small roasting pan with the oil. Add the potatoes and garlic and sprinkle with salt. Cover tightly with foil and bake 1 hour, stirring every 15 minutes. Uncover the pan and cook 15 minutes, or until potatoes and garlic are tender when pierced.
3. About 30 minutes before making the steaks, take the peppercorn butter out of fridge, unwrap, and bring to room temperature.
4. To make the basil sauce, about 15 minutes before the potatoes are done, melt the butter in a small skillet over medium heat and cook until browned. Add the veal stock and basil and boil for 1 minute to reduce slightly. Season with salt.
5. Grill or broil the steaks to the desired doneness. Cut peppercorn butter into 5 pieces. Place one piece on top of each steak, spoon some basil sauce on top, and serve with the roasted potatoes and garlic.

YIELD: 5 servings.

GOLDEN GAZPACHO WITH AHI TUNA AND HEIRLOOM TOMATOES
(Adapted from Patina)

For the gazpacho
6 large yellow heirloom tomatoes, quartered and seeded
1 yellow bell pepper, roasted, peeled, seeded, and quartered

1 Kirby cucumber, cut into 1-inch chunks

3 tablespoons extra-virgin olive oil

1 tablespoon sherry vinegar

Juice of 1 orange

Juice of 1 lemon

Sea salt to taste

Freshly ground pepper to taste

For the garnish

½ pound sashimi-grade ahi tuna, cut into ¾-inch cubes

20 tiny heirloom tomatoes (5 different colors or varieties), halved

1 bulb baby fennel, finely slivered

12 fennel fronds

20 celery leaves

20 tiny basil leaves

20 sprigs chervil

1 teaspoon finely diced red onion

1 scallion green, sliced into 12 pieces

Sea salt to taste

Freshly ground pepper to taste

1 tablespoon extra-virgin olive oil

1. To make the gazpacho, process the tomatoes, bell pepper, and cucumber in a blender until smooth. Strain through a sieve into a medium bowl. Season with the olive oil, vinegar, orange and lemon juices, salt, and pepper.
2. To serve, arrange ¼ of the tuna, tomatoes, fennel, fennel fronds, celery leaves, basil, chervil, red onion, and scallion in each of 4 large bowls. Sprinkle with the salt, pepper, and olive oil. Ladle the gazpacho over the garnish.

YIELD: 4 servings.

Stargazy Pie

~~~~~~~~~~

I N SANTA MONICA, Frank and Eddie found new friends and eventually settled in. I never did. Tom Baum, a novelist and screenwriter I'd known in New York, took over for Rafe. We had lunch all the time, endless philosophical discussions ("buttering the air," a friend called it), no political fireworks.

In a bizarre turn of events, Tom and his wife, Carol, a movie producer, bought Lee Remick's house in Brentwood shortly after she died. It was hard for me to visit them for about two years, and I regularly invited them to our house or suggested we meet at the movies or a restaurant. When I did go to their house, I felt jumpy and remorseful, though those feelings eventually disappeared. Carol would have been the producer of *Sister Sunshine*, had it advanced to the next stage. The world is the size of a pea in Hollywood.

It was difficult to work with Charlotte in the Santa Monica house. It was half the size of the one in Winston, where we could lose each other. I'd leave the office downstairs for a sandwich, and she'd be reading the paper. Passivity filled the place. She'd brought a set of bizarrely painted chairs and tables from North Carolina in hopes of selling them and starting a business for the artist who'd made them. She showed them to one person who didn't like them, and the set remained unexamined in the garage for another seven or eight years.

After a year, she landed a job as a secretary with another soccer mom who happened to be West Coast editor of *The New Yorker*. Tina Brown had recently taken over as editor, and, flush with her success at *Vanity Fair*, had fortuitously opened a small office in L.A., only three blocks from our house, just in time for the O.J. murders, an earthquake, and the Eisner-Ovitz marriage. It was a per fect jumping-off point for Charlotte, now beginning a new career. She was meant for the magazine world: literate, articulate, skilled in grammar and language, focused with ideas. Initially it was a godsend, and she'd return home at night bubbling with stories and the idiosyncrasies of her boss, a bouncy Brit named Caroline Graham who'd been a girlfriend of David Frost and a wife of Bill Graham of the *Washington Post* family. Unfortunately, Charlotte didn't advance beyond the assistant level or land a position with another magazine, and when Tina left and David Remnick took over, he de-L.A.'d the mag and closed the office, putting Charlotte out of work.

Except for screenwriting, it was a lively time to be in L.A. There were seasonal floods, annual fires, two substantial earthquakes, the Rodney King riot . . . and O. J. Simpson. Life surpassed the movies, and the place seemed to be the center of the universe, as London had been thirty years earlier. Initially, I had a run of luck: That's when Coppola called wanting to revive live television drama, with CBS's blessing and *Yanks 3* as his first project. Cable television was in its infancy then, and the vast majority of Americans still watched either the three networks or their local channels. Such exposure on network television would have made any writer's reputation. Francis talked repeatedly of the action-packed experience of directing a live TV drama on location inside a truck, and I realized it was that vision of himself pointing and snapping his fingers that made him excited about the project. As the weeks passed, I think he saw he might not get the spotlight he anticipated—unless he filmed himself directing.

I had known Laura Ziskin for several years. She produced *Pretty Woman*, *What About Bob?*, *To Die For*, and several other movies. She went on to produce the *Spider-Man* movies (taking a percentage instead of a fee!) and had been interested in developing a project with me. She currently had a deal at TriStar. I wrote a script for her about the coming phenom of afternoon television talk shows in which a young woman in the audience of a program resembling the Oprah Winfrey show lies about her misfortunes on the air, then lands a job on the show and gradually rises to the top of the show's production crew by stabbing everyone in the back and ultimately betraying the Oprah character. It had my own personal kitchen sink in it: evil and funny, New York smart and outrageous, juicy, sexy, with a lesbian twist before such things were mandatory. Laura wanted to make it right away. But the head of TriStar, Marc Platt, balked at the evil and the lesbianism and wouldn't green-light it. When she tried to set it up at another studio, he wouldn't let her, and when she was appointed head of production at Twentieth Century–Fox a year later, he wouldn't sell it to her for fear of it being a success and making him look like a fool for turning it down. In such a manner are weighty aesthetic decisions frequently made in Hollywood. Needless to say, if Marc Platt is ever found armless and legless, the local constabulary could do worse than to subpoena my DNA. At the same time, Coppola bailed out of the television project to do *Pinocchio*.

Everyone has bad luck, of course, but I also had bad ideas—or at least no salable ones. The sons of Zanuck looked at my grosses, and to paraphrase my favorite David Mamet line, they could see "the handwriting on the whatchamacallit." I consoled myself that at least I was being a good father to my children: with me as a failure, they wouldn't have the same big shoes to fill that I had had. This worked for about thirty minutes, and I quickly did what everybody in Hollywood does when discouraged: I went to a therapist.

In the nineties, southern-California therapy consisted of a mishmash of a spiritual life in which you were not supposed to attach yourself to any outcomes. If you succeeded, it didn't matter, and if you failed, it didn't matter, either. The purpose of this spirituality was unnamed, but its subtext was basically that you should avoid ever feeling bad about anything. If you got an Oscar or a wife or cancer, it didn't matter because you weren't "attached" to the outcome. This bastard Buddhism (the only four realities are life, death, pain, and suffering) embraced any belief system as long as it didn't belong to an established religion, and it allowed any sort of sexual behavior that wasn't unkind to women. In practice, it meant getting up in the morning to repeat affirmations in front of a mirror. Things like "I am perfect as I am. I draw power from the nosehead of the universe and accept my imperfections as blessings from a Greater Source" two or three hundred times until your resistance was lowered and your head shook like a tuning fork. When I complained to various therapists—I had about six over the seven years I was there—that all I really needed was a job, they would object adamantly and instruct me to attach myself to nothing. Let the outcome, if negative, slide away, and if positive, don't forget to thank the nosehead. When I asked if I was also supposed to attach myself to nothing human—like my wife and children—the response was shocked. Of course you must attach yourself to them! "But what if they die?" Then don't attach yourself. Accept all misfortunes as blessings.

The one observation I did think true came from a self-invented guru named John-Roger, most of whose other thoughts were no better than the affirmations. But he did say, and here I'm paraphrasing, "The only thing man needs to make himself happy is an idea to get excited about." And sitting in this morass of gloom and rejection, I tried to get excited.

Whether it was my cynical New York background or just common sense, this resulted in alternating periods of despair and laughter. I was so discouraged that I had trouble writing more than a page or two of anything. I'd write a line or two, then head for the nearest TV and watch first the Clarence Thomas hearings starring Anita Hill, and years later the O.J. trial starring Johnnie Cochran and Lance Ito. The latter was more addictive than heroin, completely absorbing, and professionally self-destructive. So I researched and found the foremost authority on ADD, a malady destined to be more popular than rap. Dr. Wallid Shekim first put me on Ritalin, which had no effect, then Dexedrine, which made me sad for an hour, then hyperactive for five. I tried to make him understand the difference between sad and depressed, but he seemed to think they were the same thing, so he added Prozac toward the end of the day. The Dex made me energetic, all right, but to no good end. Rather than writing, I'd run out and buy sand dabs or pompano at the Santa Monica Seafood Company or have lunch with Baum for too long or drive all the way into Hollywood to see another writing pal, David Freeman, effectively blowing the day. Dr. Shekim said, "This medicine is no good, you know, if it makes you energetic but all you do is paint the house."

So I did what I generally do when depressed: write something for the other coast. As I'd written successful movies on the East Coast, I assumed the trick to creating a successful play was to write it on the West Coast.

For relief, I became Captain New York. Having got out of town to L.A. when in New York and Winston, I now flew to New York three or four times a year to get out of L.A. Sometimes I'd keep on going, to London, where the National Theatre really revved up my soul. This was ostensibly on business, but it was clear to even the children of these therapists that I was much happier when not living where I was supposed to be living. I'd go to the theatre in New York, make notes about the plays, eat at restaurants, and make notes about them. I no longer hated the place. I didn't hate New York or Los Angeles unless I was there. Sort of like being allergic to your own skin.

The most fun I had in Los Angeles was at restaurants or on the way to restaurants listening to right-wing radio. Rush Limbaugh was only the tip of the iceberg. Later in the day, Dennis Prager would appear, and on an opposing station an old loony named George Putnam, two characters named John and Ken, Tom Lykes, and a former chapter head of NOW, a liberal lesbian turned conservative lesbian, Tammy Bruce. They were all fabulously and hilariously over the top. They tweaked the establishment Left, turning political correctness on its head. In fact, I began to think of them and the pols they bolstered as the true progressives, since all the Left seemed to want to do was advance socialism from the thirties, which seemed regressive, not progressive. These radio-talk jockeys set the bedrock for the coming Contract with America and the Gingrich revolution. When I couldn't sleep, I'd listen to Howard Stern in the morning. So did Baum, and we'd compare notes.

I cooked most of the time, if I was there. Although the kids hadn't developed much of a palate, Charlotte loved food—meat, in particular!—and I tried to make something from the *Los Angeles Times* food section every week. Despite the *L.A. Times*'s pompous, ridiculously PC editorial stance in this one-newspaper town, its Wednesday food section was more fun than that in *The New York Times*. It was livelier, more experimental, and in color. Los Angeles was celebrating California cuisine, and New York was playing catch-up, still aping Europe, and now beginning to ape the West Coast—but not initiating anything on its own. Ruth Reichl wrote the restaurant reviews for the *L.A. Times* and was sparkling, so, like the Yankees, the New York version hired her away.

During my less energetic moments with Ritalin, Dexedrine, and Prozac, I pored over cookbooks and loved picturing bizarre recipes. I found a perfect show-biz dish called Stargazy Pie, perfect because it's uncomplicated and delicious, and just looking at it will make you laugh. When was the last time dinner made you laugh? Not the guests, the food . . . ?

Nasty with unpredictability and generally greeted with both horror and delight, the sardine-packed Stargazy Pie is a darkly witty surprise and guaranteed to kindle conversation. According to the tough British food writer Jane Grigson, the pie (sometimes spelled "Stargazey") is a Cornish creation traditionally made on Tom Bawcock's Eve, two days before Christmas, commemorating the night on which brave Bawcock went to sea to find sustenance for his foodless hometown of Mousehole. Against all odds, he returned with netsful of sardines, fed the town with this pie, and wound up with a dish and an extremely minor holiday named after him. (Asking where the townspeople found the bacon and hard-boiled eggs in the foodless burg is as irrelevant as questioning how the girl who married Cain got there.)

There are several variations on it, but all versions of Stargazy Pie involve sardines, and all feature their Clupeidae heads poking up from under the crust. Grigson isn't clear whether the pie is named after the sail at the top of a mast—a stargazer—or the horse of the same name, so called because it keeps its head back, which visually parallels the sight of the sardine faces poking out from the pie. But the appearance is arresting and festive, which is why I suggest serving it to guests who have at least the hint of a sense of humor.

Stargazy Pie

(Adapted from Jane Grigson's Fish Book, *Penguin Books, 1994)*

Two 9-inch rounds short-crust or puff pastry, unbaked
8 fresh sardines, scaled, cleaned, filleted, heads on and tails removed
2 tablespoons Dijon mustard
2 tablespoons chopped fresh thyme or cilantro
2 tablespoons chopped fresh parsley
Finely grated rind and juice of 2 lemons
1 teaspoon kosher salt
¾ teaspoon freshly ground pepper
12 ounces bacon, chopped, lightly fried

4 hard-boiled eggs (do not overcook), shelled, coarsely chopped
Egg wash (1 egg mixed with 1 tablespoon water)
10 small sprigs fresh parsley, for garnish

1. Preheat oven to 425 degrees. Arrange one pastry round in a shallow pie plate or on a baking sheet. Butterfly the sardines. Brush insides of sardines with some mustard and sprinkle with chopped herbs, grated lemon rind, salt, and pepper. Arrange the sardines on pastry round equidistant from one another with filleted-side down and heads resting on edge of pastry. Scatter bacon and eggs and then sprinkle lemon juice over all.

2. Trim about ¼ inch from edge of second round of pastry and place round over sardines. Brush bottom pastry at edges with half the egg wash and press top pastry onto bottom pastry between sardines, arranging a pastry edge around each sardine neck so that just the heads peek out. Gently press pastry around the bodies of the sardines to make a wavy surface. Cut a small vent hole in the center of the top crust. Brush top with remaining egg wash.

3. Bake pie for 20 minutes. Reduce oven temperature to 350 degrees and bake 15–25 more minutes, until top of pie is a golden brown. Before serving, tuck a sprig of parsley in each sardine mouth. Or not.

YIELD: 8 servings.

GRILLED MOROCCAN SARDINES

(Adapted from The Moroccan Collection *by Hilaire Walden, Soma Books, 1998)*

2 pounds sardines, scaled and cleaned, heads and tails left on
3 garlic cloves, peeled and crushed into a paste
Finely grated zest and the juice of 1 lemon
3 tablespoons olive oil
1 ½ tablespoons chopped fresh cilantro
1 ½ tablespoons chopped fresh parsley

2 teaspoons paprika
1 teaspoon ground coriander
Pinch each saffron threads and hot-red-pepper flakes
1 teaspoon kosher salt

1. Place sardines in a single layer in a nonreactive dish. Mix the remaining ingredients in a bowl, pour over the sardines, and turn sardines to coat. Cover and let marinate 1 hour.
2. Grill or broil sardines until cooked through, about 2 minutes on each side.

YIELD: 4–6 servings.

L.A. Confidential

~~~~~~~~

WANT TO MAKE a Hollywood screenwriter really mad? Just whisper in her ear, "A Film by Rob Reiner" or "A Sydney Pollack Film" or any other misattribution of the authorship of a movie to anyone who didn't write it. Watch the top of her skull hit the ceiling, duck while her eyes shoot blood, hear the smoke rifle from her ears! Transparent lies make people mad, and screenwriters are people, mostly.

Want to make a Mexicana living in Los Angeles really mad? Just whisper in her ear that you know where to buy really good tamales. She may not have the same rampageous reaction as the screenwriter—the Mexicanas I whispered to simply looked at me condescendingly, as if I had missed the second grade—but she knows that is a lie, too.

I tried several places in search of a great tamale in L.A., beginning with a much-touted take-out shop near the airport called Corn Maiden, but either the proportions were wrong or the dough was too clunky, so I quit trying to buy them. Although I look forward to your contradiction, I agree with the supercilious looks of those Mexican women: You can't *buy* a good tamale in L.A.*

Which is not to say you can't find one. You just need to motor to the west side of town, knock on the door of a show-biz quadrillionaire or an out-in-time NASDAQer, and ask if he or she has any female undocumented workers—

---

*A matrimonial lawyer told me he regularly buys tamales for breakfast at Tito's in Culver City—though since matrimonial lawyers (euphemism for serial drug-dealing child molesters) generally feast on either human flesh or wheelbarrows full of Ben Franklin federal reserve notes and usually both, *caveat emptor*.

euphemism for "illegal aliens"—on staff, the harboring of which gave the forty-second and forty-third presidents of the United States supposedly just reason for withdrawing support from the cabinet nominations of Kimba Wood and Linda Chavez. If the quadrillionaire employs someone illegal, and I've yet to find one who doesn't, your chances of getting a decent-to-brilliant tamale are substantially increased.

In Mexico, tamales are for special occasions—fiestas, the New Year, and in honor of the dead the day after All Saints' Day. They were eaten by Mexican rulers long before Spaniards came to the New World and can be filled with just about anything except soup. Normally, they are two inches wide and two to four inches long, but Diana Kennedy, the doyenne of Mexican-cookbook authors, writes of a dusty pilgrimage she made to the tiny town of Pánuco to breakfast on a pork-filled two-footer (the three-footer was too many towns away). She also enjoyed one filled with iguana and eggs.

Making the masa, a gallimaufry of dried corn kernels, lime, salt, and the L-ingredient* all mushed together for several hours, is the most demanding aspect of preparation. But an excellent substitute is Maseca instant corn-masa mix (*not* masa harina), available in most Mexican food stores.

"It's not Christmas without tamales," Alejandrina, housekeeper for a TV producer, told me in the jumbo kitchen of one of the swanker homes north of Montana Avenue in the boonies of Santa Monica. She smoothed a tablespoon of the gluey masa over three quarters of a corn husk, then added on some *pollo en salsa verde*, nimbly folded it, and tied it at the center with a strip of corn husk. She repeated this several times, first with the *pollo,* then with *puerco,* which had been boiled in chicken stock with a full head of garlic, then sautéed with a puree of California chili peppers, the pork-boiling mixture, and more garlic. The smell is smoky and sexy. The key to the filling is in the chilies. Guajillo, jalapeño, pasilla, New Mexico—all give different smokes. "Mexican people here don't buy tamales in stores. They are not good from stores." I concur. "Now in Guatemala and some Mexican places, they wrap them in banana leaves, but this is how we do it from where I come from."

Alejandrina came from Sonora in 1981. "Like everybody who come from an-

*LARD! (Better for you than butter.)

other country, I jump from a fence over the border. They throw me out. Two hours later, I jump from the same place in the same fence and stay for five years." She begins making dessert tamales, which differ little from the savories—she adds a couple of teaspoons of sugar to the masa, dabs a spoonful of it on the corn husk, then places three or four pineapple chunks and some dried cranberries into the center, might add some chopped walnuts, then folds and wraps it as she has done with the others.

"After five years, I get sick for my parents and go back to visit them, but I cannot get back in. So I hike over mountains like everybody all night. I get very tired, but I cannot get back in. The third time I try, an American Indian with a taxi says to me, 'For fifty dollars I will take you anywhere,' so I pay him fifty dollars and take a taxi into San Diego, where Gustavo was waiting." I never found out who Gustavo was because I have to grab the tamales and run as though I, too, am crossing the border, which I am—into the deadbeat borough of Bel-Air, where another undocumented worker of another quadrillionaire was also making tamales.

Lucrecia came to Los Angeles in 1990 after her husband, a truck driver, was killed in Mexico City. She lives in a two-bedroom apartment with her five children, a granddaughter, and the granddaughter's mother. Her life back in Mexico should bring whining in America to a standstill. "My grandmother, mother, and I make fifteen hundred tortillas every day for the rich people. We get up at three in the morning to make the masa. In very big balls." She gets down on her knees to illustrate how the three women rolled out the tortillas for five hours. "We make seven hundred in the morning, in stacks this high"—she gestures three feet off the floor—"and I put them on my back. We ring the bell at each house, and we have to move fast because people need tortillas warm, and we must sell all seven hundred between eight and nine in the morning for their breakfast."

She isn't bitter but seems rather surprised by her feats—though she clearly does not wish to revisit the experience anywhere but in memory. "Then we have lunch of tortillas filled with roasted pumpkinseeds and salt. We don't have for chicken, we don't have for meat. When we have money— chicken! Meat!" She lines a steamer with empty corn husks, places fifteen tamales on top, then covers them with a dishcloth and a lid. "When we finish the lunch, we buy wood. I carry big bunch on my head! We make eight hundred more tortillas in the afternoon, and we have one hour to sell them, three to four P.M. Then is time to go wash the maize for tomorrow." The tamales steam for about an hour. "I am very glad my grandmother teach me this because I love to work." She mentions the names of the people who employ her now in Bel-Air, friends of mine, who ask to be anonymous. "I love them very much. They try to get a green card for me but it takes seven years and it cost them twenty-two thousand dollars. When my grandmother die, they send me home and they phone me every day. They have a very big heart."

An hour or so later, the tamales are ready, and the four of us—Lucrecia, her generous employers, and I—unwrap the husks and dig in. The flavor bursts through the thin dough, some mild, some smoky, some hot as hell, and the dough tastes deliciously cornful. We bolt down three each, smile big, and rub our bellies, at least metaphorically. They are right, these women—you can't buy a tamale in L.A. anywhere near as good as the ones Alejandrina and Lucrecia make. Having cleared up that lie, perhaps they could now be of help to the Writers Guild.

Undocumented Tamale Dough (Masa)

3 ½ cups Maseca instant corn-masa mix for tamales
2 ¼ cups hot water
1 cup lard
1 ½ cups warm chicken broth
Salt to taste (depends on how salty the broth is)

1. Mix masa mix with hot water to make pliable dough and let cool.
2. In an electric mixer, beat the lard on medium speed until fluffy, 3–5 minutes; then beat in masa mixture in three handfuls. Add a cup of broth until dough is the texture of buttercream frosting. Add salt, cover, and refrigerate 1 hour. Remix, adding broth if too stiff.

YIELD: thirty 4-inch tamales.

NOTE: Maseca instant corn-masa mix is available in Mexican food stores and through the website www.kitchenmarket.com.

GREEN SALSA

3 pounds fresh tomatillos, husks removed and quartered
2 jalapeño chilies, halved and seeded
2 cups roughly chopped fresh cilantro leaves and tender stems
2 small onions, chopped
2 tablespoons corn oil
About 2 cups chicken broth
Salt to taste

1. Boil tomatillos and jalapeños in 1 cup of water until soft, 2–3 minutes. Drain in a sieve or over a bowl to collect juices for 5 minutes.
2. Purée tomatillos, jalapeños, and cilantro in blender with ½ cup drained-tomatillo liquid.
3. Sauté onion in oil until almost browned, about 3 minutes. Add tomatillo purée and cook, stirring frequently, for 10 minutes, until thick, adding as much broth as needed to keep from sticking to pan. Season with salt.

YIELD: 4 cups.

RED SALSA

6 ounces Guajillo or New Mexican chilies
4–5 cups chicken broth
1 large onion, peeled and cut in half lengthwise
1 head, plus 1 clove, garlic
2 cups sesame seeds, toasted
¼ teaspoon Mexican or other dried oregano
¼ teaspoon freshly ground black pepper

3 whole cloves
Pinch of cinnamon
2 tablespoons corn oil
5 sprigs fresh thyme
Salt to taste

---

1. Slit chilies on one side with scissors and remove seeds and ribs. With tongs, briefly char chilies over an open flame, then plunge into cold water. Tear each into small pieces and place in large skillet. Cover with broth (about 3 cups) and heat to boiling over medium heat. Simmer, covered, over medium-low heat, 20 minutes.
2. Wrap onion and 3 garlic cloves in foil and place on a burner on low heat. Cook 10 minutes; turn over foil package and cook 10 minutes longer. Unwrap.
3. Add onion to chile liquid and squeeze roasted garlic from skin into pan. Mix in sesame seeds, oregano, pepper, cloves, and cinnamon, and, in 3 or 4 batches, purée, adding broth as necessary.
4. Heat oil in large skillet, add chile purée and thyme, and cook, stirring constantly, 5 minutes, adding broth as necessary to keep consistency of mixture. Salt.

YIELD: 4 cups.

ASSORTED TAMALES

1 pound beef brisket, cubed
5 sprigs fresh thyme
Salt to taste
3 cloves garlic, peeled
1 pound boneless, skinless chicken breasts
6 cups chicken broth
1 pound small shrimp, deveined
1 pound lean boneless pork

1 head of garlic, halved crosswise

Green and red salsas

30 corn husks

Undocumented Tamale Dough (Masa) (page 247)

12 ounces *queso fresco*, diced

4 ounces mozzarella, cut into thin, 3-finger-wide pieces

---

1. For the beef: Simmer beef, thyme, salt, and 1 clove peeled garlic in water to cover 45–60 minutes, covered, until tender. Drain and divide into two bowls. Salt.

2. Chicken: Simmer with 1 clove peeled garlic in broth to cover, 8–10 minutes, covered, until tender. Drain, shred into bite-size pieces, and divide into 2 bowls. Salt.

3. Shrimp: Simmer shrimp and 1 clove peeled garlic in chicken broth to cover, 2–3 minutes, covered, until just pink. Drain and divide into 2 bowls. Salt.

4. Pork: Simmer pork with head of garlic and 1 teaspoon of salt in chicken broth 8–10 minutes. Let cool in broth, then shred and divide into 2 bowls.

5. Toss half of each filling with green salsa to coat, and half with red.

6. To fill and steam tamales: Soak corn husks in warm water until pliable, rinse away all silk, and drain. With husk tops pointing away from you, spread each with a 4- to 5-inch square of masa to ⅛-inch thickness. Spoon about 2 tablespoons of meat, chicken, shrimp, or pork filling on top and fold husk over from the sides. Then either fold top and bottom of husk over the first fold or invert a second husk, fold it over the first and fold the pointed ends so that they overlap like a Christmas present. Tie with a strip of husk. Layer in a steamer, covering pot with damp towel and lid, and steam 45–60 minutes until the masa pulls easily away from the husk.

7. For cheese tamales, place 2 or 3 cubes of *queso fresco*, a piece of mozzarella, and 2 tablespoons of either salsa on top, fold, and wrap.

YIELD: 6 tamales per filling.

NOTE: Because husks add no flavor, 6-inch-wide strips of aluminum foil can be used instead, but the presentation will lack authenticity. But since authenticity is over as of 2006, according to *The New York Times*, it's okay.

Leaving Los Angeles (Without Nicolas Cage)

~~~~~~~~

E VENTUALLY, I REALIZED Los Angeles had to be left. It's no fun being unemployed anyplace, but it's the least fun of all being unemployed in Los Angeles. So much significance is attached to what you do that if you don't do anything—or worse, do something but aren't successful at it—you might as well enter your next social function with a sign saying BEARER HAS BIRD FLU. Movie folk don't generally admire the writing process because it's too mysterious—guy or gal goes into a dark room and comes out with magic or with stink—and nobody knows how it happened or what the difference between the two is. The cinematography is understandable, and the music, and the direction—but the writing is just annoyingly incomprehensible.

Freelancers in every profession are usually out of work—that's the status quo. The condition is also entrepreneurial—you can, in theory, write, photograph, or paint yourself out of failure, make up your own style, create your own empire. Picasso and Tom Clancy did; at least one screenwriter, when hot for two to three years, took on UCLA students to write his many assignments and supervised them editorially, like Rubens. So as a playwright and screenwriter, I thought of myself as an artistic entrepreneur—which, of course, runs the risk of complete failure, like all entrepreneurial enterprises—and by 1998 I had become what Darryl Zanuck had predicted. Hollywood is a town of proven failures.

Most of my downturn in fortune was due to a combination of rebelliousness and not knowing what the canon was that I was rebelling against. I never differentiated between luck and talent in the movie business, but sooner or later you have to have one or the other.

I pitched stories to people half my age—comic ideas that were received with respect but dead faces. After seven years of this masochism, nothing budged. Aside from having a couple of close friends and enjoying generally sensational weather, I felt as out of place in Los Angeles as I had at those boarding schools I'd been thrown out of. People kept telling me, "You're such a New Yorker," and I was beginning to believe them.

So I decided I should switch professions to either I'm not sure what—Dad hovered entrepreneurially—or producing. I'd long since decided that the most important skill in writing a screenplay wasn't in its content but in the ability to pitch it. The overwhelming majority of screenplays are bad, just like most movies and all but about six directors. In the eighties, it was said that one movie was made for every ninety-nine that were in development—which meant one out of ninety-nine that someone had actually paid for was produced. (There is no record of the number of screenplays written and submitted every year. It's probably two per citizen.) But those in development were backed by the studios because of reputation, track record, good luck (Nicole Kidman likes it!), good story line, or, mostly, salesmanship. I'm sure David Mamet's background in sales has helped immeasurably both in achieving a reputation and in having so many movies produced that, on merit alone, wouldn't have been. But on merit alone, almost no movies would be made.

So I went to a few sales seminars at which most of the people were interested in real estate. The principles were the same, but they didn't really address how to create and sell a story, so they weren't that helpful, either.

Finally, I attended one of Tony Robbins's seminars. Robbins gained immense fame from a series of TV infomercials through which he sold hundreds of thousands of audio and videotape packages at a few hundred dollars each. Their theme was reassuring: There is no limit to what you can accomplish if only you get your head screwed on right. He was extremely upbeat and one of the first of the truly inspired motivational coaches. His reputation became so great that when Bill Clinton was undergoing his own personal first-term doldrums, he summoned Robbins to the White House, though I'm not sure what went on there. Maybe Robbins taught him how to make Bob Dole the Republican nominee.

On Robbins's tapes, and in his seminars, he insisted that greatness was in each of us, that we were complete as we were, and that our realities were limited only by our dreams. He was dynamic and convincing, like a great evangelist, though his books and tapes weren't much different in essence from previous self-help manuals like Norman Vincent Peale's *The Power of Positive Thinking*, Napoleon Hill's *Think and Grow Rich*, and the granddaddy of them all, Dale Carnegie's *Thirteen Proven Steps to Riches*. Robbins championed a theory called neurolinguistic programming (NLP), which, in the tiniest of nutshells, claims what you do physically determines your emotional state. If you're depressed but stand up and smile and wave your arms vigorously (in the privacy of your office), you'll no longer be depressed. This actually works. You *can* program yourself physically—for about twenty seconds. It's not clear what you do after that, but as a quick fix, it works.

Robbins gave great talks, filled with energy and insight that sounded good when you first heard them. "How am I going to live today in order to create the tomorrow I'm committed to?" is one of his better-known bromides. "Using the power of decision gives you the capacity to get past any excuse to change any and every part of your life in an instant" is a little more opaque. He constantly referred to his own business success, using it as a model for us to emulate—but since his business success was in telling us about his business success, it was hard to apply it to any other walk of life except motivational speaking. I spent many freeway hours with this man's tapes in the car. I still have them. They still sound good. They perk you up. For all I know, they may have helped many people. Maybe Bill Clinton wouldn't have been re-elected had he not followed Robbins's advice. But as far as I was concerned, they had no lasting effect.

Well, they had one lasting effect. I wrote a screenplay loosely based on Tony Robbins as Molière's Tartuffe, called *Flexing the Muscle Within* (one of Robbins's bestsellers was *Awaken the Giant Within*), in which a motivational coach moves in with a depressed billionaire and strips him of everything—his money, his corporation, his home, his wife and family. The screenplay winds up with everyone walking on red-hot coals—which Robbins used to "prove" mind over matter—and Tartuffe gets his comeuppance. The billionaire (in my mind) was to be played by Danny DeVito and Tartuffe by Bill Murray, but it turned out to be too nasty or not funny enough, I forget which. But that failure got me out of L.A., so in its own counterclockwise way, Tony Robbins's motivational coaching was, for me, a success.

During so much restless downtime in L.A., I'd finished a play about race, *Stonewall Jackson's House*, which had been well received and even created something of a controversy in Manhattan back at the American Place Theatre, where my first plays had been produced. It was anarchic, and the ultimate anarchist, Wynn Handman, disagreed with every political position in the play but was a true liberal and put it on because of that. The play had a circuitous and frustrating history. On one of my many trips to Bullhead, I stopped in at the house in Lexington, Virginia, where Stonewall Jackson lived prior to the Civil War. The tour was a little cheesy, with hardly any artifacts actually belonging to the Jacksons, and the guide, a sixteen- or seventeen-year-old African-American girl, was ill-informed about her subject. In fact, a distinctly countrified couple on the tour knew considerably more about the general than the docent did and grew increasingly irritated at her lack of knowledge. The docent, in turn, became defensive.

When I got to Bullhead and recounted the incident humorously over dinner, my brother-in-law Donny said, "Sounds like a play to me." I couldn't see how, and forgot about it.

But the scene stayed with me and got funnier as I thought about it. Had there ever been a play about a house tour—particularly a second-rate house? What if the blue-collar couple actually became furious at her, perhaps having traveled miles to see the tour of their hero's home, and threatened violence against the docent. What if the girl didn't want to be in that house—after all, Stonewall was a slaveowner—and in addition was completely flummoxed by her whole life? What if another couple on the tour—making a total of five characters—felt kindly toward her and came to her defense? I didn't know where this would go but started writing it. As I tightened the screws on both the docent and the redneck couple, I conjured the girl as miserable, not only for being a guide but for being alive. Then the incendiary part came from out of nowhere: What if she were so miserable and so confused that she craved for someone to take over her life and tell her what to do? What if she begged the benevolent couple (from Granville, Ohio) to take her away from all this and let her become their slave?

I wrote the play in three weeks, and decided to chance a reading of it at the Actors Studio, where Elia Kazan, Arthur Penn, and Joe Mankiewicz had revved up a Playwrights and Directors Unit—possibly the most star-studded ever assembled. Its members included Norman Mailer, Harold Brodkey, A. R. Gurney, Eric Bentley, William Goldman, Don DeLillo, George Roy Hill, Romulus Linney, Sydney Kingsley, several recognizable visitors, and about forty others, all with opinions. The Studio was famous for its contentiousness, which was what I needed.

After a few minutes of laughs at the situation, the illustrious audience grew quietly outraged. Forty-five minutes later, the docent named LaWanda, says to Barney, the male half of the kindly white couple from Granville

LAWANDA

Do you have any openings on your farm?

BARNEY

Well, we do have openings from time to time . . .

LAWANDA

Could I fill one . . . ? I want to be your slave. I'm not talking about employment, I'm talking about slavery—uncruel but abject. You can't beat me or be mean to me, but . . . I want to be your property . . . I'll work hard for you, hard as you want. And in return you handle my money, decide what I want to do in life, do my concentrating fuh me, get me to a doctor when I needs it. Figure out which sexuality I like, pick out my clothes and friends, and bury me when it's over. I don't want to figger out taxes or parking tickets, hafta choose a HMO, keep track of my frequent-flyer miles, go to school, hunt down no jobs, or decide if Jesse Jackson's right or not. And mainly what I don't want most is to make any more decisions after this one! You own me—the lock, the stock, and the barrel.

After a few more exchanges, the couple from Ohio agrees, and the play ends.

I might as well have gone directly to B'nai B'rith and sung "Springtime for Hitler." This was a house built on social realism, if not naturalism, and the posing of tough questions about civil rights with fanciful irreverence didn't sit comfortably. Complete silence. Then all hell broke loose.

The custom at the P.D. Unit was for the author to face the audience, somewhat protected by a moderator, and have verbal fruit and veg thrown at him. Unbelievably, my moderator was Kazan.

"If you put this play on, you'll be lynched," Norman Mailer said, somewhat admiringly.

A black woman named Bonnie Greer was furious and incredulous. "This is unbelievable! Insulting!"

"What I'd like to know is, why isn't it funny?" said Eric Bentley, caustically.

Nearly everyone in the audience had an angry opinion, and all but two were at least negative and sometimes outraged. Everyone read his and her own personal experience into the play whether it had to do with race, class, or their own parental and societal disappointments, and boy were they pissed. Kazan did an admirable job of defending my "bravery," and Romulus Linney and the director Mel Bernhardt said they thought the idea was important and should be encouraged. But everyone else lambasted it for more than an hour.

After about forty minutes, I realized that I had my second act: this boiling discussion. The play brought out so many divergent feelings about victimization and seemed to have struck nerves all over the room.

I've always enjoyed controversy in the theatre, the more incendiary the better, whether I agree with it or not. Maybe because of my involvement as a student and actor with Bernard Shaw and admiration for iconoclasts like Molière and John Osborne, the gunfights between articulate ideas—providing they're dramatically presented—rivet me to a stage more than "relationship" plays (Chekhov and Shakespeare notwithstanding). Larry Kramer's *Normal Heart*, Mamet's *Oleanna*, James Lapine's *Fran's Bed* are recent examples. I admired Kazan not only for his direction of so many wonderful plays and movies—most famously, *Streetcar*, *Death of a Salesman*, *Dark at the Top of the Stairs*, *On the Waterfront*—but for taking a stand against the Communists in show business at a time when it made him a pariah. He thought them intrusive bullies in the theatre and movie worlds who frequently insisted on changing scripts to fit the party line. It's one thing to give up your career for something you believe in, but ridiculous to give it up for something you're opposed to. As dangerous and buffoonish as the House on Un-American Activities was, and he hated it, he also hated the very notion of collectivism. Had he named the names of Nazis, he would have been treated like a hero, but because the Communist party in America was something of a joke (though not in the rest of the world) he would forever after be vilified for trying to save his own skin by "ratting" on fellow showbiz folk. Far from apologizing, he took out ads after his testimony saying, basically, he'd do it again.

The next twelve years weren't kind to *Stonewall Jackson's House*. I changed the first act into a play within a play—a play that was being given a workshop per-formance by an off-Broadway theatre company to see if it warranted a full pro-duction—and the second act into scenes inspired by what had transpired at the Actors Studio session. Because of the success of *Geniuses*, most theatres around the country were eager to read this new play—but not one was willing to risk doing it. The Manhattan Theatre Club—which always says it wants to do my next play after having turned down the one before—was horrified; the Goodman Theatre in Chicago was simply afraid of the audience reaction (and subsequently did a very lukewarm version of the subject matter, *Spinning Into Butter*); George Wolfe at the Public angrily said no, even though an associate told him it was exactly the kind of play he should be doing. A theatre in Detroit said yes, then changed its mind when it learned the author was white. It was turned down by every single theatre in the country for twelve years.

I assumed it would never be produced. Then one day in 1997 I happened to send it to Wynn Handman at the American Place. I hadn't sent it to Wynn earlier because he was a well-known Liberal (his wife, Bobbi, runs the New York office of People for the American Way) and I assumed he would find it anathema.

Wynn was due for cataract surgery. He was given a drug and told not to make any important decisions for twenty-four hours after the procedure. For-tunately, he read *Stonewall Jackson's House* immediately following the surgery—within those twenty-four hours!—and phoned to say he wanted to do it. I couldn't believe it.

We had trouble finding a director; we had trouble finding an actress to play the docent—several African-American women turned it down flat. But we found the right director, Jamie Richards, who had a nice sense of the ridiculous and the sledgehammer the play required, and a wonderful actress who tore into the play shamelessly, Lisa Louise Langord. The play ran six or seven months and has been done all over the country—except in the highly p.c. L.A. and D.C.—the two cities that need it most, and where it would probably cause the most trouble. There are rules in the theatre, of course, but they're more flexible. You have to entertain the audience in some manner—but the manners are more varied than they are in the movies. And I'd finished another play, about a struggling television comedy writer at the end of his life, called *Vitreous Floaters*.

A playwright, to paraphrase Robert Anderson, can make a killing in the theatre but he can't make a living. But he is in charge of his own work. Thanks to the Dramatists Guild, he owns the copyright, not a studio or a producer, and no one can change a word or hire an actor or a lighting designer without his permission. I thought that as long as I was going to fail at making a living, I should at least fail at something that was 100% mine.

By this time, Frank was graduating from St. Andrew's and on his way to Dartmouth. Eddie was about to follow at St. Andrew's. Charlotte and I had moved to Los Angeles when Frank was eleven and Eddie eight. Frank went to Curtis, a private school, and Eddie first to Franklin, a Santa Monica public school, then Curtis and Harvard-Westlake, private ones, when Franklin turned out to be unable to keep up with him. Frank developed into a good student and a terrific athlete, Eddie into a good athlete and a terrific student. Both had scads of friends, and the only difference was that Frank and his friends tortured Eddie and his.

When Frank was ready for high school in the ninth grade, I worried at his tendency to follow a crowd endemic to all big cities but particularly pronounced in L.A.—the one with too much dough, too many cars, and way too much license. Millions of children grow into prosperous and productive adults in L.A., and I don't want to libel the entire city, but I never took to living there and both Charlotte and I preferred the educations found in the East.

You'd think I would have been prepared for any sort of wildass adolescence, considering my own, but I felt out of my shallow in curbing the suburban temptations of L.A., and Charlotte and I investigated boarding schools.

We settled on what turned out to be the single best school, boarding or day, that I'd ever experienced, and in case it's not clear, I was something of a jaded expert on the subject.

St. Andrew's, a small school of 250 students in Middletown, Delaware, was founded and thoroughly endowed by the DuPont family in the twenties and looked so much the way a prep school should that it was used as the location for the movie *Dead Poets Society*. Most of the teachers live on the campus and not only teach classes but also coach athletic teams and participate in the extracurricular activities that abound. So close do students and teachers become that it really is like one extra-large family, and in an era in which schools and colleges are scrambling away from the concept of *in loco parentis* for fear of lawsuits, St. Andrew's embraces the idea with a passion. Hardly anyone was a disciplinary problem during our eight-year involvement. There were few expulsions, fewer drug problems, and the faculty generally spoiled parents for any other academic experience by being in constant communication about their child's progress.

I took Frank to visit several schools and never urged any on him, nor even the idea of a boarding school. But when he set foot on the very first campus we visited—Woodberry Forest in Virginia—he said, "I want to go here." He then proceeded to say the same thing at every subsequent school we visited. Not only were most of the campuses beautiful, but the ease and freedom of being able to roll out of bed and onto the football field or into the comparative-religion class, without the endless driving L.A. required, made him feel less powerless. The kids looked happy and talked smart. I found Choate insufferably PC and the student body too unattended to at too early an age, but the others we visited were all contenders and all accepted Frank, who is a garrulous good interview. The choice boiled down to Middlesex in Massachusetts, Taft in Connecticut, and St. Andrew's. Charlotte and I favored St. Andrew's and at the moment of decision tried to nudge Frank in that direction, but it didn't take much nudging, and we wouldn't have minded had he chosen any of them.

But we loved St. Andrew's. At the school, he found focus, did well in classes, quickly and enduringly became part of the community, and wound up at graduation winning the prize as the best four-year athlete in the school, resulting in one very teary-eyed father. He played football in the fall and basketball in the winter and rowed crew in the spring.

The night before his SATs, during the final football game of the season and of his career, he was knocked unconscious, his only serious injury in four years. It threatened to be a concussion, so he was awakened every two or three hours during the night by the school nurse to make sure it wasn't. Despite this setback, or possibly because of it, he did well enough on the SATs the following morning to get into Dartmouth, from which he was graduated in '02, having rowed first boat for three years and majored in political science. His room was a major mess for eight solid years. He is currently fighting the investment-banking wars in New York, and I haven't checked his room recently, partly from fear and partly because I haven't been asked to.

Frank being three thousand miles away at boarding school freed Eddie from the tyranny of his older brother, and he started to find out who he was. He became an excellent and confident student, wrote beautifully, read all the time, did a few stints as a stand-up comic at school, and studiously played the piano. I'd always regretted not being forced to play an instrument because I never had the discipline to practice on my own, and Charlotte and I agreed both boys should take lessons and practice until the age of fourteen, at which time they could choose for themselves whether to continue. (Frank quit at fourteen; Eddie more or less stopped at eighteen. But at least it's in their background.) Frank was an outgoing, potentially hell-raising kid; Eddie was full of beans, too, but enormously affectionate, hugging and kissing his parents well after Frank had gone "Yewww" at the idea.

Eddie also loved nature and exploring it. He climbed trees in our Santa Monica backyard and in the Sparta forests, loved overnights outdoors, and repeatedly requested to go to wilderness camp in the summer. I tried desperately not to think of him rappelling, but he always came back alive.

Four years after Frank entered St. Andrew's, Eddie thought he, too, might want to go to boarding school, but not necessarily St. Andrew's, which he had visited with us several times. He was an attractive candidate for just about any school, and he and I toured Deerfield, Andover, Groton, Taft, and a few others. As with Frank, the trips were joyful times, as we compared notes on the schools, discussed the future, and wrestled over the amount of time he could listen to the Beastie Boys on the car radio in exchange for an hour of *All Things Considered*. I'd recommend a school-visiting trip to all parents even if their son or daughter is going to stay home. Eddie boiled his choices down to St. Andrew's and Taft.

But something happened shortly before our second trip to Taft that may have figured in Eddie's decision to go away to school: I announced to the boys that I was leaving our marriage.

I had pretty much concluded this eighteen months earlier and told Charlotte. She didn't believe I was serious—hard to blame her, since I have a history of being emphatic one moment and doing an emphatic 180 the next. But I knew there was no changing this. Although she was always a lively and provocative conversationalist and good company, we had grown increasingly separate. I realized that, aside from our children, our goals were different. I remained insanely and unrealistically ambitious about my career, and she was indifferent about both hers and mine. There were money "issues," as they're now euphemistically referred to, and in truth, there had been compatibility "issues" ever since the tortured dramas involving the townhouse in New York, which I now oversaw and leased by myself. Charlotte assumed this was another impulsive announcement on my part and urged marriage counseling, which I undertook more out of curiosity than optimism. I held out little hope for success but thought it was the least I could do after nearly twenty years of marriage. We saw a few people, all enlightening but unsuccessful.

Divorce had hovered around our marriage for years, but as the product of one, my greatest concern was the effect it would have on the boys, and so I put it out of my mind until I thought them an age at which it would be less devastating. Because I grew up with only one parent, I thought that was the worst situation, and that with each increasing year of age, the damage to the children would diminish. But Rafe's parents divorced when they were in their sixties and he was in his thirties, and he said the experience was extremely traumatic even at that age. So years may make some difference but don't remove all pain by a long chalk. I also didn't want the boys to feel this a shattering moment that would forever change their lives. I'd heard many tales of fathers announcing separations, then leaving immediately for a hotel room or, in my case, New York. With Charlotte's agreement, I waited for a vacation period when Frank would be home from school so that we could tell them and I would then stay in the house for the rest of the vacation to talk about it. This, I thought, would show them that life could go on and they would see I was still very much part of their lives, that none of this was their fault, and that their day-to-day existence wouldn't change all that much.

But Frank's spring vacations were regularly filled with crew events, and Christmas was a poor choice. Finally, he came home in the spring of '98. Charlotte continued not to believe this was happening and left the house on the night I'd decided to tell them, as though not participating in the discussion would mean it *wasn't* really happening. But unlike marriage, divorce takes only one to tango.

After dinner, she left, and I told them.

Of course these moments can be planned meticulously and then turn out haywire, like a military campaign. Frank immediately began crying and desperately tried to fix things, as he was able to with many situations at school. Eddie went limp and shut down quietly. The three of us talked and talked for two hours. Finally, when most of the factual questions had been answered and initial angles explored, I suggested they might want to talk with each other, without me, and left. When I returned an hour later, they were watching television and had accepted the facts, if not the impact, of this revolutionary turn of events in their lives. We watched TV together for a while.

At one point, Eddie said, "Well, I'm definitely going away to school next year." The prospect of living at home shattered by divorce was unbearable.

When Charlotte finally returned, she asked the boys if they had any questions.

"No," said Frank.

"Not really," said Eddie. But of course they did, and they asked them and experienced the shifting of plates beneath their feet for many years, perhaps the rest of their lives. I stayed through the spring, attempting to show Eddie how unchanged his life would be. Charlotte and I took Eddie on one more visit to Taft and St. Andrew's, and to our surprise he chose St. Andrew's.

That summer, one week shy of our twentieth anniversary, I moved back to New York, and Charlotte stayed west. We agreed almost immediately on financial terms. But because this sort of thing is genetic (at least in my blood-line), the divorce became acrimonious, and, despite our agreeing on terms, took six years. The only winners, as usual, were the lawyers, vampire teeth exposed from the first phone call. I abhor class-action suits, but if anyone ever wants to file one against divorce lawyers (or "matrimonial attorneys," as they hilariously call themselves), I've got three names. And two of them were, at least technically, on my side.

After I left for New York, whenever I saw the boys, which was as frequently as possible, I would ask them how they felt or if they had any questions about the situation. "Fine" and "No" were the general responses. I wasn't sure how deeply the knife had cut or the situation had been examined. I suspect after the initial announcement they probably concluded it made sense and weren't all that surprised. As my friend Bridget Potter said, "Children hear the grass grow."

Then, three years later, when I was taking Eddie to see colleges in the Northeast, Frank urged us to visit Dartmouth. As their final exam, he and the other students in his drama class were presenting scenes they'd written, and Frank wanted us to see his. Eddie and I drove from Cambridge, Massachusetts, to Hanover, New Hampshire, in a blinding snowstorm, unable to go much faster than thirty miles an hour, but I sensed the importance of Frank's request and risked ramming into several trees to get there. We pulled up outside his classroom—the Dartmouth theatre—two minutes before the class was to begin, and we raced inside.

We sat down just in time to see the very scene of the divorce announcement I've just described. Frank played me, and two other students played him and his brother. Though on that night I was dry-eyed, Frank, to his own surprise, was unable to keep from choking with sobs while he played me. But he finished the scene, and the rest of the students put their scenes on, in which Frank was frequently a character. I was incredulous: saddened by it and guilty at the harm I'd done. But at the same time I felt relieved that he had indeed understood what the separation meant, acknowledged it, and wanted to show his brother and me the effect it had had on him. Eddie was upset by the scene, and by seeing his brother fight back tears, but other than a serious look on his face, revealed little more. When the class was over, the brothers assumed their traditional roles of bantering combatants. The scene had been as shattering to me as the deaths of Uncle Bus and Lee.

Eddie's career at St. Andrew's was stellar. After five minutes, he was no longer "Frank's brother" but his own boy, and a superior student. He was captain of his cross-country team and an eager swimmer and rower. Throughout his four years, he was the top student in his class, but breathing down his neck was his first cousin—Charlotte's sister Elizabeth's son, Ted Unger—and, in something of a cliff-hanger, at the graduation ceremony, paralleling Frank's achievement in the athletic world, Eddie was awarded best four-year academic student and more tears from Dad. He won early admission at Princeton, where, as of this writing, he is a senior. He remains very close to his mother and, from what I can tell, anxious about her.

Although it didn't concern me much whether the boys went to prestigious colleges, it meant everything to Charlotte, whose entire family is one long Ivy League pedigree. By those standards, the boys met their mother's greatest hopes; whatever expectations their father had for them at conception, they continue to exceed them wildly.

I'VE MISSED FAMILY celebrations and the house on the parkway, but I've just about never regretted the divorce and absolutely never regretted leaving L.A. One positive result is that I don't have to read the *Los Angeles Times* ever again, although I still occasionally look at the food section on the website.

New York seemed new and surprisingly clean. Despite the knee-jerk opposition to Rudolph Giuliani spearheaded by the former and future demagogue now reduced by failure to witty troublemaker Al Sharpton, there was little doubt in my mind that the mayor had changed the town and helped it thrive. Armed with a copy of my play *Vitreous Floaters*, and a few ideas for musicals, I started out like a kid.

After a few months, I heard from my old friend and critical overseer Frank Rich, at the time an op-ed columnist for the (real) *Times*.

"The Sunday magazine is looking for someone to go in a different direction with their food section. I suggested you," Frank said on the phone. He remembered all the restaurants we'd been to and the dinners I'd thrown.

"Thank you, Frank, but I don't really write prose."

"Why don't you write just one column? Then you can both decide."

"No, I don't know anything about this."

"Just write one."

I did, and it was published in March 2000 under the title "Alice Waters Cooks Her Turkey Too Long." The editors liked it and wanted one more. After the second, they asked me to write regularly.

I COULD EXPRESS myself comfortably in letters to friends and family, but when I first started writing for the *Times*, the prose style worried me—it exercises a different lobe from the one used to write dialogue for plays and screenplays. When I told Amy Spindler, the sparkling editor of the back of the *Times* magazine, and her assistant, Andy Port, that I hadn't written this way before, they were both encouraging and said they were sure I could. Okay, but how?

I felt about most food writing at the time the same way I did about most wine writing—it was self-important and pompous and deadly, deadly earnest, as though each new innovation—like a foam—or sauce for a snapper were an earth-shaking profundity. I almost never finished reading a food article: grab the initial point in the first graf or two, then cut to the recipe, which would explain it all. The Wednesday section of *The New York Times* was guilty of this, as were most food sections of most newspapers. The *Winston-Salem Journal* was folksier, and the *Los Angeles Times*, unlike its editorial page, was less inflated, but they were exceptions. Calvin Trillin was a decided exception (I hadn't yet discovered Liebling)—he didn't take the cult of food seriously, but seemed to find it amusing, which I thought the right perspective. And when I read Nora Ephron's piece on foodies in her collection *Wallflower at the Orgy*, which actually made fun of deadly serious food professionals, I realized the subject wasn't and shouldn't be sacrosanct. This hasn't made me many friends in the foodistic world, but the approach was encouraged by Amy and Andy and, by implication, the magazine's editor, Adam Moss. After a few weeks, I took a chance and wrote about Uncle Bus and food and, when further encouraged by A. and A., decided to write about food very personally.

After I'd written about four pieces, something clicked. Maybe this was

home. Sure felt like it. They asked me to write the column weekly, but I
wanted to write another play, so we settled on biweekly. The money at the
Times was pathetic compared to movie dough. But they said no to only one
piece in four and a half years.

I bought back the remaining two months of the lease from my Jane Street
tenant and moved back into the house, complete with that ten-burner Garland range, which now had a professional reason for being, and was ready for
a second adolescence, this time, I hoped, more swinging than the first.

I dove back into New York with glee, expecting success on every front, as I
always did when changing cities. I imagined, in no specific terms, a harem, extraordinary financial success, reverence as a playwright, regular quotations on
Page Six as if I were George S. Kaufman, GBS, or Noël Coward. Young—well,
not yet old—playwright spurns Hollywood, returns to a grateful Broadway,
throws dinner parties attended by mayors and heiresses, sleeps in a tux! As
with Lee's analysis of mates, the bad aspects of the city were all out of focus
and in the b.g. Only the good ones were sharp and in ECU.

Summers in the East are hot and muggy, and there's catastrophic proto-
plasm in the air that clogs my sinuses and causes my eyes to itch for about a
month. But the first summer back I didn't even notice. As hot-button as the
Jane Street house had been during the marriage, the idea of living alone in a
twenty-four-foot wide New York brownstone had thrilled me for the last year.
I couldn't wait to cook for a dozen once a week, squire ladies to the rooftop
overlooking the Village, and, if I could get them to lean over just right, point
out the Hudson River.

Dad hadn't wanted to discourage any of his children from working, so he
left each of us just enough money to avoid starvation—to keep us from initiating a suit against his will. (Remember that: If you want to cut important relatives out of your estate, leave them *something*.)

As well as re-establishing contact with Frank Rich, I also got back in touch
with Rafe, the painter Gary Stephan, André Bishop, and Wendy Wasserstein,
and before long Oliver Clark sold his L.A. houses and moved back. Everybody
was in New York! I had even seen my old flame Bridget. She had jumped into
HBO at its inception and become an important exec. Her marriage was over,
and she was angry at her husband, who had walked out and then asked to

come back. "I miss the family," she said he'd told her, and she'd replied, "That's not good enough." She wanted him to miss *her*, and to her credit said no. In a strange star-crossing of gods and time planes, she dated Rafe's half-brother, Lewis, for several months. *Fearless*—novel and movie—had become a *succès d'estime*, and Rafe's career in Hollywood had been launched in the early nineties.

By the time I moved back, Bridget and Lewis had split up. When I told her of my plans, she said, "You're my hero."

"Why?" I said. I was feeling positive but hardly heroic.

"Because you're changing your life the way you want to." So she did, too. Bridget had never been to college, but because she was English everyone assumed she had at least a Ph.D. She always felt her collegelessness a shortcoming, and in 2002 she enrolled as a freshman at Columbia University.

Pete Gurney (the playwright, A.R.) had warned me not to come back into town expecting a play of mine to be produced just because I'd written it, but of course I'd done just that and immediately gave *Vitreous Floaters* to André, who was now running Lincoln Center Theater. I planned to write plays, then musicals, then more plays and more musicals, and, taking a leaf from Michael Caine's book, wanted to alternate supremely successful boulevard comedies with infuriating experimentation like *Stonewall Jackson's House*.

The amount of theatre available in Los Angeles had been a constant surprise. *L.A. Weekly*, the spiritual cousin of *The Village Voice*, listed forty or fifty plays in production at any given time, and the *Los Angeles Times* tried to ape the real *Times* by hiring a West Coast Frank Rich or Walter Kerr for the prestigious productions at the Mark Taper Forum or the Ahmanson, but failed. A good critic is essential to a lively theatrical environment, but the paper never managed to find one who could write. More important, the theatre didn't really matter to the general audience in Los Angeles, only to those already in show business who invariably used it as a stepping-stone to television or the movies. The Baums and I saw three or four plays by a favorite author, Justin Tanner, and at one of them were the only people in the audience. Although Marlon Brando and Aaron Sorkin never returned to it after their successes, and Gene Hackman seldom did, the theatre in New York genuinely seemed to be an end in itself, and the playwright's participation vital. There are currently four

ways to make a name for yourself as a writer: write famous novels, write famous plays, marry Marilyn Monroe, or shoot someone. Recently, the myth
that directors of television shows are as responsible for their success as their
movie counterparts are because, after all, they have the final credit, has been
debunked, and writers have actually been given predominant credit for TV,
but quick—name a TV writer! Quick—name a screenwriter other than
William Goldman! (Ummm, there's that guy who wrote *Sideways*. Actually,
two guys.) So, naturally, I assumed my re-entry into the New York theatre
would finally pay off what had appeared to be good potential only fifteen
years before.

Red

I'VE ALWAYS BEEN drawn to women of purpose, particularly professional purpose. Women who dab at work or don't do it at all make me nervous—I sense a neediness in them that resembles my mother's. She didn't work, or didn't work much—a receptionist at *McCall's* magazine for a few years, a part-time salesgirl in a tiny shop around the corner for a few years; that was it as far as I knew—and I worry I have inherited her free-floating-aimlessness gene, against which I do battle on an almost daily basis. My tendrils sense passivity at a hundred yards, and my stomach tenses.

I've always been drawn to WASPs, too. They're my favorite minority, not just because I am one, or at least aspire to being one, but because I find the duplicity of the well-behaved, well-spoken woman camouflaging underground caverns of passion and juiciness tantalizing. After experiencing a fairly raucous sixties and seventies, during which I tried to draw women of every shape, age, class, ethnicity, hair color, eye color, and number of fingers into my tent, I came to the Hitchcockian conclusion that WASPs may be cool and serene on the outside, but if you're fortunate enough to unlock the medieval stone gates someone's built to protect them, you'll frequently find them molten with yearning and occasionally nymphomaniacal on the in-. Not just sexually: The desire for experience and the delicious revelations they discover about themselves and the world after years of being told, "Don't!" can be explosive. Of course this is anecdotal, but in my experience, women who parade sexuality and candor generally are less sexual and less candid than those who conceal them, not unlike the peace-and-lovers of the sixties and seventies who were

usually filled with more violence and hatred than the button-downs they re-
belled against.

The first time I saw Heidi Ettinger (then Landesman) was in 1988; she was
walking the set she'd designed for a terrible revue produced at the Manhattan
Theatre Club called *Urban Blight*, to which I had contributed a sketch that was
eventually yanked. She had recently won Tony awards for designing the set
and co-producing the musical *Big River* with her husband, Rocco. If, on the
most superficial level, women with yellow hair seem compliant and brunettes
seem assertive, women with red hair seem defiant. "I am so not like the others, they need an additional *gender* to define me," they might as well be saying.
From the moment I saw her on that stage, commanding stagehands with
pleasant but decisive authority, I thought her red hair, aristocratic face, and
slender body hinted at an undercurrent of unbridled and possibly untapped
sexuality. When I discovered who she was, I thought she must be the feminist's wet dream of Wonder Woman: at the top of her career, the only woman
in a field dominated by men, happily married to a successful producer, three
no doubt ravishing children, and gorgeous. Oh, and unattainable.

I didn't speak to her and didn't see her again for more than a decade, but occasionally I'd flash on that image of confidence and accomplishment under
which bubbled a juiciness someone, presumably her husband, was bathing in.
I'd think how lucky she must be, particularly compared to the floundering
chaos I found myself in.

It turned out that my grass-is-greenerism was just that. When I saw her
next, at a dinner hosted by Wendy Wasserstein, who had named her Pulitzer
Prize–winning play, *The Heidi Chronicles*, after her, she was divorced, and unhappy, and her children were out of control. I was separated and happy but
looking to be happier. We hit it off immediately. For a reason I don't remember,
I revealed at the dinner table the circumstances of my NIBbing from Malcolm
Gordon—the first time I'd ever had the boldness to say anything about that
letter-writing obsession outside of a therapist's office. I was in my mid-fifties
and still embarrassed by the experience, but in front of relative strangers, in
front of Heidi Ettinger, the story rolled out of me before I could stop it.

I wish I could tell you what we had for dinner, but all I can remember
about the evening was Heidi's sympathetic face turning toward me in what

seemed like slow motion. I saw possibility in her eyes. Interest. Apparently, the story hit a nerve.

I deliberately waited a week before phoning so as not to appear overanxious, and we agreed to meet to see a movie and then skipped it in favor of a very bright Chinese restaurant on Second Avenue and Thirteenth Street for dinner. I tried my best to be glib, and she looked at me with great understanding, appreciating the effort. We walked to her house, which happened to be only seven minutes from mine. I had no idea how I was doing—she seemed tolerant and interested, but I didn't sense encouragement. We talked for an hour. When I stood up to leave, I put my hand on her cheek, she came to me, almost gliding, and we kissed. When Heidi kisses, she kisses fully, not aggressively, but giving her lips and mouth over to you, then her body. We kissed for four hours, and I left.

It was like being a teenager again. We were ravenous for each other—Romeo and Juliet if only the monks had got the message right (or Friar Laurence hadn't interfered in the first place) every night.

I'd arrived back in New York determined to lead the rock-star single life (middle-aged version) that most married men envy, and before I could even *buy* a little black book, I was cut off at the knees by "Red" (the name felt more natural than "Heidi"). I'd always been afraid of telling any woman I loved her because I think the word *love* is so weighted. Though some people throw it around like rice in a paella, to me it's always been so loaded that I reserve it for immediate family and maybe one other person, period. So it took six weeks for me to tell Red I loved her. Her response was, more or less, "Duh." She knew I loved her well before I knew.

The sexuality of the relationship only seemed to heighten, which was impossible—ask any physicist. We went everywhere together, ate everything, lapped up New York, rented a summer home, and managed our children. I cooked for her two or three nights a week, which she liked—usually fairly simple things, like chicken stuffed with tarragon and butter, and spinach with garlic, and tried to hide a chopped-up vegetable in potatoes mashed with potato water and butter so her children would have at least one vitamin to combat the tsunamis of soda. But when I could get her alone, I'd ply her with her favorite desserts, zabaglione and Meyer-lemon ice cream.

She encouraged me to write a treatment for a musical based on the year 1968, which was right up my alley, and I did. In it, a college girl joins what amounts to the McCarthy campaign, and winds up in Los Angeles for the Robert Kennedy assassination—but in my version, Kennedy lives. When we passed around the first-act treatment, there was much interest, particularly in seeing how the second act would turn out. However, my politics ran away with the second, and the result was an America turned fascist—not exactly what the producers (or indeed, much of the audience) was dying to see musicalized. Still, it was a heady exercise.

Obstacles cropped up. Charlotte, basically agreeing to the terms of the divorce, wouldn't sign anything that would advance it. A year dragged by, then another and another. My divorce lawyer said it was a first for him—usually the injured party was screaming for the money and the settlement and the more loaded spouse was fighting tooth and nail to protect his/her resources. But here, I was trying to force money on her, and she wouldn't take it. He brought the case up in front of his law class, which was just as dumbfounded as he was. A new law was passed in California regarding prenups, which we had, so I attempted to move the case there, where she still lived, just to get it moving. But the California lawyer I took on made misjudgment after misjudgment—except when sending his bills, which were quite meticulous. Another year went by.

In the meantime, I was writing my *New York Times* food column. Red and I ate and traveled to the South and the West and, memorably, to Paris and London whenever she could take time away from her three children, who were living with her and undergoing sometimes painful adolescences. Frank had graduated from Dartmouth and moved in with me for six months while chasing down an apartment and a job. Eddie had graduated from St. Andrew's and, after a summer of rappelling and braving the wilds of another wilderness camp, moved in at Princeton.

My relationships with women have been simultaneously impulsive and cautious. I'm much more fun in pursuit than as a steady diet. But with Red it was different. It was provocative all the time. This didn't prevent me from finding other women appealing, just as she found other men appealing, though I hope not ravishing. Ideally, you don't retire from life when you get married.

Return to Henley

～～～～

I N 1997, MY SON Frank, then seventeen, was invited with his high school crew team to row in the annual regatta at Henley-on-Thames in England. The Henley Regatta is more or less the World Series of rowing, and St. Andrew's, fresh from a season it dominated in the eastern United States, manned (or boyed) an extremely strong boat. On the very first day of the regatta, the eight-man crew powered its way through nearly 2,000 of the 2,112-meter course, well ahead of its only competition, the English school Canford (all the races at Henley are two-boat races). But about ten strokes short of the finish, one of the rowers made a mistake, crippling the boat and causing it to slide impotently onto the wooden barriers bordering the race lane. Canford crept ahead and won.

Rowing is a precision sport, requiring synchronization not unlike that of a symphony orchestra, acrobats on a trapeze, or the Rockettes—one slip and the cymbal falls, the 'bat hits the circus net, the chorus line collides in disarray, which is what happened in that race. One boy "caught a crab"—dug his oar so deeply into the water that he was unable to get it out in time for the next stroke—resulting in the rest of the rowers scrambling in chaos as their oars whacked into one another.

The scene back at the rowing sheds afterward, which only twenty minutes before had been one of ecstatic optimism and jubilant testosterone, was, while perhaps lacking the dimension of full tragedy, among the saddest I've ever seen: eight young men on the verge of adulthood suddenly returned to their cribs by the crushing disappointment, some crying, all bewildered. As a show of solidarity, each had shaved his head the night before; and now here they were, childlike baldies wondering what had happened. And what had? After fourteen weeks of intense practice—the last two, for six hours a day in England—arguably the strongest team in its category was instantly out of the running (one loss and you're through at Henley). To twist the sword, the boat St. Andrew's was ten strokes away from whipping so soundly went on to the finals.

So when Frank phoned four years later and said he and Dartmouth, his college team, had been invited to the regatta, I took the news with a sense of both hope and dread.

FOR FIFTY-ONE WEEKS a year, Henley is a picturesque countryside town along the River Thames, lying roughly equidistant between the glorious city of Oxford and the tawdry city of Reading. For fifty-one weeks a year, nothing particularly newsworthy happens in this town of 11,000. Then, in early summer, Henley welcomes some 250,000 visitors over a period of five days—which would be the same as if New York suddenly played host to 200 million. Almost like Brigadoon, Henley springs to life, transforming itself into an Edwardian sporting event–cum–costume show that rivals the World Cup as a tournament and Ascot and Wimbledon as a social event.

For those with the gnawing suspicion that they were born in the wrong century—say, the twentieth or twenty-first—the regatta at Henley-on-Thames is a paradise. It is not only the dress code established by the stewards of the Royal Regatta that makes the scene look like a mass audition for *The Importance of Being Earnest*—no trousers on ladies, dresses and skirts must be at least two inches below the knee (and are generally to the ankles); gents must be blazered and necktied or cravated. It is also the *choice* of those attending the posher section of the viewing areas. Frequently, the men outdo the women: Nearly mandatory Panamas and straw-boaters festoon the pink-cheeked faces of present-day Evelyn Waughs, often competing for color with their bright rowing-club jackets piped with opposing hues. Although most of the 1-mile-550-yard strip that parallels the course is open to the public, the regatta organization owns and administers the last 500 yards or so nearest the finish, and it is here, in the Stewards' Enclosure, that the regatta looks put together by Merchant and Ivory's production designer.

This time, Red was with me. She and Frank and Eddie were on good, if somewhat formal, terms. She and I discussed her coming to Henley because Charlotte would be there, then asked Frank if he'd like it, and he said he would. She and Charlotte were cordial, and Red stayed in the background, not wanting to upstage the boys' mother before and after the races. But she reveled in the Henley experience and loved dressing up in ankle-length blue silk and a broad-brimmed straw hat.

Dartmouth's rowing season had been a disappointment in 2001, and though its hopes were high for the regatta, no one expected the team to do particularly well. The two leading contenders were Yale—to whom Dartmouth had lost twice in the regular season—and the expected winner, Princeton, which placed first in the Eastern Sprints to Dartmouth's eighth. We outsiders prayed only that Dartmouth would win once, to prove that it belonged in the regatta, and I personally hoped the St. Andrew's curse would not revisit the river. That disaster had become somewhat famous in rowing circles—the expression "They're a St. Andrew's crab away from winning" was a reminder to those who knew about it that one little misstep could turn certain triumph into sudden catastrophe. Several onlookers remarked that they had either been present at or heard about the afternoon when the "strong, tough team" of high school boys in '97 had caught a crab after leading so decisively. And so touched with superstition and foreboding was the event that Eddie, also a rower and by this time attending St. Andrew's himself, refused to videotape it because that's what he'd been doing at the Great Humiliation four years earlier.

So I watched with unalloyed joy as the Dartmouth eight creamed its first draw, the Hollandia Rowing Club from the Netherlands, by more than two lengths—a substantial win in rowing measurements, as you'll see. I hurried back to the sheds to find the team relieved but hardly callithumping. The men (no longer boys) were already preparing for the match the following day with the dreaded Yale, who had won their race handily, and the oarsmen looked even grimmer than before the race. All were purposeful, too serious for college athletes. Or were they?

The days of the fun-loving, beer-drinking three-letter jock faded into the sunset sometime in the seventies: College athletics have demanded dedication bordering on fanaticism for decades now, and not just the more glamorous ball sports, which lead to all the lucrative contracts, exorbitant fame, and illegitimate children that eat up so much newsprint and clog so many airwaves. Rowing, in fact, differs from most sports because it promises no professional future, is hardly ever televised, and, even in England, gets very little space in the press. But as with any college sport, it demands three to four hours of exhausting practice every day for at least nine months of the year (and you better not get out of shape the other three), which, if you are juggling a rigorous academic schedule, can burn out the most driven of undergrads. A college athlete's schedule pretty much precludes a social life or sufficient sleep, not to mention the more hallowed extracurriculars like yearbook-editing and meetings with the Young Cartophiles. When Frank was in grade school and showed promise as an athlete, his headmaster advised me that crew would be perfect for him. "It's hard to get hurt, and if you can stick it out, it's indication of genuine inner strength and character that colleges admire." So perhaps the Dartmouth victors *weren't* taking the Yale race too seriously.

The following day, Charlotte and I rode out in the umpire's launch, which trails the two racing boats, accompanied by two imperious men, one of whom wore a blue blazer and was certain of Yale's victory. I am sometimes—many would say "always"—obtuse and prattled on with him about the various teams and even repeated the story of the St. Andrew's curse. His chatty confidence continued until halfway through the race—about three and a half minutes—when Yale had fallen behind by half a boat length. After seven minutes, a much less imperious man in a blue blazer stepped out of the umpire's boat, a forced smile straining his face. Dartmouth had pulled off the unthinkable—beaten Yale by more than a length!

I whooped and hollered like an Arkansas hog caller and told the stranger it was a great upset, and a great day for Dartmouth, and a terrible one for Yale. I'm sure he must have thought me the perfect fool—and in this case, "perfect" is appropriate. Charlotte said after we'd hit the shore, "Do you know who that was?"

"No."

"The Yale coach," she said. My mouth dropped open in mortification . . . and then we started laughing. It made the victory positively glucoid.

Again, the sheds were a tableau of intense, almost military concentration, not rapture. If you hadn't seen the race, you would have thought they'd lost. Again, the team returned to its lodgings (all in the private homes of rowing buffs in town) to eat pasta, meditate, and watch tapes of *The Simpsons*. As well they should have. There was no possibility of beating the invincible Princeton, and on the trophy for which they were competing, called the Ladies' Challenge Plate, there is no room for the name of the second-place finisher. And Princeton had just whupped Syracuse by two full lengths. But at least Dartmouth had shown it deserved to be at Henley.

On the twenty-seventh Sunday of the year (the day the finals at Henley are always held), what *The New York Times* called "the most exciting race of the day" broke into action at a cloudy, cool 2:40 P.M. One third of the way, Princeton led by a half-length, then by a three-quarters-length, and seemed to be breaking away. Then gradually, Dartmouth gained. They were never ahead or even even with the Princeton boat as the two teams hit the halfway mark, then the mile-and-an-eighth, or a hundred yards from the end. But at the very last moment, now neck-and-neck, the upstarts from Hanover, who were supposed to have been out of the contest on the second day and possibly the first, somehow pulled across the finish line first, winning by what is called a "canvas"—about two feet. They had defeated the best team on the Atlantic Coast! It was thrilling.

The enthusiastic but normally restrained onlookers burst into whoops and applause—not because they necessarily backed one team over the other but because the race had been so brilliant and exciting. Though I had been trying to videotape the race, with so many people jumping up and no clear angle, I mostly captured feet and hats, but cheered in the best British manner with everyone else when the results were known.

Back at the sheds, havoc erupted at last. We cheered the boat as it docked, and the victors peeled out—one rower with a chronically bad back had to be lifted from the scull, another rolled over onto the dock in agony, a third leaned over to throw up into the river. What appears to the casual spectator as an elegant and graceful activity—boats gliding silently by in beautiful surroundings under Constable skies—belies the effort and strain the sport requires. But most were simply exultant—they embraced, cheered, threw themselves and one another into the Thames. After they climbed back on the docks, a new realization set in—they had actually won! Frank cried in his mother's arms, Eddie in mine—they are emotional boys, thank God, and unafraid to show it, at least to us—and even the team's customarily reserved coach, Scott Armstrong, struggled to fight back tears. Nuclear tension was lanced and relieved—and the St. Andrew's crab exorcised.

The hoopla lasted nearly an hour, as first the coxswain, a young woman, then the coach, were tossed into the drink. A small boat motored by, and a group of Brits hollered, "Three cheers for Dartmouth!" Several other crews ran by to congratulate. The Princeton team came to the docks and everyone lined up and shook hands. Except for a canvas—those two feet!—this delirium could have been happening at another dock. I am told—and the size of Frank's headache the next day substantiated it—that the neighboring pubs were visited well past their normal closing hours that night.

If you can go to Henley, do; if you can make it during the regatta, the competition and the *mise-en-scène* are well worth it. If you can stay an extra week, Henley holds an annual festival, which recently featured Kiri Te Kanawa on a floating stage and the cellist Julian Lloyd Webber, among several other performers. And Red reminded me several times of the hunk multiplicand—the sight of hundreds of young men competing in perfect physical condition wearing what amounts to spandex underwear elicits in some the sensations similar to those of young girls at rock concerts.

The ubiquitous and unofficial official drink of the regatta, Pimm's (formerly Pimm's *Cup*) is sold everywhere in town, particularly during the regatta, but I found its best incarnation on the regatta grounds because the mixer isn't too sweet. The drink is basically Pimm's liquor topped off with lemonade, slices of cucumber, lemon, and orange, and a sprig of mint. Although Pimm's used to come in several varieties—Pimm's No. 1 was gin-based, No. 2 was vodka-based, No. 4 brandy, all the way up to No. 7—now all but No. 1 have disappeared. The drink used to be flavored with the herb borwich, but simplicity of preparation now leaves that out.

The secret of a successful Pimm's, it seems to me, is in the lemonade. At the Red Lion Inn, the drink was unhappily sweet because the lemonade was sweet; inside the Stewards' Enclosure, Schweppes bitter lemon was the mixer, and it turned out better. You might experiment with various lemonades the next time you're sporting rowing cap and club blazer if you want to imagine yourself back on the Thames, but basically, the less sweet the better.

STEWARDS' ENCLOSURE PIMM'S CUP

1 sprig of mint
1 slice cucumber
1 slice orange
1 slice lemon
50 milliliters Pimm's (or Pimm's No. 1)
One 8-ounce glass of ice
One 150-milliliter bottle of Schweppes bitter lemon

1. Bruise the mint and macerate it and the cucumber, orange, and lemon in the Pimm's for 15 minutes, or up to 2 days.
2. Pour the mixture over the ice in the glass.
3. Fill with Schweppes bitter lemon.

YIELD: 1 serving

If the tournament becomes overwhelming, nearby are the towns of beautiful Oxford, the very tatty Stratford-upon-Avon, and the truly modest Ayot St. Lawrence, home of the merriest prankster of the English language, George Bernard Shaw.

Pajama Food

~~~~~~~~

Isn't it redundant to call anything you put in your mouth voluntarily "comfort food"? All food is comforting, or we'd be eating nothing but hot dogs at Shea and warm tar (indistinguishable in a *Times* blind-testing), with possibly a few vitamins thrown in. Unless you're on some kind of nasty medical diet or undergoing a fraternity initiation or briefly lapse into Joan Crawford territory with one of your sons, there is no such thing as "punitive food." And at no time in my memory did the need for palate-pleasing palliatives seem so urgent as during the aftermath of the destruction of the World Trade Center.

Red and I were in Sydney, Australia, the last two weeks of August 2001. She was producing and designing *A Little Princess*, a musical based on the Frances Hodgson Burnett story, which has been made into about 360 movies, the most famous of which starred Shirley Temple. Australian investors wanted a look, so she and the director Susan H. Schulman put together a workshop of the first act, which was quite promising. The Australian stage star Anthony Warlow wanted to play the young girl's father, which thrilled the investors.

Red and I then spent a few days in the Hunter Valley, a winemaking area two hours outside Sydney. When she went back to town, I stayed on two more days to write about it for *Travel & Leisure*. We returned to New York the first week in September, and Red moved into my house with her youngest son, Dodge, then ten, because contractors were renovating hers. On September 4, her son Nash, fourteen, arrived from a trip abroad late at night and didn't have a key. He rang my bell around midnight, and Red flew down the stairs to let him in. At the bottom of the staircase, she twisted her ankle badly and sprained it. The following day, Dodge began school across town at Gateway, located at Fourteenth Street and Second Avenue. Red and I put him on the bus and then spent hours in doctors' offices having her ankle X-rayed and being told nothing much could be done about a sprain except staying off it for a month.

A week later, September 11, 2001, Red got up at seven to put Dodge on the school bus. I was half asleep, flipping through radio stations, which I often do between five and eight in the morning. The companionship of strangers keeps my mind off me, and, depending on the program, either makes me mad, makes me laugh, or puts me back to sleep, my goal. I regularly listened to Howard Stern, who, despite his adolescent obsession with human discharge, remains the most imaginative and funniest personality currently on terrestrial or satellite radio. I don't know if he's as creative or as hilarious on satellite radio, where he is allowed to say "fuck" and "cunt" as much as he wants, the terrestrial prohibition against which led to much of his humor (not unlike movie comedies of the thirties and forties, which had to use wit to circumnavigate the ludicrous censorship of the Hays Office instead of having the freedom to say or show anything commerce would allow, as they do now). When Stern hit a dull patch, I would switch to Imus, then at his commercials, NPR, then, when they get into fund-raising pitches (more aggravating than other commercials), to Curtis and Kuby (Curtis Sliwa and Ron Kuby, Right and Left politically) and possibly to WBAI for a few additional laughs and some nostalgia for my brief flirtation with sixties radicalism.

Unlike most grown-ups (or most who will admit it), I heard about the attacks on the World Trade Center from Howard Stern. While Red was preparing to go to the dentist, Stern announced that a plane had crashed into the World Trade Center. He and I both thought it a bizarre accident but nothing more. When he announced the second tower had been hit by a second plane, I, like the rest of America, figuratively flew out of bed.

Red phoned Trevor Day, Nash's school on the Upper West Side. The school wisely assured her it would keep everyone there. She then phoned Gateway and was told to pick up Dodge immediately—the school wouldn't keep the students there, a gross error in judgment, adding to the panic and congestion of the city, especially downtown.

I had always thought I'd be an embarrassment in a crisis but was surprisingly calm, though every sense was alert to the slightest ping. Frank was safely in New Hampshire at Dartmouth and Eddie in Delaware at St. Andrew's. Increasingly agitated, Red decided she had to rescue Dodge and finished dressing. I saw there was no way she could make it to the curb with her sprained ankle, let alone all the way to Second Avenue. It was ten extra-long blocks, which would have taken twenty minutes by bus on the best of days. I told her I would collect Dodge.

I grabbed my radio and walked fast to Greenwich Street, looked downtown, and could see plumes of beige and black smoke from the financial district. There wasn't a chance it would ignite anything this far north, at least not yet, and from this distance looked benign—another New York fire. Birds continued to sing on Jane Street, oblivious of the devastation less than two miles away. Didn't affect *them*. I looked for a taxi, and of course there were none. I headed for Fourteenth Street and jumped on a bus. It inched. I flipped between Howard Stern, CBS, and WINS, the all-news station, and Stern actually did the best job of reporting the events. Completely gone was the adolescent, and in his place an adult journalist who neither exaggerated nor panicked as many of the regular reporters did. Others wondered aloud whether the date and our national emergency phone number were a coincidence or intentional and whether the meaning of choosing United and American airlines was a clever, if literary, irony. Howard stuck to the story.

After twenty minutes and still between Seventh and Eighth avenues, I realized the entire city was gridlocked and quickly jumped off and headed east on foot.

I remembered the panic that had swept the nation in the seventies, when the Symbionese Liberation Army kidnapped Patricia Hearst and threatened to attack and blow up America. No one knew how large that army was but responded for a few days as though it were the entire Soviet Union. I wondered if this would turn out to be the same ridiculously small number of zealots or if another shoe would drop at any second. I marveled at the ingenuity of using our own planes against us. In this age of electronics and intricately complex plots shown nightly on television and at the movies, here was a perfect plan anachronistically low-tech and dirt cheap.

I finally made it to Second Avenue and picked up Dodge, who understood something bad had happened but was primarily cheerful because he didn't have to go to school that day. I tried to phone Red, but cell service was still overloaded. I found a pay phone—soon approaching the antique—and got her.

"I've got Dodge. He's fine. We're headed back."

"Where are you?"

"Third and Fourteenth. We'll be there in a few minutes." She didn't sound worried any longer. We had a pleasant stroll home to Jane Street. It was a beautiful day, but each step, for me, was becoming graver and graver. I knew none of us and our country would be the same again but didn't know how. Only the day before we thought ourselves envied, but on this day it was clear we were hated, which had never occurred to us—whether by a thousand or a billion would become clear later. Our belief in our invincibility and in our specialness in the eyes of God would be no more.

We returned home, and Red was calm and happy to see her son. We went to the corner café—the Tavern on Jane—which was jammed with people, everyone sober in every sense of the word, the television excitedly repeating facts, rumors, predictions. The number of dead rose and fell. Mayor Giuliani seemed like the one man—perhaps besides Howard Stern—who not only knew the truth but was telling it. The three of us ordered cheeseburgers and silently began to miss the days, now gone forever as of three hours ago, that could have been described as deliriously, if selfishly, carefree.

When we returned home, a message from Eddie at school sounded fearful. Another from his adviser said he was distraught, assuming I'd been in or near the World Trade Center during the attack and was dead. I was so caught up in events that I thoughtlessly forgot to call him and his brother to assure them I was all right. I phoned Eddie immediately, and we laughed with some relief. I phoned Frank and was reassured to find him still the optimist—he knew damn well I wasn't in any danger. In this case, Eddie got my gene and Frank his mother's.

It's NOT EXACTLY that we were eating abrasive food before September 11. Far from it. Diners scaled the zenith of decadence nightly, often at home and certainly in restaurants around town, where meals for $100 a person were almost considered thrifty. It was precisely that merry extravagance that felt not only unwelcome in the days immediately following the attacks, but also like something we didn't deserve.

It seemed no one would ever, ever go out again, and until our predicament could at last be joked about weeks later, pajamas were the perfect garments for those uncertain times—at once commodious and self-expressive, sloppy, and potentially elegant, perhaps the least self-conscious clothes in all fashion for eating in in. And they already had a cuisine to match.

Pajama food doesn't require caloric conservatism. Ideally meant to be eaten with one leg draped over the arm of a chair or sofa, pajama food can also be taken lying in bed on Sunday morning with *The McLaughlin Group* or at midnight with the door to the fridge wide open and a pair of chopsticks in your hand—or at any other time. The only real requirement is that it give you pleasure. This usually means it's soft. And since you might be half asleep, it shouldn't be complicated to prepare. (Make complicated things earlier, then nuke them in your jammies.) Although the all-stars of pajama food are probably peanut butter (practically illegal for adults to eat until the eighties), ice cream, and just about any form of mashed potatoes, pj food is, of course, entirely subjective. Customarily, it's a dish you had as a child, abandoned as childish when those things began to matter, and then re-embraced when you realized that, say, macaroni and cheese wasn't something to be ashamed of.

Most often, pajama food is eaten with one hand because the other is busy holding the container, whether it's the just-delivered Sautéed Spicy Whole Green Pepper (Mao's favorite) from Grand Sichuan International or the cauliflower risotto from Lotus or the mashed potatoes made with a pound of butter, the potato-cooking liquid, a full udder of cream, and slices of sautéed cabbage that's found at my place alone. They all reheat beautifully. The rumor that pj food must be white as well as soft was debunked not only by a friend from North Carolina who claimed that any kind of sausage will make her "admit to everything," but also by none other than Alain Ducasse, whose closet snack is a hot dog with everything on it. Eric Ripert, the chef at Le Bernardin, has no guilt about his midnight food: "I get excited about eggs. I think there's something sexy about them. Maybe I should see a doctor, I don't know, but I love to see egg yolks running." The simple bistro dish eggs *en cocotte*—in which two eggs are sandwiched between 2 tablespoons of cream, crème fraîche, or any sauce, then baked in a 375-degree oven for 7–10 minutes in a boiling-water bath—allows myriad enrichments. "I really like them on top of warmed ratatouille or tomato *concassé*," he said.

For the cholesterolically untroubled, it's hard to do better than a perfectly grilled rib-eye under a pair of gorgeous and silky sunny-side-up quail eggs. A chicken's will also do.

Except for steak and eggs, anything that needs cutting with a knife doesn't really qualify because the whole thing becomes hard work. (*Eating* with a knife is fine.) Unfortunately, this rules out my own personal favorite, osso bucco, as too messy. Pajama food, I decided, should be relatively neat. And it should be easy to make, like my longtime guiltiest pleasure: a midnight bowl of Cracklin' Oat Bran and heavy cream, for which I frequently need a jailer with soft handcuffs to prevent a second helping.

It goes without saying that puddings of all kinds are perfect. Wendy Wasserstein liked Jell-O because "it's colorful, it moves, and it goes down easy."

For many years, it seemed that a new Civil War might break out over the question of grits, the ground dried corn that visually resembles cream of wheat when cooked but outperforms it gustatorially. Northerners felt they were as inedible as poi, while southerners took pride in preparing them every which way: boiled, baked, fried, souffléed, boiled *then* baked, savory with butters and cheeses and garlics, sweet with honey or maple syrup. Though a Yankee, since my first grit as a child, I've found they cool my hot head and make me want to stay put.

I've concluded the only rule for pajama food is that there are no rules—except the one mentioned above, that it should please you. And, as if you needed to be told, you don't even have to wear the threads to eat the chow.

CHEESE GRITS WITH GARLIC

6 cloves garlic, peeled
1 teaspoon salt

¼ pound butter

1 cup grits, preferably white, preferably stone-ground

2 cups really sharp, shaved Cheddar cheese

1 teaspoon Worcestershire sauce

4 eggs, separated

1. Preheat the oven to 350 degrees. Grease a 2 ½-quart baking dish.
2. Using the side of a knife, mash garlic and salt until a paste forms.
3. Melt 1 tablespoon of the butter in a skillet and stir in garlic paste. Sauté over medium heat until golden, about 2 minutes.
4. Boil 4 cups of water in a saucepan. Stir in grits. Add garlic. Cook until thick, about 6 minutes, stirring constantly.
5. Add ½ cup of the cheese, remaining butter, and Worcestershire sauce.
6. Off the heat, beat in the egg yolks. Beat the egg whites in a bowl until they are stiff and then fold them into the grits. Spread mixture into casserole, top with the remaining cheese, and bake for 30 minutes.
7. Serve in pajamas or not, as your solo dish or accompanied by just about any protein or anything remotely breakfastlike.

YIELD: 8 servings.

MIDNIGHT CRACKLIN' OAT BRAN

2 cups Cracklin' Oat Bran, dry and crisp (refold the liner bag)

1 cup heavy cream, or to taste

1 TV

1. Wait until 11:55 P.M.
2. Pour cereal into a bowl and moisten, cover, or drown with heavy cream.
3. Turn on the TV; throw the rest of the cereal box away.

YIELD: 1 serving.

Corn Pudding

½ stick butter
4 eggs
¼ cup masa harina or flour
2 cups heavy cream
One 18 ½-ounce can of creamed corn
1 teaspoon salt
1 ½ cups fresh or frozen corn
½ teaspoon cayenne

1. Preheat the oven to 375 degrees.
2. Melt the butter in a 1 ½-quart casserole.
3. Beat the eggs with a whisk till foamy.
4. Sift the flour into a large bowl and then stir in the cream until thickened. Add the beaten eggs, followed by the creamed corn, salt, fresh or frozen corn, and cayenne, stirring thoroughly after each addition.
5. Pour the mixture into the buttered casserole and stir to incorporate the butter. Bake for 10 minutes, then stir; bake another 10 minutes, stir; and another 10 minutes, stir. Finally, bake an additional 30 minutes without stirring. Serve almost immediately—when cooled just enough not to burn your tongue.

YIELD: 6 generous servings.

THERE WAS A POSITIVE result from the destruction of the World Trade Center: America was suddenly forced to recognize the rest of the world. Since the collapse of the Soviet Union and the crumbling of the Berlin Wall, we had retreated into a smug little cocoon, confident that we were the best, had the most, lived the justliest, and were far from all harm except small-town drugs, Howard Stern lesbianism, and board scores good enough for Brown but not Princeton. Other continents were for visiting on vacation and doing business with. The Hard Left continued to champion the European form of social democracy ("Christian" was excised for the folks back home), as it had the communism of an earlier era, and will probably continue to do so long after the model has failed—as it has begun to with the failure of the E.U. Constitution—just as it did with the former Soviet Union long after it was exposed as unworkable. Under the Clinton administration and the astonishing prosperity of the nineties, we inched toward the European ideal with guaranteed this and that until Newt Gingrich put a stop to it. We thought, to paraphrase the popular Las Vegas slogan, "What happens on the rest of the globe stays on the rest of the globe." We didn't need anything or anyone else. The Middle East was ignored the way finding an alternative to oil was—or used for bombing practice. While I hope I don't have to say I wish the attacks never happened and the people in the buildings never destroyed, in fact they shocked us into the state of mind much of the rest of the world had been living in for a generation: terror. When President Reagan pulled soldiers out of Lebanon, when President Clinton withdrew from Somalia and then refused to retaliate against the terrorist acts against our embassies and the S.S. *Cole*, it seemed that evil would be confined outside our borders. It was despicable, blah blah blah, but wouldn't really touch us personally or interfere with our jogging and single-minded pursuit of self-esteem unless a loved one happened to be involved in one of the events. September 11 changed all that, at least for a while. We suddenly, if briefly, discovered uncertainty and fragility—which the Europeans had been well aware of for years, if not centuries—and for about fifteen minutes finding the nearest parking spot at the mall wasn't a national priority. The day after the attacks, a Greyhound bus was hijacked, and it appeared the invaders might be everywhere and had a well-thought-out plan to cripple all our transportation systems. The peculiar and as-yet-unsolved anthrax mailings made us feel, as Don Imus is fond of saying, "that the wheels were coming off" the country.

The gloom was palpable, as though everyone were carrying an extra thirty pounds of free weights. We were all in this together, and there was the bond of a shared disaster, which led to a further bond of shared defiance. But almost immediately, we began patting ourselves on the back. While it took weeks for anyone to make a joke about the attack and the potential future attacks, the "we New Yorkers are so resilient" campaign began within two days. Yes, I thought, we're resilient—for a day. But real resilience could be found in

Palestine and Israel, both of which endured smaller versions of this assault almost daily. Come back to me after six months or a year of perpetual bombings and destruction, *then* you can say we New Yorkers are resilient—if we have been.

As THE INVASION of Iraq was ramping up, a jingoistic sense of excitement overflowed American satellite dishes and Internet sites, as did a sense of dread in Europe. For those of us who favored pre-emption over the tired (and unhelpful) yakking about the Middle East over the last several years, and were buoyed by what then appeared to be a quick and comprehensive victory in Afghanistan, there was hope an invasion would establish a second bastion of western principles. However, years of inner-child orientation palliated many into believing there was no such thing as a bad child and no such thing as evil—only misunderstood infants and equally valid differing points of view. Violence was never, ever a solution to anything, this lazy line of argument went—hadn't Phil Donahue and Oprah promised us that all disagreements could be talked through if only we poured compassion over them like syrup over morning pancakes? Weren't people the world over basically reasonable, and don't we all share pretty much the same values?

A few weeks before the invasion, a good-natured screaming match with dinner guests swung toward vituperation—I was the one in the room who thought the Middle East needed an intervention or the relentless terror there would continue for God knew how many years, and that our presence in Iraq would not only put the terrorists on the defensive instead of us, but put us right smack in the middle of everything geographically. Furthermore, politics being the art of the possible, Iraq looked easier to invade than Iran, regularly reported to be on the brink of youthful revolution, and more important than Syria.

"But, Jonathan," Pete Gurney said, "we have no business there. It's playing right into the hands of the terrorists."

"Not if we win right away. Look what happened in Afghanistan."

"The Bush people believe the Iraqis are going to welcome us with flowers!" Pete said. "That's ridiculous."

"No they don't," I said, giving the administration more credit than it turns out it deserved. "I was around for the Bay of Pigs, and so were they—they can't believe that. They have a plan."

"Which is what?" Rafe said.

"Who knows? They didn't tell me."

"That's always your problem—you never know." As mentioned, Rafe and I have a history of scratchy political discussions.

"Look, you were sympathetic to the Soviet Union, and still haven't admitted you were wrong."

"I never supported the Soviet Union," shouted Rafe.

"Then I'm wrong," I said.

"You're always wrong," he said.

"I'm never wrong," I said.

The wives and wives-to-be tsk-tsked. It's not easy being conservative in New York and it's against the law in show biz—even if you're conservative on only a few issues.

There was excitement in the American air, all right. The anticipation of instant vindication—as had been the case in Afghanistan—promised payback against the bastards who cheered on 9/11 (and for all the nightmares they had created since). It reminded me of the boys going to war at the beginning of *All Quiet on the Western Front,* filled with hope, romance, and bravery.

None of the evidence about "weapons of mass destruction" or a connection between Saddam and Osama bin Laden was convincing to me, and Colin Powell's testimony at the United Nations was pathetically transparent. I didn't think it mattered. I thought the Bush administration held a more farsighted view, but that announcing we were going to war to establish a threatening—and balancing—stance in the Middle East, which would warn against anyone doing us harm again, was too abstract to expect the American public to get behind. We needed an attack, or at least the threat of an attack. So the administration popularized one—that Iraq had weapons of mass destruction ready to be used—which it felt it could explain away after a quick and triumphant victory. And had the administration been successful *fast,* it could have. But I learned for about the thirty-eighth time that one can never overestimate the incompetence of the government, Democrat or Republican (the thirty-ninth time came when Hurricane Katrina devastated the Gulf areas of Louisiana, Alabama, and Mississippi). It never occurred to me that no one had a strategy for the post-invasion victory. Perhaps spoiled by movies and TV, in which our government was technologically superior, agile, and intelligent, I was suckered into believing the administration. But the nay-sayers had no convincing arguments.

One of the difficulties the anti-invasionists failed to surmount was its lack of countervailing ideas. I had no certainty an invasion would succeed and earnestly sought other possibilities. Everyone was articulate and vehement in their anti-war stances, but when asked before the invasion what an alternative might be, no one I knew or read or saw on television had anything to offer except "to talk" or to further involve the United Nations, which had recently nominated Libya to chair its Human Rights Commission. But talking and relying on the U.N. had helped us arrive at 9/11. Reagan's retreat in Lebanon and Clinton's generally passive strategy to deter terrorism were failures—though they continued to be the only ones offered. They're *still* the only ones offered. Three years after the invasion, I asked for an alternative to it during an argument, and all I got back was, "We should have continued to pressure them"—whatever that meant—but not to establish a forcible presence. With two symbolic acts, the retaliation against Qadafi and Libya for the Pan Am bombing and what seemed at the time to be the ridiculous invasion of Grenada, Ronald Reagan actually did more to prevent terrorism than any amount of rhetoric or diplomacy.

Michael Moore's film *Fahrenheit 9/11* also suffered from a lack of strategies. Though brilliant, if facile, at criticism and a moving antiwar film, it wasn't specifically an anti-Iraqi-war film: The bereaved American mother who had been such a loyal military supporter and then did an about-face when her son died could have been any mother in any war; the recruiting tactics lampooned could have been from any recruitment; the distraught Iraqis, moving as they were, could have been from any country; the connection between the Bush family and the Sauds wasn't convincingly proved to be evil, just conveniently political.

My support for invasion was pragmatic and hopeful, certainly naïve, based on a quick resolution, which didn't happen. With my perfect hindsight, I wouldn't have opposed the invasion, but would have embraced Colin Powell's strategy of overwhelming force. And I sure as hell oppose most of what's happened since. It wasn't long before governmental incompetence was so staggering. I soon wished the execs at Wal-Mart were running things.

In ten years, if the situation is resolved, it may appear to have been quick, after all, but right now it's beginning to look more and more like the end, not the beginning, of *All Quiet on the Western Front*, with soldiers returning home damaged and disillusioned, forever changed right along with their country.

IT TOOK WEEKS for humor about 9/11 to appear. The first instance I remember now was a sketch on *Saturday Night Live* in which actors playing the World Trade Center and Pentagon attackers had a change of heart and were in a cave begging Osama bin Laden for a slight postponement. What made it particularly funny was that it was performed in what sounded like the low-key, very reasonable English translation of the Arabic we'd grown accustomed to from the bin Laden videos.

The fear that we might be invaded by a large force vanished quickly when it became clear how cleverly and inexpensively the attacks had been accomplished, and a greater fear set in: If fewer than fifty people could pull this off, how much damage could sixty do? Or five, or ten? Despite a few crackdowns, we continued to have a liberal immigration policy and fenceless borders. Anyone with ill intent could certainly get together with a few friends and cause disasters on subways, in theatres, Grand Central Station, and ballparks. The enemy clearly had superior weaponry: It had suicide bombers, and all we had were puny old useless nukes.

As the second anniversary of 9/11 approached, The Fear subsided somewhat. The intellectual knowledge that all around us could be exploded and crushed RIGHT . . . NOW!! continued, but the airplane engine overhead or the backfiring truck down the block no longer made us sit up in bed.

Cooking for friends and my magazine column at the *Times* brought a new sense of intimacy. People became less demanding and more cheerful, except for Rafe, whose wife, Margaret, had contracted bladder cancer and was slowly dying. He was experiencing a personal tragedy within the national drama, and by and large most of us were experiencing just the national drama. Life went on or stopped, as before.

The Cafeteria Factor

THE LITTLE-KNOWN PREDICTIVE that decides every political race, high or low, has nothing to do with policies, war strategies, pro or contra stands regarding pan-gender marriages, photogenics, or economic success. Every presidential victor since Truman, save one (the exception that proves the rule)* has been blessed with it. It's a complex theory substantiated by much sociology, Sunday-morning-TV tooth-gnashing, and several doctoral theses. Narrowed to its marrow, it's known among us professional pols as the "Cafeteria Factor."

You don't have to be Kevin Phillips to appreciate that the one quality Americans admire most is the same one they resent the most: other people's wealth. Take Michael Bloomberg, both Presidents Bush, Senators Kerry and Edwards, self-appointed poobah Trump: Your average citizen (me included) dreams about, obsesses about, or at least pines for the kind of wealth any one of them has and at the same time luxuriates in their public downfall, on the assumption that they deserve it because they are wealthy. Mayor Bloomberg is, by definition, "out of touch" because he's wealthy; President H. W. was out of touch because he was so wealthy he didn't know what a grocery scanner was (despite the fact that most of us yearn to be so wealthy that we never *have* to know what a grocery scanner is); W. may be in touch, but it's the wrong kind of touch because he's wealthy, too. And the hottest places in public-resentment hell are reserved for those who've inherited their wealth, like the Bushes, the Trump, and the Kerry.

*Richard Nixon

In the 2004 presidential race, all the final candidates and incumbents were at least millionaires except Dennis Kucinich (and Al Sharpton probably would have been if only he'd pocketed some of those lavish personal-appearance fees instead of spending them on hotels and jets; still, he lived like one). Senator Kerry got something of a pass because he served so endlessly honorably in Vietnam, and for a while voters didn't seem to mind that Edwards reached that exclusive club by silver-tongued ambulance-chasing, one of whose jury summations included an imitation of a baby in its birth canal. And of course Ralph Nader, who still gives all his money away, was the only one familiar with the verb *to iron*, and looks as though he *lives* in a cafeteria, was excused. Americans suspire for money—but vote for those who don't look as though they've got any: LBJ, Nixon, Carter, Reagan, and Clinton didn't look rich. Hence, the Cafeteria Factor: Regardless of fortune, how comfortable did each candidate look sliding a brown, rectangular tray down a stainless-steel track in front of a glassed-in steam table?

Although they're an artifact of the American past—perhaps exemplified by Horn & Hardart, long out of business—cafeterias may be making something of a comeback. For an example of the original, nothing beats Smith's Bar at Forty-fourth Street and Eighth Avenue, which has been around forever and is just what a cafeteria should be—friendly and loud, linoleum floor peeling slightly, not that recently painted, glassed-in steam tables, choice of hot meats and chickens that have been cooking for three or four years, big fat meat sandwiches, a full bar a few steps away. W. would probably fit in best here, eating lamb shanks as good as any in town with his fingers, slapping the barflies on the back, and nicknaming all the bartenders. And though it's hard to picture Ralph Nader ever relaxed, at least he'd feel guiltless about the prices. The Kerry rectitude might suffer in this jovial, sloppy hangout, and it would test Senator Edwards's noted pan-classism.

Providing the comestibles are delicious, there's little that's more liberating than a cafeteria: You get to pick your own food by pointing at it, and, master and commander of your own culinary fate, bring it to a table you select, eat it on the tray or not, and never, ever have to tip.

Certainly one of the wilder lunchtime scenes takes place at Veronica, right in the middle of the button-and-bead district on West Thirty-eighth Street. It is, believe it or not, an Italian cafeteria featuring all sorts of specialties, from stuffed shells to Monkfish Francese, and attracts roughly a billion customers between eleven and two.

"I'm a newcomer," says Veronica's head chef, Andy, beaming. "I've only been here thirty-six years. And this woman here, she's my boss." He gestures to his wife, Ceil. "Veronica was my mother's name." Did Veronica start the restaurant? "No, she started his appetite!" laughs Ceil, patting Andy's stomach, evidence that he at least tastes what he cooks. "But she was a good cook, and I grew up knowing what was good food and what wasn't."

This food shouldn't be confused with Felidia's or Babbo's—it's strictly steam-table fare, each dish cooked earlier, then warmed up specially for you in a microwave, which is historically tough on pasta. And someone with glove size XXXXL administers the bread crumbs, so that finding the veg in egg-plant parmigiana is heavy going (but you can't put "Breadcrumbs Parmigiana" on the menu).

Still, it's a festive place, and by God the food is nourishing. The people on line all seem to be Italian, or at least inflect with Italian gestures, and they're half the reason to go there. To get filled up is the other half. I'd say all the candidates would have done well here except Mr. Nader. The noise might make him retreat farther into his shell.

But the junior senator from Massachusetts would have positively shone at the Condé Nast cafeteria. The striking, almost Brahmin, design by Frank Gehry—featuring smoky-blue transparent panels, curved and overlapping—defines three eating spaces, and the pickled floor and elliptical orange-topped tables comforted by puffy caramel banquettes encourage a brief rest, if not exactly an afternoon stay. I'm not suggesting W., Mr. Nader, and Senator Edwards aren't architecture buffs, but here Mr. Kerry could at last find a place where he didn't have to pretend to "get down."

Stations are arrayed at which you can order tailor-made stir-fries, burgers, and sandwiches, and two large steam tables serve domestic and "international" fare. Miracle of miracles, a burger ordered rare actually turns out that way—a feat most restaurants that *aren't* cafeterias seldom accomplish. And I would rush to the station from which came the yummy, jammy raspberry pudding and the scrumptious peach-crumb pie, both of which belong in any self-respecting crib right next to your copy of *Goodnight, Moon*.

The one drawback of the cafeteria is that you can't get into it unless you work for Condé Nast or know somebody who does. So this might be the time to wheedle friendships with Trillin, Wintour, or Steingarten, even if you're just opportunistically using them for a crack at the Black Forest cupcake.

In summary, the class-straddling Senator Edwards would probably fit most photogenically into all these places. On the other hand, one shouldn't underestimate the social dexterity of cowboy boots; W. might have won a second term simply by strolling in and rolling up a pant leg.

The Democrats wound up nominating one of the least interesting candidates, Senator Kerry, whose onscreen persona was moneyed but aloof, sometimes nasty, and though it radiated intellect, often came across as phony. Most things he said and did seemed calculated for effect, and though President Bush's were undoubtedly calculated for effect, too, they didn't seem so obvious, and consequently Kerry appeared stiff. He implied enormous intelligence but refused to release his Yale transcript, was declared a hero in Vietnam but refused to release his war records. Five months after the election was decided, he released his college records, and it turned out his grades were no better than those of the president, whom detractors regularly referred to as a moron. Senator Kerry was certainly a skilled debater, but his heroism, followed by his criticism of Vietnam in the sixties, followed by simultaneously trading on his heroism *and* that criticism for the sake of the election, made him seem either dishonest or at the very least confusing.

Meanwhile, President Bush had revealed himself to be the worst public speaker of anyone in the White House since the invention of recorded sound, and that included his father, who was also a marble-mouth public speaker, and his father's vice-president, Dan Quayle, who made "deer in the headlights" a popular descriptive, and appeared to be understudying Tommy Smothers at his dumbest (but Smothers's stupidity was an act). But because W. didn't appear to be pretending he was something he wasn't, supporters found his frequent tongue paralyses evidence of authenticity, which was as big a buzz word in political circles as it was in food circles. He was also upbeat and positive, and Senator Kerry, despite a pretense of optimism, seemed dour and eager to reimport the restrictive European social democracy that the Democrats had embraced since the sixties and had been rejected by the electorate so many times since the heady deceptions of Lyndon Johnson. It was a clash of personalities: the Brahmin Kerry versus the country-boy Bush—though both were from prestigious and wealthy families and Kerry had married way, way up. Kerry was the wealthiest man in Congress and certainly wealthier than the president. Both had gone to Yale, and it's probable that Bush won at least partially because he didn't let it rub off on him.

If it was a snap to dislike Kerry as a person, it wasn't easy to like Bush as a politician. Aside from his boldness in attempting to reshape the Middle East, he curried to the witless elements of his party. His staunchest campaign platform was to oppose all science, whether it be stem-cell research, any kind of abortion, an accurate depiction of the state of the environment, or Darwinism. He insinuated he might be a Creationist and opposed the legalization of any aspect of homosexual relationships. He allowed his FCC to censor radio and television personalities by fining the companies that employed them; he clearly had no idea what to do in Iraq after the initial military victory, and will probably continue making it up as he goes along until he's out of office.

Unfortunately, Senator Kerry had no alternative to President Bush's Iraq strategy. He backed the soldiers (Who didn't? It would be like saying, "I can't stand the environment!"); claimed, as Nixon did in 1968, to have a plan for ending the war but wouldn't let us in on it—either before or after the election. For me, the overriding issue was Iraq. I was certain the country as a whole wouldn't make abortion illegal, that some country would undertake stem-cell research, and that sooner or later, the revulsion against homosexual unions—whether called "marriage" or something else—would abate, and that Howard Stern would go on to satellite radio, where he could say whatever he wanted. So it wasn't an easy choice—until I happened to see a discussion between Christopher Hitchens and Andrew Sullivan on Tim Russert's show, which took place on MSNBC September 25, 2004, just five weeks before the election. This, for me, was decisive.

Hitchens and Sullivan framed the issue cogently: Regardless of other important domestic concerns, the war in Iraq was of primary consequence because it was bound to affect us directly sooner or later. The enemy was Islamo-fascism, or what might be called, for the sake of symmetry, the Islamic Right, and the conflict was who would control not just the Middle East, but larger and larger populations. "I think the United States needs to be defended against the forces of jihad," Hitchens said. "There is no possibility of having a moral-equivalence discussion here—I won't listen to a bar of that song." He regretted not realizing how serious and terrifying this war would be when his friend Salman Rushdie was threatened with a fatwa in 1989. "We are headed for a confrontation with Islamic totalitarianism. There's a civil war going on in the Muslim world. We must not let the tyrannical side win there."

Sullivan went further. "I don't want this to be a war between the Christian Right and the Islamic Right but between fundamentalism and liberal democracy."

They both agreed on the administration's incompetence, but the mixed messages sent by Kerry—for Vietnam, against it, for it, against it—and the blunders he made, exemplified by his saying that he voted for a bill before voting against it (what one Republican strategist joked was "the gift that kept on giving") made him seem unfirm and weaselly.

"It's a campaign of the irresolute versus the incompetent," Hitchens said. Sullivan hated that Bush wouldn't tell the truth about what was happening on the ground and was furious that such a noble enterprise was being handled so clumsily. But Hitchens had just returned from Afghanistan and found that it worked and would really work if only the United States would give up its idiotic war on drugs so the farmers might flourish. "We burn the only crop these people have and then tell them we're trying to win their hearts and minds. We should be *paying* them to grow this stuff. Painkillers have to come from opiate." He was so encouraged by Afghanistan that he hoped the same, eventually, for Iraq.

They took Christianity, Judaism, and Islam to task for so many of history's wars, and Hitchens pointed out the irony of the Left in the Middle East generally backing the Iraqi regime-change because it meant a tilt toward secularism in the region while the Left in the United States by and large opposed it. The roles were similarly reversed for the Right in both areas.

The discussion was more complex than my summary, but both agreed that in the end they supported Bush because he would take responsibility for the war he started and was the less likely of the two to give up on it, which both agreed would be disastrous for us and for the Middle East and a major, major victory for the dark forces of jihad.

Red went to her voting booth, and I went to mine.

RASPBERRY PUDDING

(Adapted from the Condé Nast cafeteria)

2 cups fresh or frozen raspberries
1 cup raspberry jam
2 ½ cups sifted cake flour
2 ½ teaspoons baking powder
½ teaspoon salt
12 tablespoons unsalted butter
1 ½ cups sugar
8 large egg yolks
1 teaspoon vanilla
1 teaspoon lemon juice
½ cup milk

1. Preheat the oven to 350 degrees.
2. In a small bowl, stir raspberries and jam together. Put the mixture into a 9-inch round cake pan.
3. Sift together cake flour, baking powder, and salt. Set aside.
4. In a mixing bowl, cream butter for 30 seconds. Gradually add sugar and beat this mixture on high speed 3–4 minutes, until light and fluffy. Set aside.
5. In another bowl, beat the eggs, vanilla, and lemon juice on high speed until they are thick and a pale yellow.
6. Beat the egg mixture into the butter mixture, making sure to scrape the sides as you go.

7. Add the flour mixture ⅓ at a time, alternating with the milk mixture, ½ at a time.

8. Pour the mixture on top of the berry mixture.

9. Place in the oven and bake 30–45 minutes.

10. Use a toothpick to test the cake. If the toothpick comes out clean, you have a beautiful raspberry pudding.

VARIATIONS: If you are in a super hurry, you can always use a yellow box cake, angel-food cake, or chocolate-cake mix. They are all superb with raspberries.

YIELD: 8–12 servings.

RED IS THE THIRD of six children (one was killed at twenty-four in an automobile crash when Red was twenty-two), and grew up privileged in northern California. She went to Miss Porter's, the exclusive girls' school in Farmington, Connecticut, at fourteen, then to Occidental College in L.A., where she majored in theatre and art, then to Yale for a master's degree in stage design, where she met Rocco, who was teaching there. She married him at twenty-six and divorced him at forty-three. "I married too young and divorced too old," she told me once, martini in hand.

Her grandfather was the co-founder of Prentice-Hall, at one time the leading textbook publisher in America. His son, Red's father, was the heir apparent, but in a fit of rebelliousness told his father he really wanted to be a farmer. He didn't want to be a farmer but no doubt enjoyed the effect it had on his old man. Needless to say, he didn't take over Prentice-Hall as he was supposed to. "My grandfather was cold and ruthless and ambitious—sort of like your father," Red said once, same martini.

"And he was disappointed in his son?" I asked.

"Oh, yes. He never thought his son was very bright." Red's father died of lymphoma in 1994, the same year she got her divorce. A terrible year for her.

Her children are all show-biz babies. "I had North in eighty-five, when I designed and co-produced *Big River*. I cut the show in the hospital," she laughed. "I had Nash during *Into the Woods,* and I had Dodge during *Secret Garden*— which proves there's no point in planning anything." Amazingly, she remains close to her ex, valuing his friendship and professional advice. I speak to Charlotte perhaps twice a year—her desire, not mine—but Red and Rocco talk almost daily. They have disagreements—mostly over whose weekend it is to take the kids—but otherwise are pretty much best friends. For a significant birthday recently, his current wife, Debby, asked him whom he'd like to have at dinner. "You and Heidi," he said.

Rocco recently became really rich. As president of the Jujamcyn Theaters in New York, he made a deal with the owner, James Binger, to buy the five theatres at then-market value upon Binger's death. Binger died in November 2004, and the theatres were then worth considerably more than Rocco had to pay. Although he and I are both in the theatre, our worlds couldn't be farther apart. His interests are largely, though not exclusively, financial and mine unfortunately aren't. And there is some closeted, if benign, competition. In 2004 he said to Heidi, comparing himself to me, "But I am smarter, right?" And if smarts are measured by business success, I'd say, "Way."

Red has two sisters and a mother on this coast, a brother and a sister on the other, and when I threw her a surprise fiftieth one year late, I asked her who her best friends were. "Actually, my best friends are my family," she said, and that's who showed up.

But first . . .

Six Redheads and a Fjord

IF YOU WANT to know how to capture the rapt attention of five redheads ranging in age from two to sixteen, take them forty-five minutes by boat from the high-end Solstrand Fjord Hotel just outside Bergen, Norway, across the Bjørnafjord to the island of Tysnesøy. This is where Eystein Michalsen and Nina Havn have set up a meticulously rustic retreat called Kubbervik. Eystein will take these redheads out on a boat, yank in the nets he has laid the night before, and, with luck, bring in a couple of cod (one weighing more than twelve pounds and worthy of gasps from several would-be Cousteaus) together with dozens of red and clear jellyfish, about which he will claim, "These are not good." He will then gut the cod to the wonder of all, describing each of the organs as he goes along, and toss the inedibles back into the fjord, where they'll be immediately dive-bombed by a trio of friendly seagulls and one graceful tern. Game Boys and Walkmen will be silenced and earphones pocketed as the kids (and, I might as well admit it, another ten or so adults) will be transfixed by his surgical skill in filleting the cod, which he does in under two minutes. Who would have thought marine biology so much fun?

In the summer of 2003, Red and I traveled to Norway with her family—three children, a mother, two sisters, their spouses and children, and so many cousins, aunts, and assorted friends that I began to feel like Sir Joseph Porter aboard H.M.S. *Pinafore*. The number, I think, got as high as twenty-six, and in ten days never fell below eleven. My sons couldn't make the trip—Frank was slaving at a law firm, Eddie going native in Italy.

Red is mother to two redheads and aunt to three—and is one herself. The occasion was the sixtieth birthday of her brother-in-law Sven, and it was a logistical undertaking worthy of Joel Silver on location. Sven is a native Norwegian, though he grew up on the Kenai Peninsula of Alaska and lived in Seattle from the age of six, and he and Barbara, Red's sister, had arranged an exhaustive—though mercifully voluntary—schedule of excursions to acquaint us with several high points of his homeland. Many of these included indigenous food, and there is little that five redheaded kids greet with more apprehension than victuals that stray from the domestic familiars of burgers and 'zza. So Eystein and Nina had their work cut out for them.

If you're lucky, you'll be able to visit Kubbervik, which is open from April through November, when it's overcast or rainy; if you're blessed by an even higher power, you'll get to see it when the sun is out. Approaching its wood boathouse in a drizzle, we could see a long pine table laid for lunch, the candles of the silver candelabra blazing like a scene from *Babette's Feast*. Eystein, who is handsome enough, and Nina, who is the paradigm of the Norwegian knockout, are married, and for four years, the former economist and the advertising executive have been reconstructing four cottages that sleep a total of twenty, none with electricity—and, oh, there is no road—for vacation hideaways that authentically replicate the primeval Norwegian countryside.

At the moment, the complex of six buildings—two of them dismantled at another location, transported here, then rebuilt—are rented out for corporate bonding and "team spirit" retreats. But we were the only ones retreating that day, and despite the light rain, the food, walks, and miniature fishing adventures, were comfy.

Even those who seriously don't like fish—four out of six redheads, one of whom had proclaimed, "I don't *do* fish," the day before we left New York— were swayed by the chowder that Eystein and Nina made for lunch: just fish stock, white wine, cream, butter, and the previous day's catch of flounder, pollock, and cod. We looked out over Bjørnafjord (*bjørn* means bear) as the rain softly plinked on the surface, and it couldn't have been more familial, safe as we all were under our sloping tile roof, with candles, strengthening soup, and a fortifying white Burgundy.

The kids, of course, eschewed soup superlatives and eventually grew rest-less, leaving the table to explore the grounds as the rest of us curled up like slugs for naps in front of the fireplace in the main house or delved into some of the hundreds of books (many in English) from a backless birch bookcase hanging nearby. Eystein took me on a brief tour of the house. "I just made those beds," he said, pointing proudly to two brightly painted blue wood pedestals lying foot to head, with protective gingerbread cutouts that prevent sleepers from rolling off and busting their pates. And he didn't mean he'd tucked in the sheets; he meant he nailed and screwed the boards. Concerned about dinner, he shipped out once more, scraped a few mussels from rocks nearby, and began preparations for our seafood orgy. As the afternoon pro-gressed, the ever-inventive redheads started a game of charades, cheating wildly by adult standards. ("No, no, it's a *movie*," one actor-out corrected his team of guessers, then, on a later title, announced, "No, no, it's *MALCOLM in the Middle*.")

In the kitchen, Nina sautéed fresh, fat scallops in a little butter, removed them, and made a simple but exquisite saffron sauce by adding a little stock, cream, and a few pink peppercorns for color. Eystein dipped monkfish chunks into an elemental flour batter for quick sautéing.

I've never subscribed to the marketeers' description of monkfish as the "poor man's lobster"—it's like the Chicken Liver Council claiming its product is foie gras for the homeless. I usually find monkfish combative in texture and only mildly toothsome. If you see a whole monkfish at the market, you'll think its massive mouth scarier than a shark's. And it's devious: It sits on the bottom of the ocean passively, opens its Godzilla jaws, and waits for poor unsuspect-ing fishies to swim right into it, not unlike the latest recipients of W's capital-gains cuts. So it has in common with lobster only reprehensibility of character. But Eystein had the novel idea of freezing it first—even though it had been netted the day before—to improve its texture, which indeed it did. Perhaps this technique should be used on all passive-aggressives, human or piscine: freeze them first to soften their fibers, then cut them into pieces.

As everyone assembled at another long dinner table, activity in the kitchen increased, and the spirit grew jolly. Nina's team of attractive high school girls bearded the mussels, and Eystein steamed them simultaneously with fistfuls of toothpick asparagus. He poached two-inch cubes of the newly gutted cod in lightly lemoned and salted water, simmering them for a brief two to three minutes as Nina decorated each plate with superb wild salmon that had been juniper-smoked locally. It's more intense than Scottish but less blunt than Nova.

At the long dinner table, redheads young and old gathered 'round. Dodge, who was twelve years old at the time and a daring eater, zapped around the table begging other people's mussels and racking up twelve or fourteen shells on his plate; Nash, the sixteen-year-old fiske-a-phobe, moved his scallop around his plate with a fork and ultimately slipped it to an uncle. The younger ones looked suspiciously at their plates and were finally granted hamburgers. But the rest of us feasted and feasted—mussels, cod, salmon, monkfish, asparagus, the ubiquitous boiled potatoes—till the last sliver was done. It was nine at night by the time we finished, so naturally, the sun came out and stayed till midnight.

Kubbervik Scallops

3 tablespoons butter
12 fat sea scallops, with coral attached, if possible
Salt and freshly ground pepper to taste
1 ¼ cups dry white wine
2 tablespoons Fish Stock (see page 307)
1 ¼ cups heavy cream
1 tablespoon lemon juice
½ teaspoon saffron threads
¼ cup minced chives
Cracked pink peppercorns, for garnish

1. Melt the butter in a large skillet over high heat. Season the scallops with salt and pepper and sauté until lightly browned, about 1 minute per side. Remove the scallops and set aside. Pour the remaining butter and liquid into a medium-size saucepan.

2. Add the wine, stock, cream, lemon juice, and saffron to the liquid in the saucepan and reduce over medium heat by about half, until you have a rich sauce. Season to taste with salt.

3. Gently reheat the scallops in the sauce and stir in the chives. Serve immediately, sprinkled with the pink peppercorns.

YIELD: 4 servings.

Fish Soup for a Rainy Day

4 tablespoons butter
4 tablespoons flour
5 cups Fish Stock (see page 307)
1 cup dry white wine
1 cup clam juice
1 ¼ cups crème fraîche
1 ¼ cups heavy cream
1 large carrot, peeled and julienned
1 small celery root, peeled and julienned
5 scallions, green part only, cut into half-inch slices
5 cups coarsely chopped spinach leaves
1 teaspoon sugar
Salt and freshly ground white pepper to taste
2 pounds skinless, boneless white fish such as cod, flounder, turbot, or
     catfish, cut into ¾-inch chunks
30 mussels (optional)
3 tablespoons chopped chives

1. Melt the butter in a large soup pot over medium heat. Stir in the flour and cook, stirring constantly, for 3 minutes. Stir in the stock, bring to a boil, and boil for 5 minutes, stirring occasionally. Stir in the wine, clam juice, crème fraîche, and cream. Reduce the heat to a simmer.

2. Add the carrot and celery root and cook 2 minutes. Add the scallions,

spinach, and sugar. Season to taste with salt and pepper. Add the fish (and mussels, if using). Cook for 3 minutes, or until the mussels open. Ladle the soup into bowls, sprinkle with chives, and serve immediately.

YIELD: 6 servings.

FISH STOCK

Bones and trimmings from 1 large white-fleshed fish
3 quarts water
¼ head celery root, rinsed and peeled
1 carrot
¼ leek, rinsed and chopped
Juice of half a lemon
Salt and freshly ground pepper to taste

1. Rinse the bones and place them and the vegetables into a stockpot. Add water and bring to a boil. Lower the heat and simmer for 20 minutes, skimming off and discarding any foam that forms on top of the liquid.
2. Strain the liquid, discard the solids, and return the liquid to the pot. Continue to simmer until reduced to 6 cups. Add the lemon juice and season to taste with salt and pepper.

YIELD: 6 cups.

Reform Reform'd

~ ~ ~ ~ ~ ~

O NE OF RED's great attractions is her ambition. She's not Sammy Glick and she's not a wild-eyed dreamer, but hardheaded and realistic about her career and, fortunately for me, about mine. For herself, she wants to design one musical a year—that's all. Doable and manageable, what with me, three sons, and two stepsons to deal with.

I arrived in New York from California in '98 with *Vitreous Floaters*, in which an aging sitcom writer lures a much younger woman to front for him to sell a series to the age-conscious network, and while it made the rounds, Red led me through the writing of the musical '68. She then saw to it that producers I didn't know read it. When the assignment from the *Times* came up, she persuaded me to embrace it. ("But I'm a playwright," I said. "You're a writer," she said. "This is writing. And it pays.") Then she contributed ideas, accompanied me on trips, and as of this date has read every single column I've written for that and every other magazine I've written for. She suggested the battery of nominators that secured me a Guggenheim for playwriting (André Bishop, Robyn Goodman, Pete Gurney, Frank Rich). Since knowing her, I've felt part of a professional team, which I'd missed—with Charlotte I often felt I was the tumbler in a dangerous trapeze act and my catcher was missing.

In the fall of 2002, Red announced that Carole Rothman, the artistic director of the Second Stage Theatre, wanted to do a one-man show of my columns, starring . . . me. It was Red's suggestion, of course.

She had mentioned the idea before, but usually in an offhand way—"Might be interesting to see your columns onstage," she'd said casually—as though she'd said, "Wouldn't it be fu

feeling as though I'd been tr

ence in which a director airs

for a few minutes until the p

rector gives up on it. So I was

let alone won Carole's green

food writing for the *Times* ma

sional autobiographical tak

Spindler and Andy Port enc

didn't want to be, and didn't

So when Red floored me

wanted to put me back onst

ternating layers of wet terror . . . and curiosity. What would it possibly be like? I mean, if it didn't go well, I could always claim a heart attack on opening night, couldn't I? It's in my family.

Carole founded the Second Stage with Robyn Goodman in 1979, initially to give second productions to good plays that had received bad ones the first time around. Robyn left to become an independent producer (recently winning a Tony for *Avenue Q*), and over the years Carole maneuvered the theatre into one of the leading not-for-profit companies in the city. Carole has been so successful that she and her board built a handsome new theatre on Forty-third Street just off Eighth Avenue.

"This should only include autobiographical stories," she said in her office. "And Heidi could put an entire kitchen onstage," she added. She knows Red by her professional name, Heidi Ettinger, and they have been friends for more than twenty-five years. Once a month or so they used to call a meeting of the Red Meat Club, at which Red, Carole, and Wendy Wasserstein would devour obscene amounts of highly prime beef.

"Got to have a deep-fried turkey," I told Carole.

"Deep-fried turkey? On a stage? Can we do that?" she said, and loved it. A *coup de théâtre*, all that bubblin' oil crackling when the raw yellow bird went in, oohs and aahs when it came out forty-eight minutes later, glistening and golden brown. I volunteered that my character could cook a five-course meal while rattling off these vignettes.

Wrestling

310

"Really? Five courses?"

"And we can feed the aud

three hundred . . . I guess

Every bit of it sounde

wasn't exactly frig

other actor to

"I don't

would

B

ience! Onstage! Or, let's see, theatre capacity is

we couldn't feed everybody and still make money."

like fun . . . except the part about my being in it. I

tened, but was certainly hesitant. "What about getting an-

lay me?"

ink so," she said firmly. "I mean you're not exactly famous—what

e the point?" She was sympathetic but intransigent.

etween columns for the *Times,* I wrote the show over the next eight months—more difficult than I thought it would be. Turning reflective prose into action and dialogue snaps you to attention. I understood why only one of America's great playwrights—Thornton Wilder—was able to master both forms. The director, Peter Askin, grew up in a well-to-do New York real estate family and also came from a private-school background, so could relate to my travails, as narrated in the play. Peter has made a specialty of one-performer shows—John Leguizamo's, *The Vagina Monologues, Hedwig and the Angry Inch,* among others.

We had many sessions working on the script, which though part of a director's job, is generally misunderstood by anyone who hasn't actually done much stage work. The best directors, like the best editors, have a serious understanding of the play and don't attempt rewrites. They try to help the author clarify and dramatize what he wants to say—rearranging and cutting the blubber, which often means persuading the author to get rid of his favorite passages.

Peter is a soft-spoken, sandy-haired man in his fifties, married twice, with one set of grown children and another of smalls. He's so reserved that if you were a bully you'd think you could walk right over him, which would be a mistake. "Get rid of as many of the *he said*s and *she said*s as you can," he said quietly at one of our first meetings. "Instead of ' "I'm hungry," she said,' *become the person* and say, 'I'm hungry.' Put it all in the present tense, so it's active." I did, and at the next meeting, he said, "Get rid of as many of the *he said*s and *she said*s as you can."

"I thought I had."

"Uh-huh," he said, which meant I hadn't. I again brought up the possibility of another actor. "Brian Cox's very good," he said. I couldn't tell if he was going to pursue the English Cox, a LAMDA alum, or was forcing me to say, "Hey, he can't play that part! It's mine!" but it made me quit talking about a different actor.

Toe in the water, but not full leg, I thought for my own protection that the show might play better with an additional actor and so invited Peter and Carole and Red and two fellows on the tech crew to lunch, during which I'd deep-fry a turkey with my friend Oliver Clark, the actor who'd tricked me into believing we were writing an original musical. Lunch would be a two-man show featuring our kitchen banter. Peter had a cold and ate lightly, but the "performance" was a success, though I didn't tell Oliver the lunch's ulterior motive in case it didn't work out. In fact, I've never told him. He's learning it for the first time reading this, but it's not payback for *Redhead*.

Afterward, Peter phoned and said, "I like the way you two interact. Would you like to do it with Oliver?"

"I think I would, yes."

"Well, let's think about it overnight," he said softly.

I thought having Oliver onstage would be easier for me and possibly the show would be more fun but that it was also sort of cowardly. The next day, I phoned Peter. "You know, I think having someone else onstage would dissipate the story. Like it or not, it's about me."

"Well, that's true," Peter said. Man, was he making me work.

Typically, I harrumphed and rationalized and came up with all sorts of reasons why it should be a two-man show and why it shouldn't. Finally, Peter put a stop to it.

"Uh-huh, okay," he said. "So you would like to do it by yourself."

"Ummm . . . yes." At last, he'd heard a commitment! I had wormed my way backward into a one-man show, and Peter understood the anxiety.

"Uh-huh. Okay. Now I really think you should cut out as many of those *he saids* and *she saids* as you can."

I don't know to this day whether Peter thought there should be one or two men on that stage, but he didn't gloat and he didn't object. Just straight ahead.

He urged me to cut indulgent passages that were significant to me but not to the audience. If I didn't by the next meeting or rehearsal, he'd bring up the cut again, quietly . . . and again and again and again until I had. Of all the cuts and suggestions he cajoled, I think only one three-line section remained by the time we opened. I mean, I had to protect my manhood somehow.

I began memorizing the script in September, a month before rehearsal. My old summer-stock teacher Alvina Krause believed an actor rehearsing with a book in his hand was just wasting time. So I calisthenically learned a page and a half of dialogue every day, and at first rehearsal had the whole script under my belt.

Red designed a wondrous and fanciful kitchen, cut it back when the budget was reduced (as it always is), framing me with transparent walls, a whimsical arch of gleaming copper pots, a fantastical cornucopia of produce gushing forth from the wings, and a magical dining table that suddenly slid in, fully laid, a second before the final curtain. And of course, everything on the stage was functional—running water, stove top, ovens, machinery. I wrote in music that was important to me—"Moonglow and the Theme from *Picnic*" because of Kim Novak, "All Right, Okay, You Win," sung by Joe Williams and played by the Count Basie Orchestra, because Uncle Bus used to take me to Birdland to see them.

Red and the techs set up a working kitchen for rehearsal. I showed up on the set feeling as if I'd never left the stage and just sort of bulldozed my way through the next thirty days and slept through the accompanying thirty nights with only marginal help from Sonata. There's a line in the play referring to Lee Remick's death: "Denial is murder in a relationship but sometimes can be one of the more useful weapons in our psychological arsenal." In my case denial was just the insulation I needed.

Although I acted the role of being an actor—outwardly nattering and worried, seeking consolation and approval from everyone 24/7, like every actor I've known—in fact, at the center, I was relatively unruffled. Perhaps because there was so much writing at night and so much arithmetic during the day— the potato soufflé has to come out of the oven *here*, so it has to go in *here*, so the potatoes have to be mashed *here*, the cardoon chopped *here*—this nifty negation set in, not unlike the time I underwent a massive general anesthetic for a sinus operation and just ignored the possibility that all the things I knew could go wrong in a hospital would. Only after the operation did I really focus on what had happened and what could have happened and decided never to get sick again. I did wonder which, if any, of the seven rules for seducing a woman through cooking her dinner (reduced from ten) would get laughs (three invariably did, sometimes four; never seven) and if I would be able to make it through the descriptions of Uncle Bus's death—I was making a Reuben's apple pancake—and of Lee's cancer—during which I drained the braising cardoon—without tearing up.

The dreaded first night of *Dinner with Demons* came and went with attendant but short-lived panic: There were too many tasks to perform in this play! I looked out at the audience—which I couldn't see individually, and began peeling tomatoes, as planned. The words flowed out, the tomatoes got peeled, the turkey glistened, Lee died of cancer, I welcomed my demons to dinner. BLACKOUT. Applause.

Aside from the second performance, when I got lost and called offstage, "Where are we now, Kyle?" to the production assistant, and one very brief fire—squelched with a tea towel—I never had a problem with the technical aspects of the lines or the performance. I could have been deeper or funnier or more this or that, but the lines came out one after another in the right order for eight straight weeks, and the cooking came off without a slip—a deep-fried turkey, tomato sorbet, braised cardoon, a potato soufflé, and a splendid Reuben's apple pancake theatrically flipped, like a circus trick, just before the final curtain—and the running time always ended within a minute or two of its desired length. So I could do it! I never quite got rid of the voice inside my head that said, right while I was talking, "You could forget this line! This one might not be funny! That guy in the front row isn't moving—is he listening, asleep, or dead? Someone there in the middle laughed where there's never been a laugh before . . . and now, where there's always been a laugh, nothing! Hey, why is Kyle reading a book—what if I go up? Watch it—you're going to fuck up!" Battling this internal CD was the most exhausting aspect of every performance. But I got through sixty-five of them without falling off the stage or giving in to the voices. The show became better, the script tighter, my performance more relaxed (or so I'm told—I couldn't tell because the CD never shut off).

Red came often but left early, too nervous to watch for long, she said. Nancy came five times and laughed at the mention of her ballet days and memories of our mother. Frank and Eddie each saw the show twice—once bringing friends, so I knew I hadn't embarrassed them too much. Don Junior flew in from Tulsa with his wife, Rose, and said tears came to his eyes when I played our father tersely appreciating a fried catfish I'd made for him—about the only appreciation he'd ever shown either of us. When my Uncle Bus's widow, Margaret, came with her children and husband, I got teary during the sequences about Bus and again during Lee's death, imagining their responses. When Rafe came with his wife, Margaret, who was dying of cancer, I thought I might not be able to make it through Lee's cancer, worrying how it would affect them.

Oliver saw it twice—I recognized his laugh when I imitated my mother smoking, and a bunch of chums from Denison enthused over the sequence where one of them and I got arrested for trespassing at Kim Novak's. I heard Wynn Handman, the cantankerous and wonderful force behind the American Place Theatre, which had produced my two one-acts, *Yanks 3 Detroit 0 Top of the 7th* and *Rubbers*, as well as the catastrophic *Tunnel Fever, or The Sheep Is Out*, and the controversial *Stonewall Jackson's House*, laugh at a matinee. Andy Port and Michael Boodro, two *Times* editors, came on a chilly afternoon and kept everyone awake.

There were other rewards. The reactions of the pros who saw it swelled my head. Mario Batali said it was the best thing he'd seen all year—and the year was almost over! Eric Ripert was flatteringly incredulous that I could say all those words while prepping a five-course meal. Rocco DiSpirito, in the middle of media hell because of his TV show, came backstage and effused. *This* was thrilling.

WOULD I DO IT again? I can't say I ever looked forward to the performance every day, nor was I sufficiently at ease on the stage to completely enjoy what

I was doing: It was work, first and last; discovering a half-full and unrespon-sive house on a freezing December-January matinee was uphill work; I never felt particularly refreshed by the applause and in fact told Peter that I'd be happy to forgo a curtain call if it would make the show better. He said, "I've never had an actor volunteer that," and then "no." The money was lousy. But after each performance, when the CD shut up and friends and strangers ap-peared backstage, all warm, all positive (fortunately, people who feel negative about a play seldom come backstage or, if they do, they lie), was the second most sublime moment of the day.

First most sublime was the eleven o'clock martini and many forms of mus-sels with Red at Café de Bruxelles on Greenwich Avenue, which also serves the best French fries in town. That made it worth doing. For a million dollars and those experiences, I'd do it all over again in a fingersnap.

POTATO SOUFFLÉ
(Adapted from Potatoes *by Annie Nichols, Ryland Peters & Small, 2003)*

For the almond parsley pesto
1 bunch flat leaf parsley, washed, stalks removed
⅓ cup almonds, skin on, roasted till golden
1 cup extra-virgin olive oil
¼ cup grated Parmesan
Salt and pepper

For the soufflé
3 tablespoons unsalted butter, melted
⅓ cup bread crumbs
3 pounds floury potatoes, skins on
¼ cup unsalted butter
⅔ cup milk, warmed
2 large eggs plus 1 large yolk
Salt and pepper

½ cup grated Parmesan

4 ounces mozzarella, drained and cubed

4 ounces Fontina or Emmental, cubed

---

1. In salted water to cover, boil potatoes till soft, about 30 minutes. Drain and peel. Preheat oven to 350 degrees.
2. Grease and coat soufflé dish with half the melted butter and half the bread crumbs.
3. Mash the potatoes and add unmelted butter and milk, then mix in eggs and egg yolk. Season with salt and pepper, then add Parmesan and mix again.
4. Spread half the mashed potatoes on bottom of the soufflé dish, creating a ½-inch lip headed up the sides. Lay the cheese cubes evenly over the potatoes, then cover with the remaining potatoes.
5. Brush with remaining melted butter and sprinkle with remaining bread crumbs. Bake at 350 degrees for 20 minutes, then at 425 degrees until golden, about 10 minutes.
6. While baking, prepare the pesto by grinding parsley, toasted almonds, and 2 tablespoons oil in a mortar or food processor until fairly coarse. Blend in Parmesan and remaining oil and season to taste.
7. To serve, spoon the soufflé onto plates with ribbons of pesto over it.

YIELD: 4 servings.

Stolen Moments

I WASN'T VERY NICE to my mother in *Dinner with Demons*. Although what the play says is true, it omits the concern and sense of helplessness that made her, like most people, paradoxical. She was a single parent with a hefty divorce settlement and so befuddled about her two children that she frequently overreacted with almost-comical extremes of punishment. But there were other moments.

Two days after a Christmas in the early fifties, she planned to take me to a classical piano concert and, as a special treat, dinner at Schrafft's, the upscale chain of restaurants that infiltrated New York in numbers rivaling the fire hydrant—at one point there were nearly fifty of them.

I didn't look forward to classical piano at all and didn't even look forward to Schrafft's—too stuffy for my taste. Furthermore, she had been particularly generous at Christmas and I had bought her almost nothing, so I felt considerable guilt.

The day before the outing, I walked by the neighborhood jeweler's window and fell in love with a gold-plated cigarette lighter completely covered in mother-of-pearl. Although it would look more like a souvenir of Las Vegas to my eyes today, when I was eight or nine it was the most dazzling object I'd ever seen. Mother loved to smoke Pall Malls, long unfiltered cigarettes that no doubt helped lead to her death.

On an allowance of sixty cents—thirty-five of which went toward the Saturday kids' matinee at the Trans-Lux around the corner—I hadn't saved a nickel, and the lighter cost twelve dollars.

So I stole the money for it.

From her.

She left her purse lying on the bureau every night, and late Friday, I popped it open while she was frying chicken for my sister and me and hurriedly grabbed a wad of bills. Early the next morning, I went to the jeweler and bought the lighter, its pink, turquoise, and lustrous white finish changing magically in front of my eyes. She was astonished and thrilled. "It's beautiful! How thoughtful of you," she said in true amazement. Within a minute or two, she had sussed out the situation and began the tenderest of third-degrees. "How ever could you afford it?"

"Oh, I have some money."

"It's the sweetest thing, and I'm filled with gratitude. But I know how much allowance you get. Where did the money come from?"

I decided to face the suspicion head on. "I didn't steal it!" The more I protested, of course, the deeper the hole I dug.

Just before the concert, I lacquered on a handful of Wildroot cream oil, despite instructions that urged only a dab. "Mmmm, there's so much of it," Mother said with a scowl, noting the shiny, greaseball helmet that had previously been my hair.

"I like it like this," I said and then, tightening my own handcuffs, "I didn't steal that money!" This time, she didn't respond.

We went to the concert, and I tried to sleep with my head on her shoulder, but she gently pushed it away because of the Wildroot bear grease. "This is new," she whispered of her houndstooth suit jacket. I dozed off, waking just in time to head for Schrafft's.

Schrafft's was by then an institution of middle-class comfort. Its first "store" (as they were always called) opened on Broad Street in 1906, thanks to Frank G. Shattuck, who had previously been the top candy salesman for W. F. Schrafft & Sons. It lost money until his sister Jane was recruited from Syracuse to create a brief menu with distinctly homemade dishes.

"It was Jane's idea of what a kitchen should really be," his great-grandson Frank M. Shattuck told me recently in his small tailoring shop. "It was a much more genteel time then—everyone wore hats and handmade suits. And if you were a lady, it was safe to go in there, sit at the soda fountain, and drink gin from a teacup." Frank M. has never been in the restaurant business; he is an actor and a tailor specializing in dashing $5,000 suits that he designs himself. One day in 1980 he went into the last remaining Schrafft's—"It wasn't really a Schrafft's, just a pizza place with a dirty sign"—and made off with 2,500 recipes from the safe. "I asked the guy there if it was okay to take them, and he said yes, and a week later I sent him a bottle of Jack Daniel's."

Frank M.'s uncle Gerald worked at several of the stores. "It all came out of the Victorian era," he said over the phone. "Menus changed every day—we didn't want people to get bored. My grandfather was very concerned with quality. He paid top price for every ingredient. And it was clean, which is not so unusual today but was then. The most popular dishes were Lobster Newburg, Creamed Chicken on Toast, Fillet of Sole, and of course the hot fudge sundae." It might be said that Schrafft's was bricked and mortared with chicken; of the 187-and-counting recipes for hot chicken dishes alone, more than a quarter were fricasséed, creamed, or dumplinged in some fashion, including such exotica as Creamed Chicken and Sweetbreads on Southern Spoon Bread, Spiced Peach and Peas. Seen that on a menu anywhere lately?

"We also had a wonderful cheese bread," Gerald said. "And a fresh fruit salad with our own dressing. And pies! Lamb pie, lobster pie, tuna fish, all cooked on Hall china so they wouldn't break in the oven. And our steaks would have put Peter Luger to shame. We were such big purchasers of beef that during the Second World War, we supplied the Carlyle, the Waldorf, and the Pierre. Toward the end, we had what's his name who did the soup cans—Andy Warhol—painting our ads."

These deluxe emporia had such devoted customers that some left their favorite waitresses money in their wills and often waited in line for their favorite waitress and table rather than be seated at any available spot. The employees may have been treated even better than the customers: They were also profit-sharing partners and were kept employed even during the dark days of the Depression. Primarily rosy-cheeked young Irish women straight off the boat, they voted down unionization three to one. They were lined up in military fashion for daily inspection and were proud of their work. "The same waitresses worked there year after year," George C. Shattuck, Frank M.'s father, told me on the phone. "Sometimes two or three generations of them. We really were a family." At one point, more than seven thousand large.

What made it so beloved? "Consistency of quality and friendly service," George said. Why did it go out of business? "Times change," Gerald said. "New York became quite a dangerous place in the sixties. Our main competitors were Longchamps and Childs, and we all stopped about the same time. Schrafft's lingered for quite a few years as an ice cream company. Then Pet Milk bought it, pretty much abandoned it, and eventually probably sold the land alone for more than the purchase price."

I didn't know about the store's history when I sat down with Mother after that piano concert; I knew only that it seemed hoity-toity, and the chopped steak with brown gravy I'd had on a previous visit wasn't as good as its down-market counterpart at Hamburger Heaven. *Plus* you had to wear a tie and sit up straight even though you thought you already were. Mother ordered the lobster pie.

"You'll have to return the lighter," she said quietly. I didn't fight. The jig was up.

"But I want you to have it."

"I know, dear, and it's the sweetest present I've ever received, but it wasn't your money."

"I could save up for it."

"Of course . . . but you need to return it now. When you have the money, then you can buy it." She knew me. I managed to save up a few cents for a couple of weeks, then Dubble Bubble got the better of me.

"Try some of this lobster." I screwed up my face. Nunh-unh. The Irish stew I'd ordered was exotic enough and, except for the turnips, warmed up the winter outside. Mother had a dark rhomboid on the shoulder of her new suit.

"What's that?" I said, slurping the gravied warm veggies and lamb chunks.

"You went to sleep. Your hair is very greasy." I didn't understand—wasn't she trying to keep my head *off* her shoulder? "Well, yes, but you looked so tired, and you're my son."

I took a bite of her lobster pie. It was thick and sweet, with the brilliant briny flavor of real lobster, and it was the first comfort food I can remember.

SCHRAFFT'S LOBSTER THERMIDOR

4 cooked lobsters, about 1 ¼ pounds each
6 tablespoons butter
1 shallot, minced
1 tablespoon lemon juice, plus more to taste
¾ teaspoon paprika
Pinch cayenne
Salt and pepper to taste
6 ounces small white button mushrooms, sliced
3 tablespoons flour
1 ¼ teaspoons powdered mustard
1 ½ cups chicken stock or mild seafood stock, or a combination
⅔ cup heavy cream
½ cup grated Parmesan cheese

1. Preheat oven to 450 degrees. Split lobsters down the middle and remove and reserve meat from tail and claws. Discard everything from the head and remove the front legs, without detaching the cartilage that holds the head and tail together. Rinse and dry shells and set aside.
2. Cut reserved meat into ½-inch dice. Sauté 2 tablespoons of the butter in a medium-size pan and add shallots, lemon juice, paprika, and cayenne until warmed through. Season with salt and pepper. In another pan, sauté mushrooms in 2 tablespoons of the butter until tender.
3. Set aside mushrooms and lobster meat. Melt the remaining butter in the pan the lobster was cooked in. Stir in the flour and mustard and cook for 2 minutes. Slowly whisk in the stock, then the cream, stirring constantly, until thickened, about 5 minutes. Add the lobster and mushrooms and cook 2 more minutes. Season with more salt, pepper, and lemon, if desired.
4. Spoon mixture into the shells, sprinkle with cheese, and bake until the cheese is lightly browned, 10–12 minutes. Serve immediately.

YIELD: 4 servings.

SIMMERING IRISH STEW WITH DUMPLINGS

For the stew
2 tablespoons vegetable oil
3 pounds lamb-stew meat, cut into 1 ½-inch cubes
12 cups water
1 teaspoon salt, plus more to taste
¼ teaspoon pepper, plus more to taste
6 carrots, peeled and cut into 2-inch pieces
2 turnips, peeled and cut into 1-inch chunks
1 small onion, sliced ⅛-inch thick
3 potatoes, peeled and sliced ¼-inch thick
4 tablespoons flour
Butter as needed

For the dumplings
1 ½ cups flour
2 ¼ teaspoons baking powder
¾ teaspoon salt
½ cup parsley
¾ cup milk
2 tablespoons butter

1. Heat oil in a large pot over high heat and brown the meat in two batches. Return meat to the pot and add water, 1 teaspoon salt, and ¼ teaspoon pepper. Simmer for 1 hour.
2. Add carrots, turnips, and onions and simmer for another hour. Place potatoes in a small pan and ladle enough broth over them to just cover. Simmer potatoes until just tender. Pour stock back into meat, leaving just enough to keep potatoes moist. Season with salt and set aside.
3. When vegetables and meat are very tender, strain the stew. Let the broth set until fat accumulates on top. Skim fat off and measure out 4 tablespoons (if you have less, use some butter).

4. Heat fat in the pot over medium heat. Add flour and stir for 2 minutes. Whisk in the broth. Cook, stirring, until mixture thickens. Add meat and vegetables and reduce heat to a simmer.

5. Whisk together flour, baking powder, and salt. Whisk in parsley. Heat milk and butter in a saucepan until butter melts, then stir it into the flour mixture until just combined. Drop rounded spoonfuls into the simmering stew. Cover and cook for 10 minutes. Serve with reheated potatoes.

YIELD: 6 servings.

Red All Over

~~~~~~~~~

I'VE NEVER MET a human or a pet or a fish who wasn't dogmatic about his food. Let's face it—my taste buds are only mine, not yours or anybody else's, and as such deserve no special accolade just because they temporarily have access to a printing press. This is helpful to remember not only in matters culinary, but in matters artistic, financial, and romantic. For instance, if somebody said she thought the 2002 Pulitzer Prize–winning drama was the emperor's new clothes, featuring some nice dialogue but essentially a play without a point or any forward action and would be considered racist if written by someone white, or trivial and pretentious if written *about* someone white, well, that would only be HER taste buds about *Topdog/Underdog*, not yours or anyone else's. And if another person added that although the seriously credentialed Pulitzer committee occasionally gets it right, the guiding criteria are invariably ones of safety and correct politics, why that would also be just ONE set of taste buds, no more nor less valid than any other.

Similarly, your broker's recommendation to buy or sell MerkDizneySoft options is only one person's opinion; and one woman's droolful hunk will inevitably be another's appalling brute. And if I tell you that the food at the Venetian hotel in Las Vegas modeled after the city of Venice is considerably better than the food in Venice itself, that's only my opinion—even though in this case it's right. And if I add that the food in that Italian city is the Most Mediocre and Overpriced in the World (not the Worst—that belt is still comfortably worn by Shea Stadium), well, that again is entirely subjective and a potential field day for the deconstructionist.

It's harder to be dogmatic about people than it is about food unless you love them. Legally free to remarry at last in 2003—yes, the divorce took six years—I was shy about marriage because the barbaric divorce industry has made the prospect so treacherous and commercial. The practitioners practically demand prenuptial agreements, then make sure they are dismissed if challenged. Its lawyers have their most intense cosmic orgasms when people are at their most vulnerable, like buzzards—or is it vultures?

I can't think of a more despicable profession.

So infuriating and debilitating was this divorce that I was sure I'd never marry again. But when I saw the hope and delight for our future in Red's eyes, even the Hannibal Lecterian figure of the Los Angeles bar faded away. Who was going to determine our lives—us or the crummies?

2003–2004 had been an active season for us. Yale University Press finally published Nancy's book, *No Fixed Points: Dance in the Twentieth Century*, which she'd been writing with Malcolm McCormick for twenty years and which received genuine raves from the *Times*es on both coasts as well as all the major dance magazines. My column was proceeding smoothly, and *Dinner with Demons* had been a confidence-builder. Red's designs for the otherwise incomprehensible musicalization of *Dracula* were among her best. Art nouveau in style, they visually resembled what Gaudí might have done had he designed the show. They slithered on and offstage from the wings, flew down from the flies and popped up from the traps cinematically in a spooky evocation of time and place that would have made Bram Stoker shudder with approval if he ever got out from under his seat. And then there was Red offstage.

I was so intrigued by the mystery of her femininity, sexually beguiled by her deep and ambiguous WASP deviousness, and just happy, downright happy, to be around her, that over Christmas of 2003 I asked, and she said yes. She is flinty and straightforward when angry, cushy and pliable when in love, and laughs freely at just about everything I say, but brutal if she doesn't like what I put on paper.

A comparison of the improbable is "That's like Heidi saying no to her children." She spoils them mercilessly, either from guilt at being a single parent or at being a professional or from her own permissive upbringing or from living through the seventies or a combination of everything, but so far they thrive on it, though I wish they'd learn Spanish. Most important, she loves them, and her relationship with my sons is affectionate and relaxed.

Once we decided to get married, we agreed to tell all five boys together at a special dinner at "21." I was concerned about Eddie's reaction—he continued to be dutiful toward and protective about his mother, so I told him ahead of time. He sighed, then said, "I thought that was what this dinner was about. I'm happy for you, Dad."

My grand and theatrical plan turned out to be a miscalculation bordering on the farcical. Dodge, Red's twelve-year-old, burst into tears at the announcement, worrying aloud that this would mean he'd never see Rocco again. He left the table, crying. His brother North consoled him, then Red did. Nash looked stunned, no doubt wondering what this meant about his room—would he get to keep it or was everybody moving? Frank, to my surprise, was himself surprised. He hadn't seen this coming, despite all the arrangements for clearing calendars made for this one dinner. Eddie was good-humored but sober, worrying, I think, how Charlotte would feel. In short, the reactions ranged from misery to sobriety. All five boys wondered what this meant in terms of their own lives and real estate, and all were somewhat annoyed at being told something so shocking in public. The waitstaff didn't quite know what had happened: Why were three boys looking stunned and one crying hysterically? It had all begun so happily.

I had told Charlotte by phone beforehand and Red had told Rocco, neither of us wanting them to hear it from anyone else. Charlotte thanked me and was sweet about it, but the irreversibility of our split sank in.

Both Feet on the Ground?

Love is lovelier, the second time around.
Just as wonderful, with both feet on the ground.
— "Second Time Around"

RED AND I got married in May of '04 (sorry, boys), and if you haven't recently but are interested, there are a couple of ways to go about it. Of course you can always take the stressless, inexpensive, and most direct route by bringing a thirty-five-dollar money order to City Hall (1 Centre Street, actually, second-floor southwest, no blood test needed) to get your license and twenty-four hours later swarm the hallways with a much friendlier, if smaller and apolitical, United Nations, waiting for a JP.

But if you believe argument, anxiety, and financial deprivation make for a colorful introduction to your new life together, you can exercise your culinary and aesthetic vision by doing what we did: invite everybody you know and throw a party. To add *frisson*, make sure your Beloved is designing sets for the *Dracula* and *Little Princess* musicals, both due at roughly the same time—two weeks ago. Then try to get your publisher to phone and say, "You know that deadline of January '05? It's now July '04." And if you're tired of sleeping deeply without aquavit beforehand, you can intensify the time contingency to, say, two months.

We struck gold almost immediately. After visiting a handful of reception venues—mostly low-ceilinged, gold, "tasteful," and hideous, we stumbled upon the Angel Orensanz Foundation, a funky palace on Norfolk Street on the

Lower East Side with mile-high ceilings and a faint odor of religiosity, ruin, and Eastern Europe. It's the oldest extant synagogue in the city and is now used for events, parties, and, occasionally, as a synagogue. There was no runner-up to the Angel. But what were we going to eat there?

Wait a minute—first things first. Red and I, both lapsed Episcopalians (Red severely lapsed, as in atheistic, me still wondering, "Well, if he rose from the dead, isn't that pretty persuasive? And if he didn't . . . likewise, only the reverse?"), agreed to see a few churches on the theory—mostly mine—that you're not really married unless it's sanctioned by someone a little loftier than Governor Pataki. After rejecting Heavenly Rest's *Fountainhead* interior and the Gothic splendor of Grace because I'd already been married there, we wound up at what may be the loveliest treasure in the diocese: the Church of the Ascension on Tenth Street and Fifth Avenue. Designed in the Gothic Revival style, the church is adorned with an enormous canvas mural by John La Farge (once the largest painting in North America) and a Tiffany-style stained-glass window, and, most important, radiates an unpretentious sincerity of mission. All but the opportunistic are welcome. As the rector, Andrew Foster, implied, "This isn't a stage set for rent; we have to know you are serious of purpose." And thus, between food planning, wine tasting, heated discussions about music, photographers, transportation, invitations, dresses, suits, length of honeymoon, set designing, column writing, and book finishing, we met with Father Andrew weekly for a gentle exploration of the essentials. How did we feel about each other's children? Where were we going to live? What were we planning about money? What would our religious participation be? The process was surprisingly enlightening, and it forced us to focus on the marriage itself.

By this time, I'd contacted several caterers with serious reputations for hosting things like J.Lo's next three weddings and Madonna's Kabbalah ordination. All came up with menus that featured what I consider the teeny-tiny fussies: little phyllos with baby somethings, squirts of goat cheese, pancakes folded nine ways and drizzled with trendiness, taquitoettes stuffed with an *emincé* of cedar-planked shrimp loin embedded in a Meyer-lemon remoulade—the sort of preciosity that makes me want to run around the corner for a good pulled pork.

All bids were ambitious (on our behalf, of course) and expensive (on theirs). As one friend said, "When caterers hear the word 'wedding,' they start adding on the zeros." You might want to tell them you're planning a wake and see what happens.

Because I'm cheap, and like being cheap, and like even better being *thought of* as cheap, I phoned them all and asked them to cut their prices in half. One said he would and never phoned back, another never phoned at all, and another was suddenly busy on the day.

We wanted a menu that would surprise, mixing high—to show we could—and low—so that people might relax and smile. I conjured sea urchin juxtaposed with corn dogs, Osetra caviar next to mini-cheeseburgers, maybe little bags of those superb fries from Bruxelles with ortolans akimbo, or a fried meat pie from New Orleans, where North was enrolled at Loyola, with gratinéed cardoon wedges. And since cooking is so often performance (as I'd recently demonstrated), perhaps a station at which a chef would make bouillabaisse in front of your eyes, and the gent with the stainless cart from Fifty-third and Sixth Avenue would throw together his chicken curry in a pita (with the aluminum foil and all those mystery sauces, of course) accompanied by celeriac shoestrings.

From left field, enter Scarsdale.

Scarsdale? Lynn Sobel, an ebullient party planner, recommended a firm named Standing Room Only (SRO). A caterer from Scarsdale? How un-chic, how reverse-droll, how . . . *suburban*. But also how reasonable in both expense and control, how eager to please, how energetic! Sharon Snyder welcomed the challenge—even the requests to replicate the smoked duck from Grand Sichuan Eastern and Madhur Jaffrey's incomparable mango soup. We motored to Scarsdale to sample.

Snyder's chef, Herb Lindstrom, spun a superb sea-urchin cerviche by infusing it with lemongrass, chilies, and lime, excellent gingered green beans (to be served upright, in glasses), and brilliant little finger-food lamb chops (teeny-tiny, but not fussy), their bones wrapped in scallion blades. We discussed, made notes, drank wine, and threw some darts at the menu. We decided that with cocktails we'd pass the sea urchin, green beans, fries in bags, and lamb chops, plus pencil-thin sausages in square glass jars, warm fresh figs with honey, and little macs and cheese; that we'd serve wedges of iceberg with Roquefort and the mango soup at the table; that everyone would then visit stations, where bouillabaisse, lamb tagine, and smoked duck would be assembled in front of their eyes, and a street cart would sport pitas and chicken curry. If anyone was still standing, out would come a carrot wedding cake and bowls and bowls for banana splits.

We asked only that the duck be smokier and that physics be defied by standing the mac and cheese on its own, without redundantly starchy pastry or ramekins—impossible, of course—and fled to the city for the finale.

The clock ticks grew louder. The original florist with an estimate of $18,000 was replaced by someone who charged $6,000 and came up with original, almost confrontational arrangements consisting of boxes of grass; we found a mos' danceable band called the Manhattan Rhythm Machine (they'd sing gospel outside the church and doo-wop outside the Angel); Red arranged for double-decker buses and pedicabs to get us all from church to reception; the photog was engaged. We decided against the full Ascension choir and Handel's "Zadok the Priest" (usually reserved for English coronations and therefore, I'd thought, fitting), and in favor of Purcell strings. Sharon rushed into town with two carrot cakes under her arm for us to try—we chose pecans over walnuts—then zoomed back to Scarsdale. As we panicked, Lynn Sobel took over like the driver of one of those out-of-control stagecoaches in an old Western. Red's three boys and my two were suited and pink-tied alike so they could usher and act as givers-of-the-bride and best men respectively.

And suddenly we were at the altar. I don't remember any of it except that I knew I was doing the right thing and Red looked resplendent in a Gabrielle Carlson gilded oyster dress. I'm told Wendy Wasserstein and Oliver Clark read humorous marital quotes I'd assembled ("No man should marry until he has studied anatomy and dissected at least one woman"—Balzac) and that two of Red's sisters read Shakespeare's "Sonnet 30," and that my brother and sister read a few verses from "Song of Solomon" (not the usual ones). One hundred and fifty people filled the pews, Whoever Is in Charge arranged for a beautiful day (Red is reconsidering her atheism), and Father Andrew calmly wrapped our ringed hands in vestments. We kissed, and it was fact.

Out the church we headed, to startling applause, then everyone mounted the double-deckers and pedicabs and headed for the Angel, waving our hats. Pedestrians stopped to applaud as we went by.

Not everything came off exactly as planned. The band played "Moonglow" but not "Moonglow and the Theme from *Picnic*," and there wasn't enough rouille with the bouillabaise. But the variety and surprise of the food and the happiness in the ether made the guests laugh (or so they reported), and Sharon miraculously managed to get the mac and cheese to stand on its own! Lynn oversaw the works with her mighty sword, and the band played till eleven, and two years later, the bride and groom are very pleased with each other.

Of course, marriage, child-rearing, adolescence, death, birth, and life in general are excruciating and never quite work out. I'm amazed at how well they have for me so far, gripes, bitches, and a bad review in the *Times* for *Fighting International Fat* notwithstanding.

Two people together for a lifetime seems a sensational idea—providing one of them lives only to age thirty-six. In my experience 91% (or thereabouts) of the marriages I know about wind up either in divorce or as some version of *Who's Afraid of Virginia Woolf?* or with the participants eating dinner together in silence. It's almost never been *Love Finds Andy Hardy*. That doesn't mean all the people aren't eventually happy. Single lives, separate lives, remarried lives, are only failures in the eyes of those inside the box. But it doesn't mean Judge Hardy was a fool, either. And Red and I make a hell of a racket at dinner.

Sea-Urchin Cerviche

3 cups Tropicana orange juice

1 large shallot, finely chopped

1 tablespoon chopped ginger root

1 stalk lemongrass, split and cut into little pieces

2 chiles de arbole

3 garlic cloves, finely chopped

Juice of 1 ½ limes
½ bunch fresh cilantro, finely chopped
Salt and cayenne pepper to taste
6 sea urchins

1. In a medium saucepan, reduce orange juice, shallots, ginger, lemongrass, chilies, and garlic by two thirds over medium heat. Strain and cool.
2. When cool, add lime juice, cilantro, and seasonings.
3. With a pair of scissors, cut the top of each sea urchin and discard any shell that might have broken loose.
4. With a small spoon, detach the urchin from shell, taking only the pale roe.
5. Lightly toss sea urchin with the orange sauce and marinate 15 minutes.
6. Clean shells and fill with cerviche.

YIELD: 6 servings.

VERTICAL MAC 'N' CHEESE

1 pound elbow pasta
1 quart heavy cream
2 quarts shredded cheddar cheese
¼ pound shredded American cheese
Panko (Japanese) bread crumbs

1. Prepare a day in advance. Cook pasta until al dente in well-salted boiling water (do not add oil). Drain and allow to dry.
2. In a medium saucepan reduce heavy cream by half over medium heat. Stir in both cheeses and purée with immersion blender until smooth.
3. Add cooked pasta to cheese sauce and return to stove. Cook on high heat, constantly stirring, until very thick.
4. Pour mixture into a greased half sheet pan, filling it to the top.
5. Refrigerate overnight.
6. Preheat oven to 350 degrees.

7. Using a 1-inch ring mold, cut rounds of mac 'n' cheese and dredge in Panko (Japanese) bread crumbs.
8. Bake 5–7 minutes, or just until warm inside.

YIELD: forty-eight 1-inch rounds.

MARINATED GRILLED NEW ZEALAND BABY LAMB CHOPS WITH SEA SALT

1 rack New Zealand baby lamb, trimmed and Frenched
Sea salt and pepper, to taste
½ pint extra-virgin olive oil
3 cloves garlic, chopped
Leaves from 2 sprigs fresh rosemary, chopped
7 scallions, green-part only, cut long enough to cover bones

1. Preheat oven to 350 degrees and generously season lamb with salt and pepper.
2. Mix olive oil, garlic, and rosemary and spoon half over lamb.
3. Grill 1 minute on each side, then place on a sheet pan, pour remaining marinade over it, and roast 12–15 minutes, until lamb reaches internal temperature of 120 degrees.
4. Rest lamb for 5 minutes, then slice off individual chops, cover each bone with the scallion leaf, and serve with a ramekin of sea salt for dipping.

YIELD: 8 servings.

Acknowledgments

~~~~~~~~~~~~~~

FOR FIVE YEARS, I had about the best food-writing job of anyone since Petronius. In addition to biweekly exposure, *The New York Times Magazine* allowed me unusually free rein over subject matter, style, and opinion, all the while supplying me with ideas ranging from inspired to zany. For this I thank primarily the late, joyfully combustible Amy Spindler and my own special champion, Andy Port. Andy, a woman whose "invisible editing" and metaphorical handholding improved every single piece of mine she worked on and made me feel I was the best writer on the magazine, though there was plenty of evidence to the contrary.

Adam Moss, then editor in chief of the magazine, encouraged or allowed Amy and Andy to allow me that free range and is now eating everyone's lunch at *New York* magazine. His successor, Gerry Marzorati, made me feel welcome, too.

Frank Rich not only suggested me to the *Times* but more or less insisted I take the assignment when I was too dim to realize its possibilities. I'm most grateful for his prescience.

I had wonderfully sympathetic and incisive line editors at the *Times* in Michael Boodro and Maura Egan, and learned much from two accomplished and extremely patient recipe testers, Mary Johnson and Alice Thompson.

This book could not have been possible without the extraordinary skill, cooperation, and frequent touches of genius from the chefs whose recipes are included herein. Since that week on the S.S. *France*, I've admired the art and craft of serious cooks; but it surprised me when I began writing the *Times* column and other pieces for other magazines—but surprises me no longer—to discover how generous chefs are as a breed. I've never been turned down for any request by any chef, whether it involved printing a recipe or profiling them or didn't, and believe me, it wasn't because of my good looks. Well, there was one, a woman who runs a fashionable kitchen in the East Village, and that may have something to do with my looks. But every other serious cook was helpful, expansive, creative, and kept no secrets.

My agent, Kathy Robbins, tirelessly shepherded a ragged bunch of columns into just the right corral, and my team of editors—Daniel Menaker, Dana Isaacson, and Joan Benham—molded them into the manuscript that became this book. The cynical might add, "My God, what must this have been like without them?" and they'd be right.

Although I haven't yet met A. J. Liebling, Jane Grigson, and Calvin Trillin, I urge anyone interested in food or writing of any kind to read them, and to read the late and irreplaceable R. W. Apple, whom I did met—as who did not? I assume the first word out of the pope's mouth on learning one works for the *Times* to be, "You work for the *Times*? Did you know Johnny Apple?" No one was kinder or more encouraging.

I would like to praise the courage and patience of my sons, Eddie and Frank, for putting up with years and years of unreasonable food combinations, including fish liver, pig cheeks, and oatmeal topped with spinach and a fried egg that frequently drove them from the table but fortunately not from home. I'm pleased to see their palates are now more adventurous than mine. And I have deep appreciation for the culinary frustration I put my stepsons, North, Nash, and Dodge Landesman, through, exemplified by one of them saying, "Can't we ever eat anything normal?"

But I wouldn't have drawn a single happy breath nor written a single column without my wife, Red, professionally known as Heidi Ettinger, the cardinal editrix who pored over every single word of every single column before anyone else, focused pieces when they went haywire, and read three versions of this manuscript when some may have trouble with one. She is the center of my life for many reasons, thank God, not the least of which being that she inspired the first paragraph of *Lolita* without ever having met the author.

JONATHAN REYNOLDS is a playwright, actor, screenwriter, author, and television producer. His biweekly column on food appeared for five years in *The New York Times Magazine*. His plays include *Dinner with Demons*, *Stonewall Jackson's House*, which received a Pulitzer recommendation, and *Geniuses*. He lives in New York with his wife, the theatrical designer and producer Heidi Ettinger. He has two sons, Frank and Edward, and three stepsons, North, Nash, and Dodge Landesman.